Law and Philosophy Library

Volume 126

The Law and Philosophy Library, which has been in existence since 1985, aims to publish cutting edge works in the philosophy of law, and has a special history of publishing books that focus on legal reasoning and argumentation, including those that may involve somewhat formal methodologies. The series has published numerous important books on law and logic, law and artificial intelligence, law and language, and law and rhetoric. While continuing to stress these areas, the series has more recently expanded to include books on the intersection between law and the Continental philosophical tradition, consistent with the traditional openness of the series to books in the Continental jurisprudential tradition. The series is proud of the geographic diversity of its authors, and many have come from Latin America, Spain, Italy, the Netherlands, Germany, and Eastern Europe, as well, more obviously for an English-language series, from the United Kingdom, the United States, Australia, and Canada.

More information about this series at http://www.springer.com/series/6210

Lorena Ramírez-Ludeña • Josep M. Vilajosana
Editors

Legal Conventionalism

Springer

Editors
Lorena Ramírez-Ludeña
Pompeu Fabra University
Barcelona, Spain

Josep M. Vilajosana
Pompeu Fabra University
Barcelona, Spain

ISSN 1572-4395 ISSN 2215-0315 (electronic)
Law and Philosophy Library
ISBN 978-3-030-03570-9 ISBN 978-3-030-03571-6 (eBook)
https://doi.org/10.1007/978-3-030-03571-6

Library of Congress Control Number: 2018965182

This Springer imprint is published by the registered company Springer Nature Switzerland AG
The registered company address is: Gewerbestrasse 11, 6330 Cham, Switzerland

Contents

Introduction

Lorena Ramírez-Ludeña and Josep M. Vilajosana

The existence of a convention in a given community requires the presence of a recurring behaviour, the belief that the existence of this behaviour is a reason to follow it, and a set of expectations generated by the common knowledge of these circumstances. This characterization is already found in the seminal work of David Lewis, and has been adopted, with some variations, as the starting point of the current discussion on legal conventionalism.

The defence of the existence of a connection between legal conventionalism and legal theory has generally been carried out within a positivistic framework. Legal positivists attempt to explain the existence and content of legal systems by making reference to complex social facts. According to them, such facts are dependent on the acceptance of rules, which involve, among other considerations, the adoption of certain conventions on how to recognize or identify those rules. In this respect, the Hartian rule of recognition can be understood as a convention.

Taking the previous ideas into consideration, the present work will analyse some of the problems in legal conventionalism, including defining the main features of conventions, the possibility of understanding the rule of recognition as a convention, its role with respect to the existence of legal systems, its normative nature, and the role that conventions play in legal interpretation. All these problems intersect with each other throughout the following chapters.

The first part of this book contains the writings of Bruno Celano and Verónica Rodríguez-Blanco, who deal more directly with the problems posed by the notion of convention.

In his paper, Celano argues that there are conventions of a peculiar sort that are neither norms nor regularities of behaviour, but both at once. After a brief analysis of the meaning of "convention", he provides examples of the kind of phenomena he has in mind: bodily skills, know-how, taste and style, habitus (P. Bourdieu), and

L. Ramírez-Ludeña (✉) · J. M. Vilajosana (✉)
Law Department, Pompeu Fabra University, Barcelona, Spain
e-mail: lorena.ramirez@upf.edu; josep.vilajosana@upf.edu

L. Ramírez-Ludeña, J. M. Vilajosana (eds.), *Legal Conventionalism*, Law and Philosophy Library 126, https://doi.org/10.1007/978-3-030-03571-6_1

"disciplines" (M. Foucault). He then puts forth arguments supporting his claim: (a) considerations about the identity conditions of precedents (D. Lewis) and the projectibility of predicates in inductive inference generally (N. Goodman); (b) thoughts about rule-following (L. Wittgenstein); and (c) an examination of some of J. R. Searle's ideas about the "background" of intentionality. He concludes with some remarks about the time-honoured antithesis *nature v. convention*.

According to Rodríguez-Blanco, there are many key distinctions that play an important role in mapping out plausible ways of thinking about law construed as a social practice. Among the varied dichotomies, the one that has probably been most influential is the distinction between a description of an action and the normative characterisation of an action. The former aims to explain an action without resorting to the values or principles of the agent, while the latter aims to show how actions are part of a normative landscape, where values, principles, and other normative standards play a key role. The focus might be on values, principles, and standards of the agent or on values, principles, and standards that are objective. In previous work she has defended the view that the primary conception of intentional action is normative all the way through. There are no "brute" or "pure" facts about actions, and therefore actions cannot be grasped primarily by descriptors of the world either mentally, physically, or of a similar sort. She has argued that in order to make intentional actions intelligible, we need to resort to the values, principles, or good-making characteristics that the agent aims to bring about in the world. We also need to understand that the values, principles, or good-making characteristics of the action provide a unity and intelligibility to the various bodily movements of the agent. This is a complex and occasionally difficult understanding of agency but one that, in her view, is sound. The core elements of this account of agency are that (a) there is a parallel between practical reason or deliberative reasoning and intentional action; (b) practical reasoning involves practical knowledge that is non-observational; (c) the error of an action stems not from what the world looks like but from the performance of the agent; and (d) intentional action is primarily from the first person or deliberative point of view and therefore it is forward-looking. In her contribution to this book, Rodríguez-Blanco focuses only on (d) and argues that this feature provides the key premise for the conclusion that a characterisation of actions in social practices, including law, cannot be carried out on the basis of descriptions. She first shows that (d) is true and she then describes the best account of actions in terms of descriptions provided by legal philosophers in recent years: the idea that actions and resulting social practices can correctly be grasped as "deep conventions". Finally, Rodríguez-Blanco shows that conventions *sensu stricto* and deep conventions require (d) to be intelligible.

The second part of the book contains five texts that focus on analysing whether the rule of recognition, first postulated by Hart, can be understood as a convention. In particular, the first three texts are mainly concerned with whether the rule of recognition is a constitutive convention.

According to Marmor, many critics have held that Hart did not provide any good reason to think that the rules of recognition are conventions, and in any case, no conventional understanding of such rules is plausible. Others, including Marmor himself, defend the conventional character of those rules, albeit on different grounds. His main aim in this essay is to clarify his position and provide further arguments in support of the view that constitutive conventions are within the foundations of law. In particular, he tries to show, in the face of criticism that his proposal has received from Postema, that it is still necessary to postulate the constitutive character of the rule of recognition. Indeed, Postema has argued that it is sufficient to extend the notion of coordination employed by Lewis and himself at some earlier time (he now prefers to speak in terms of "cooperation") to argue that it is not necessary to take Marmor's step. In contrast, Marmor argues that there are innumerable conventional practices, which would be wrongly described as solutions to pre-existing coordination problems. In his view, insisting on coordination belittles our talent and inventiveness as human beings. Our sophisticated social practices are not limited to solving the problems in which we find ourselves. People create practices and activities that they consider valuable, one of them being the law.

The second text of the second section, written by Rodríguez, is precisely intended to criticize the position that Marmor has defended in previous works. Essentially, his criticism is that a convention cannot be constitutive, and therefore the rule of recognition cannot be a constitutive convention. According to Rodríguez, the concept of convention employed by Marmor is too weak and would lead to considering a rule to be conventional even though all the members of a community follow it because they consider it to be correct. The rule may not be conventional, though everyone is following it because others follow it. Moreover, it seems pointless to speak of constitutional conventions inasmuch as, according to Rodríguez, the idea of the arbitrary character of conventions is incompatible with the constitutive character of a rule. Consequently, Marmor's view is affected by an internal inconsistency because, by its own definitions, the constitutive character of the rule of recognition would be incompatible with its conventional character.

The third text, by Vilajosana, is intended to show that the existence of law in a given society requires a unitary practice of rule identification (a rule of recognition). It is also argued that the best way of understanding this rule is to see it as a constitutive convention, which allows for the autonomous identification of the law of a particular community. According to Vilajosana, "just as the existence of money requires the belief that it exists, the existence of a legal system depends ultimately on a set of beliefs shared by the relevant persons". After developing this position, a series of recurrent criticisms against conventional conceptions is revisited with the aim of rejecting them. These criticisms include that the rule of recognition as a convention does not account for the normative nature of the convention, nor would it account for the presence of principles in legal systems, nor the disagreements between lawyers. Finally, the problem of the arbitrariness of the rule of recognition and its alleged banality is addressed.

The second section ends with the contributions of Sánchez Brigido and Ratti. According to Sánchez Brigido, after abandoning the idea that the rule of recognition is a coordinative convention in Lewis's sense, Postema offered a new, more sophisticated version of conventionalism. According to this new version, the rule of recognition should be understood not as a coordinative convention, but as a cooperative convention. The paper examines Postema's account of cooperative convention. It claims that it is unsuccessful for a crucial reason: certain features of officials' practices may be constitutive of a rule of recognition, but there need not be any cooperative problem to solve, and uncertainty, interdependence, and mutually conditional preferences (the conditions that define a cooperative problem) need not be present. The paper also suggests that a correct account of the rules of recognition should recognize that the practice constituted by such a rule should be understood not as a cooperative convention but as a special type of institutional practice.

Ratti explores some possible applications of some elementary notions of set theory (such as "intersection", "union", and "difference") to two age-old and intertwined problems of legal philosophy: the identification of law and the rational reconstruction of an ultimate rule of recognition. The main results of the inquiry are the following. (1) Contrary to a widespread view, "law" does not denote a unitary set of rules, but rather a family of sets, the main relations among which are examined in the paper. (2) Contrary to what the strong version of legal conventionalism advocates, there is a conceptual space to regard the rule of recognition as the overlapping of several sets of criteria of identification that are used within a certain community. Amongst other things, this thesis renders the famous Dworkin's critique against conventionalism harmless.

Finally, in the third section the reader will find articles that relate debates on legal conventionalism with legal interpretation.

According to Arena, Dworkin famously argued that Hart's practice theory is unable to provide an account of legal duties and therefore is a poor theory of law. Conventions were then proposed as substitutes for the practice theory, and were capable of demonstrating the existence of legal duties. In his paper, he examines two different conventionalist strategies that have been proposed in answer to those criticisms, Marmor's constitutive conventionalism and Postema's constructive conventionalism. He claims that both proposals remain captive of Dworkin's premises. Dworkin's argument is based on the premise that a good theory of law should explain the existence of legal duties. Conventionalists accept this premise. The reason for this acceptance is that, according to Dworkin, not explaining the existence of legal duties would makes a theory unable to explain two essential features of law: (1) the fact that judges claim or assume that there are legal duties and (2) the fact that judges disagree about the content of those duties. Arena argues that the explanation of these two traits does not require proof that such duties exist. He claims that judges' statements of duty are merely a projection of their attitudes and that their discourse can be preserved under a quasi-realist schema. Thus, when a judge claims that "capital punishment is forbidden", she is voicing her attitude in favour of a state of affairs in which capital punishment is not used. However, judges do not make such statements freely; they ground them in interpretative methods. If our judge favours textualism, she would be expressing a positive attitude towards deciding a case in that particular way (e.g. declaring capital punishment to be constitutional–hooray!) on the grounds that there is an existing interpretative convention amongst judges that one should take into account the literal meaning of the provision. First, Arena introduces Dworkin's criticism and the premises on which it is based. Second, he examines how conventionalism has answered such criticisms and shows why they are unable to escape from Dworkin's premises. Third, he shows why Dworkin's premises are wrong and how this opens an alternative for conventionalism in which a legal realist thesis is endorsed, one he calls "sceptical conventionalism".

According to Ramírez-Ludeña, an intuitive view of language is frequently assumed. In this view, competent speakers relate words to descriptions that determine reference. This view is generally understood as conventional in the sense that it emphasises the existence of conventions that determine what descriptions are relevant. However, this descriptivist approach is shown to be problematic in reconstructing our linguistic practices. In contrast, the Causal Theory of Reference (CTR) provides a plausible account of our uses of words. CTR is, however, understood as providing a non-conventionalist approach to language and as being committed to an implausible version of essentialism. In her paper, Ramírez-Ludeña presents a version of CTR that deflects the criticisms that are normally addressed to it. She also shows that this version of CTR is advantageous when compared to the traditional descriptivist model. In the legal field, CTR has been associated with non-positivistic conceptions about law. However, since CTR is not committed to essentialism but takes into account the way in which a community uses words, the author also demonstrates how the proposed model is compatible with conceptions in legal philosophy that emphasise the conventional character of law, such as Hart's.

In the last chapter, Shapiro makes reference to the problem of legal disagreements within the framework of his theory of law as a plan. In his account, Shapiro emphasizes the relevance of social facts while rejecting the relevance of interpretive conventions. Like Dworkin, he understands that in order to provide an explanation for theoretical disagreements, it is essential to take into consideration the purpose of legal practice. In addition, both agree that the most appropriate interpretive methodology in a legal system depends on that which best fits its objectives. Unlike Dworkin, however, Shapiro does not consider that the attribution of a purpose requires an exercise in moral and political philosophy, but rather an inquiry related to social facts. In this sense, the task of the legal interpreter is to detect the political objectives that were intended by the designers of the system so that the relevant purposes are those that explain, and not justify, the practice. Consequently, such purposes may be morally deficient. To uncover these objectives, the interpreter must analyse the institutional structure and determine which objectives and values best explain the system. The correct interpretive methodology for the system that which best harmonizes with the objectives of those who designed it.

This book has its origins in the publication of "Convencionalismo y derecho" (Marcial Pons, 2015) and in the seminars that were held at Pompeu Fabra University (Barcelona) in later years. We thank the support of Marcial Pons and the Ministry of Economy and Competitiveness (Ref. DER2016-80471-C2-1-R) to carry out this project.

Part I
The Notion of Convention

Pre-conventions. A Fragment of the Background

Bruno Celano

Abstract In his paper Celano argues that there exist conventions of a peculiar sort which are neither norms nor regularities of behavior, partaking of both. He proceeds as follows. After a brief analysis of the meaning of "convention", Celano gives some examples of the kind of phenomena he has in mind: bodily skills, know-how, taste and style, *habitus* (P. Bourdieu), "disciplines" (M. Foucault). Then he groups some arguments supporting his claim: (i) considerations about the identity conditions of precedents (D. Lewis) and about the projectibility of predicates in inductive inference generally (N. Goodman); (ii) thoughts about rule-following (L. Wittgenstein); (iii) an examination of some of J. R. Searle's ideas about the "Background" of intentionality. Celano concludes with some remarks about the time-honored antithesis "nature" *v.* "convention".

> [...] because in every one habit [*ethos*; Bekker: *consuetudo*] is a matter of importance, since it soon becomes a second nature [*physis*]—Aristotle, *Problemata*, XXVIII

1 Introduction

I will argue that there are entities that can be plausibly called "conventions", which are neither mere *de facto* regularities, nor rules (norms), but that—in a sense to be specified—have both the character of *de facto* regularities, as well as a normative character: they are, literally, "normative facts". This paper attempts to isolate these entities.

The matter is delicate. Philosophers usually distinguish, and with good reason, between rules and regularities, between facts and norms. In each pair, the two

---

Translated by Marco Segatti. The Italian original of this text was published in *Ragion Pratica* (2014) 2, pp. 605–632. A previous version of this contribution in English was published in *Revus* (2016) 30, pp. 9–32.

B. Celano (✉)
Law Faculty, University of Palermo, Palermo, Italy
e-mail: bruno.celano@unipa.it

L. Ramírez-Ludeña, J. M. Vilajosana (eds.), *Legal Conventionalism*, Law and Philosophy Library 126, https://doi.org/10.1007/978-3-030-03571-6_2

concepts are thought of as mutually exclusive. The distinction is intuitive, and it appears, at first sight at least, incontrovertible. The entities that we are trying to isolate are, mostly, at the edge of our visual field—and delimit it. For this reason, they usually go unnoticed, and to see them we need to try and look at them from the corner of our eyes. (These are only metaphors, of course). Usually, whenever we discuss particular moral, legal, or political problems, we distinguish between a *de facto* regularity, and a rule; on the one side we have facts, on the other, norms. We do well to distinguish between them. Confusing facts and rules *is*, indeed, a cardinal sin.[1]

The entities that I will discuss are, as I said, conventions. I do not mean to suggest, of course, that what I will try to pin down is the only meaning of "convention"; nor, even less, the "true" meaning of the word (whatever that might mean). The term "convention" has, simply, more than one meaning. For this reason, it is appropriate to begin with an exploration—albeit only amateurish—of its semantic field.

2 The Word "Convention": Some Meanings

As a first approximation, it is safe to say that, in Italian (as well as in similar languages),[2] the semantic field of "convenzione" (the word usually translating "convention") is divided into two distinct areas. In a first sense, the term refers to an explicit agreement, which is conscious and deliberate, between multiple parties; or, to the result of such an agreement (sometimes, an assembly which is assumed to have the task of reaching an agreement of this kind). In a second sense the term refers instead to social norms, customs, ways of behaving, that are consolidated by tradition. The elements that are common to the two areas are:

(1) The idea of an "agreement", using this term in a very generic and vague way: a generic "*con-venire*", "being together", "going together to the same place (or in the same direction)". A very sketchy idea, nothing more.
(2) The idea of arbitrariness: a convention might have been (at least partly) different from what it is, without significant changes (with respect to some criterion, more or less precisely defined). When X—a rule, a sign, and so on …—is conventional, it is, within certain limits, immaterial (not necessarily *completely* immaterial) whether X has certain features rather than others; what matters is that those, and not others, are the features that are commonly accepted.

This is, however, only a first approximation. In the semantic field of "convenzione", one should distinguish between two further areas. On the one hand, there is the idea of an agreement—which can be either explicit or tacit—informed by the "perception of a common interest", in Hume's words[3]; that is, the reasoned pursuit,

[1] Celano (1994).

[2] What I say in this section does not necessarily apply, in unrevised form, also to the English word "convention" (stemming, of course, from the same Latin root as the Italian "convenzione").

[3] Hume (1777), p. 257.

by each of the parties involved, of their own goals (in this case, I will speak of a "rational explanation", or of a "train of reasoning" explaining the behavior of the relevant parties; this reasoning, too, may, in turn, be tacit or explicit).[4] On the other hand, the idea of a shared, and established, manner of doing things, a way of thinking or acting, which is not explained by a train of reasoning, be it tacit or explicit.

This distinction produces an ongoing ambiguity in the use of the term. If one emphasizes the agreement-aspect (an agreement explained by a train of reasoning), leaving aside the antithesis "tacit" *v.* "explicit", one ends by oscillating between *contract* and *convention*,[5] or by recording a tight connection between *convention* and *custom* (according to some of the many meanings of the word "custom").[6] But apart from this ambiguity, one should keep in mind the possibility of conventions—both explicit or tacit—that are not explained by a train of reasoning (that is, conventions which are not amenable to a rational explanation).

The semantic field of "convenzione", in short, is articulated through two axes of differentiation: the antithesis "rationalizable" (explained by a train of reasoning) *v.* "non rationalizable", and "tacit" *v.* "explicit".

If we now try to follow the thread of this double articulation, isolating these different conceptual possibilities, we move beyond a mere exploration of the semantic field of the word. Rather, we are engaged in the search for an explanatory redefinition of the term—more precisely, a rational reconstruction of a plurality of different concepts of convention (or "convenzione"; from now on, I shall use the two terms indifferently).

3 Convention: A Family of Concepts

If we cross these two axes of differentiation, we obtain a matrix with four boxes, corresponding to four different notions of convention.

The entities that I will try to isolate occupy—but do not exhaust—one of these boxes. The main modern and contemporary theories of conventions occupy one of the remaining boxes. Let us see.

The box which results from the combination of the two traits: 1. "train of reasoning", and 2. "explicit"—that is, conventions that are explicit agreements, backed by a train of reasoning—is occupied by phenomena such as contracts, multilateral promises, treaties, and the like. The relevant theories try to account for these phenomena as the product of self-interested behavior by rational agents; in their extreme forms, they explain conventions as agreements that are reached by subjects whose

[4] The mere *possibility* of reconstructing the relevant actions as having such a structure is not enough. This would make the notion too generic.

[5] This is how one may come to the paradoxical interpretation of Hume as a contractarian (Gauthier 1979, pp. 3–38).

[6] Celano (1995), pp. 173–231 and Celano (2014), pp. 597–667.

behavior maximizes expected utility. (The crucial problem for these theories is to account for the principle *pacta sunt servanda* in terms of rational choice).

To date, the most influential theories of conventions are those of David Hume[7] and David Lewis.[8] These theories try to account for conventions that are agreements (in the generic sense; see above, Sect. 2), backed by a tacit train of reasoning. Hume and Lewis—and, in their wake, others—provide an explanation of conventions as the result of decisions by rational individuals pursuing their own interests, in the absence of an explicit agreement (and in the absence of an authority that enforces it).

There remain, in addition to the two boxes marked by the presence of a train of reasoning (explicit agreements: contract; and tacit agreements: conventions *à la* Hume, or Lewis), two boxes left. Here, I will not deal with explicit agreements that are not backed by a train of reasoning. Social groups usually have explicit conventions that are not, or at least do not seem to be, amenable to rational decisions by the individuals involved.[9] The phenomena that interest me occupy the fourth box: tacit conventions that are not backed by a train of reasoning.

This covers different possibilities. The idea that interests me is this: convergent behavior (behavior which is in "agreement", in the generic sense indicated above, Sect. 2) which is not a biological regularity, and is the result of learning, but which is also automatic: it is spontaneous (unreflective), rapid, fluid, *effortless*.[10] Therefore, it may as well be particularly rigid, mechanical, blind, dumb. Conventions—to use yet another metaphor—that are part of the body, in the flesh, so to speak, and have become as natural as breathing, a "second nature".[11]

All of this, of course, stands in need of clarification. I will proceed as follows: in the next section, I will provide some examples of the phenomena I have in mind. Later on, I will present some arguments supporting the conclusion that there exist, indeed, conventions of the relevant sort, conventions that are "embodied", and that these are normative facts. The arguments themselves are not mine; but the light in which I present them is, it seems to me, somewhat original—specifically, the idea that these arguments may illuminatingly be viewed as all leading to the same conclusion, and the spelling out of this conclusion.

[7] Hume (1740).

[8] Lewis (1969).

[9] Proponents of an inflexible rational choice-based methodological individualism will (implausibly) deny this. But I shall not go here into the controversy between advocates of *homo economicus* and defenders of *homo sociologicus*. It is enough for my purposes that the one indicated in the text is in fact a coherent conceptual possibility—even if the concept turned out to be an empty class.

[10] These are, by and large, the traits that Kahneman (2011) attributes to the workings of System 1. I say "by and large" because the workings of System 1 include biological phenomena as well.

[11] See—albeit confusedly—Murphy (2007), especially at p. 54: "custom /…/ must be analyzed into two more basic notions, habit and convention" ("customs are habitual conventions and conventional habits: custom naturalizes conventions just as it conventionalizes human nature"). (Here, "custom" expresses the notion of convention I am interested in). Notice the usual ambiguity between "custom" and "convention" (noted in Sect. 2, above).

4 Pre-conventions: Some Examples

Before going on, however, I should note a difficulty which is implicit in what has been said so far. I said that one of the axes articulating the semantic field of the term "convention" is the antithesis "tacit" *v.* "explicit". I pointed out that the entities that I am trying to isolate are "tacit" conventions, "tacit" in the sense of automatic: regular convergent behavior that, while not a biological regularity (e.g. breathing), is spontaneous, unreflective, fast, fluid, effortless. The difficulty is this: human beings are made in such a way that everything, or almost everything—even the demonstration of Gödel's theorem, or the selection of an efficient allocation of scarce financial resources on a certain market—can, by virtue of a learning process, become automatic. Anything, or almost anything, that can be learnt can become "second nature". This fact threatens to undermine our reconstruction. Thus, for example, it is possible that those who follow a convention *à la* Lewis (a tacit agreement supported by a train of reasoning; see above, Sect. 3), and for which this convention has become obvious, have a "tacit understanding of it, which they cannot easily articulate to outsiders".[12]

This is an endemic problem when dealing with intentional phenomena. So, for example, each one of us has, in every moment of her life, countless tacit beliefs (I believe, for example, that the apartment that I live in is on the fourth floor); but it is not easy to identify the features that distinguish a belief of this kind from other similar entities, which are in some sense tacitly present in us, but that it would be quite odd to call *beliefs*—such as, for example, the "belief" that the Earth existed before I was born.[13] Of course, if I were asked whether or not the Earth existed before I was born, I would answer, yes (that is what I'm doing right now), just as I would answer yes if I were asked whether or not I live on the fourth floor. But is this enough to say that "The Earth existed before I was born" is, and was, the content of a *belief* of mine, albeit a tacit one? If so, there will be no limit to my tacit beliefs (do I have the tacit belief that I am not a worm?). Similarly, returning to the case of those who follow a Lewis-convention which has become for them "second nature" we can say, of course, that what they are doing is implementing a train of reasoning that is "within them", in a tacit and non-articulated way—just as a tacit belief proper. But it is unclear what that might mean, if not that they behave *as if* they were doing this. But this appears to be question begging. When the convention has become "second nature" what guides their conduct is, in some sense (see below, Sect. 6), what they actually *do*.

These considerations show, I think, that it is necessary to distinguish two senses of the adjective "tacit". In the first sense, it is used to refer to a tacit belief proper ("I live on the fourth floor"); in the second, it refers to entities that can only improperly be called "beliefs" ("The Earth existed before I was born"; "I'm not an earthworm"). Or, returning to our case, one should distinguish between the sense in which a "train

[12] Sugden (1998), p. 379.

[13] See in general Lycan (1986), pp. 61–82. The example is taken from Wittgenstein (1969).

of reasoning" supporting a Lewis-convention can originally—i.e., when the convention comes into existence—be called "tacit"; and the sense in which it can be called "tacit" when the convention has become "second nature". The entities that interest me are agreements which are "tacit" in the latter sense. (The crucial point, as we shall see—below, Sect. 7—is that the entities in question are not intentional phenomena).

Let us now consider some examples of the kind of phenomena I have in mind. Not all the things that fall in each of the areas that we shall now review are conventions. But in each of these areas there is room for the conventional.

Consider learning a sporting skill such as front crawl.[14] What is *the correct swimming stroke* in front crawl? Human life is full of things like that: a certain way of walking, of sitting … these things are not sets of rules. We can certainly, in many such cases, identify or conjecture relevant rules—rules that maybe we cannot formulate. But *the correct stroke* in crawl (not, of course, *a* stroke, a token, but the type), the way of walking we call "marching" etc., are not, in themselves, sets of rules.

Nor are they, on the other hand, *de facto* regularities. Granted, when one or more individuals swim the crawl, or march, their behaviors are, under some respect, regular. But *the correct stroke* of front crawl, or the way of walking we call "marching", are precisely the respect under which their behaviors are regular, and what *guides* these behaviors.

The essential point is that these things are abstract entities (not an actual behavior, but its form); but they are *in the body*: those who know how to swim the crawl, or march, have these forms in their body. *The correct stroke* of front crawl or the way of walking we call "marching" are tacit bodily schemes, which are intermediate between an image (e.g., a mental picture of somebody swimming, or marching) and rule[15]: embodied diagrams that establish what to do, what is the *correct*, the right or proper way to proceed. And in these diagrams, or at least in many of them, there is a more or less conspicuous conventional component. Human biology sets the limits, a frame. But within these limits we then indulge our whims; and the limits themselves can, sometimes, be manipulated. What front crawl is, is—in part—an arbitrary agreement (in the generic sense introduced above, Sect. 2).[16] Because of this conventional component, these wired-in forms (forms in the body, that is) are, inseparably, both natural (a "second nature") and cultural[17] (I return below, in Sect. 8, to the antithesis "nature *v.* culture").[18]

---

[14]The example is taken from Casey (1998), pp. 208–212.

[15]Casey (1998), p. 211.

[16]If these things were rules, we should say that they are "constitutive conventions". (This notion has been worked out by Marmor (2009), exploiting Searle's notion of a constitutive rule). But they are, in fact, constitutive conventions which are not rules.

[17]Casey (1998), p. 212.

[18]A comment is in order here. As remarked above (see Sect. 2), Hume's account is usually regarded as the paradigm case of an account of "conventions" in the sense of tacit agreements backed by a train of reasoning. Hume's well known example of the two rowers (1976, p. 490) who mutually

The point may be further clarified by recalling familiar experiences, e.g. learning to ride a bike. John Searle provides an illuminating description of this kind of process:

> As the skier gets better he does not internalize the rules better, but rather the rules become progressively irrelevant. The rules do not become "wired in" as unconscious Intentional contents, but the repeated experiences create physical capacities, presumably realized as neural pathways, that make the rules simply irrelevant. "Practice makes perfect" not because practice results in a perfect memorization of the rules, but because repeated practice enables the body to take over and the rules to recede into the Background /…/ On my view, *the body takes over* and the skier's Intentionality is concentrated on winning the race.[19]

The central idea is aptly captured by the phrase *the body takes over*. What the body is doing, from now on, is not a mere *de facto* regularity, but something that is in between a norm and a regularity: A way of doing things, the way in which "one does" this or that.

We shall examine later on (below, Sect. 7) Searle's argument. But I should indicate a point of crucial importance now. L. Wittgenstein, as we shall see (below, Sect. 6), has shown that similar considerations apply also to that particular kind of human ability that is the mastery and use of concepts, or rule-following.

G. Ryle[20] famously distinguishes between two kinds of "knowing", or knowledge: *know-that*, or propositional knowledge; and *know-how*: knowing how to do something, even if you are not able to say which are the rules one should follow in order to do it. The content of "know-that" is propositional: it can in principle be expressed—even though it is not necessarily conscious—through a declarative clause (a *that-clause*). This may be a descriptive proposition, or a set (possibly, a system) of propositions of this kind; or a rule, a directive, or a set of rules. To "know-that" is, in this sense, knowledge of a set of propositions.

The basic idea is that "know-how" is heterogeneous with respect to, and therefore irreducible to "know-that"—in opposition to the idea that, e.g., to know how to play chess is not different from knowing the rules of chess, and that playing chess is nothing but to be guided by these rules[21] (below, in Sect. 6, I will focus, following Wittgenstein, on the apparent simplicity of "rule-following"). Not only in the sense that it may well happen that I know how to do a certain thing, and I do it, without knowing the rules that I have to follow in order to do it, or without knowing many of the relevant facts—general or specific–, or even having erroneous beliefs

---

adjust the pace of their rowing, however, is an example of the exercise of a physical ability. True, the two rowers' actions are guided, as Hume says, by the perception of a common interest: the two want the boat to proceed, and to proceed as fast and smoothly as it can; and they realize that, in order to accomplish this, they need to synchronize their rhythm. But what they do—synchronizing their actions, that is, their convention—consists in a bodily activity that, in it and of itself, does not—not necessarily—include a train of reasoning. Hume's account has a wider scope than it is usually believed.

[19] Searle (1983), pp. 150–151. Italics are mine.

[20] Ryle (1949).

[21] Fantl (2012).

thereabout. But also in the sense that, often, those who do not know how to do a certain thing are able to state—they know—the same propositions about what doing such a thing requires, as those who, in addition, know how to do it. So, turning back to the example cited above (the cases discussed in the present section, sub 1), are, in fact, cases of "know-how"), someone who cannot ride a bicycle may well be able to say the same things about how you go cycling, as someone who can do it ("One must keep in balance", "You must push one pedal, then the other"). The difference between the two seems to consist precisely in knowing how to ride a bicycle.[22] It may even happen that the former has propositional knowledge which is much more complex and in-depth than the one the latter has (e.g., knowledge of the physical laws that govern the complex processes we call "cycling"), but does not know how to ride a bicycle (unlike, e.g., a child who has not studied physics). To put it with Searle once again, at some point in the process of learning, *the body takes over*.

The question of whether "knowing-how" is indeed irreducible to any form of "knowing-that" is controversial. Proponents of an, as they say, "intellectualist" account of "know-how" reject non-reducibility. Proposals for reduction, more or less ingenious, have been numerous. I cannot here adjudicate the merits of this debate. I shall limit myself to two observations.

(A) From a conceptual standpoint, reduction proposals, even though sophisticated (sometimes precisely because too sophisticated), appear implausible.
(B) Recent studies in cognitive psychology[23] tend to corroborate, experimentally, non-reducibility.

Activities that can be the subject of "know-how" may be of a more or less conventional kind—e.g., to swim front crawl, or to play chess. Which acts constitute "playing chess" depends on arbitrary (in the sense indicated above, Sect. 2) agreements (in the generic sense indicated above, Sect. 2).

We say of a person that she has style, or that doing this or that is in her style. The same may sometimes be said of groups, variously identified. Style does not so much depend on what one does, but on how—the "way" in which—one does it. And often it is style that makes the difference: worth—better, worse, admirable, unseemly, etc.—is often a matter of style.

What is style? Taste is a similar phenomenon. Tom has "good taste" (or "bad taste"), in general or, more plausibly, in this or that field (wine, cinema, etc.). Maybe Harry has learnt that tasteful people appreciate *x*, *y* and *z* (this or that wine, for example), but when it comes to choosing between new options, which are not already included in the list, he mistakes disastrously: he does not have good taste (a person of good taste would have never preferred *q* over *w*).

Style and (good) taste are notoriously not sets of rules. In two ways: first, purported codifications of style or taste in handbooks or manuals ("The Art of …") have something hopelessly contrived and cloying. It is not so much that the rules are too complicated to be compressed in a handbook—the very idea of a codification

---

[22] Fantl (2012).

[23] See for example Wallis (2008), pp. 123–153.

(of style, or taste) betrays a misunderstanding (someone who engages in the project of codification does not understand, in fact, what is at issue; the very idea of reducing style, or taste, to a set of rules betrays a certain lack of style, shows bad taste). Second, someone who has style, or has good taste, does not choose this or that by applying rules but spontaneously (those who follow the manual will be, at most, a boor who tries to pass himself off as a person of good taste). Granted, in the relevant fields (be it wine, cinema, or any other) there may be rules, of various types, that cannot be violated by those who have style, or taste. But style and taste, in themselves, are precisely what exceeds the mere application of rules—or, if you will, they are the right way of applying them.

And this takes us to the other side of the coin. Style and taste are not, as we have just seen, sets of rules. But neither are they, on the other hand, mere *de facto* regularities. Of course, he who has style, or taste, chooses certain things regularly. His is a *disposition* to choose in a certain way. But this is not a disposition of the same kind as, e.g., the disposition to close one's eyes in the presence of a strong light source, or a conditioned reflex. It is a disposition to choose in the *right* way—where, as we have just seen, which way is the right one does not depend (solely) on rules. Therefore, it is a *normative* disposition—again, an embodied norm (*the body takes over*).

And it is plausible, if not obvious, that this territory—who has style, what good taste requires—is also occupied by arbitrary agreements (in the generic sense; above, Sect. 2), i.e. conventions.

Style and taste are parameters of social differentiation, and of classification and hierarchy within social groups. This idea was developed systematically by P. Bourdieu.[24]

Differences and hierarchies of social class, or of gender, are embodied in styles: one's gestures, posture, or the way one eats, or walks, and so on. "Taste, a class culture turned into nature, that is, *embodied*, helps to shape the class body /…/ the body is the most indisputable materialization of class taste".[25]

In order to account for these phenomena Bourdieu works out the concept of *habitus*. An *habitus* is a set of dispositions (inclinations, tendencies, proclivities), acquired (most of them inculcated when we were children), consolidated, which are "*a way of being, a habitual state* (especially of the body)",[26] and operating as "generative schemes":

> principles of the generation and structuring of practices and representations which can be objectively "regulated" and "regular" without in any way being the product of obedience to rules.[27]

---

[24] Bourdieu (1979).

[25] Bourdieu (1979), p. 199.

[26] Bourdieu (1977), p. 214.

[27] Bourdieu (1977), p. 72.

An *habitus*, therefore, is not a set of rules. Rather, it is a set of dispositions that have been acquired and have now become natural ("history turned into nature"[28]), fixing the *right* way (an embodied norm) to proceed in new circumstances: the "generative principle of regulated improvisations".[29]

M. Foucault[30] developed the concept of "disciplinary power". Disciplinary power is a form of power which, according to Foucault, has been a common feature of European society since roughly the eighteenth century (the reliability of Foucault's historic claims does not concern us here), modeling and shaping the bodies on which it is exercised—its correlates are "docile bodies". It works, that is, through continuous, uninterrupted coercion, in the form of indefinitely repeated exercise, and examination; each exercise becomes a phase in a perpetual examination, and *vice versa* each exam is an exercise. Disciplinary power does not seek to bring about the performance of actions, or omissions, via the threat of punitive sanctions in case of breach of directives. Its typical form is, instead, training. In this way, it aims to model the bodies that are its object to the most minute detail, in what they do, in their attitudes, their gestures, their looks, tone of voice, and so on; and this for every moment of the performance of the activities that are so regulated—at its extremes, the entire life of the subject. In barracks, colleges, schools, prisons, hospitals, factories (and, as always, in convents) disciplines transform farmers into soldiers, unruly children into school-kids, criminals into prisoners, sick people into patients, and so on, through uninterrupted training, affecting every detail and every moment of the life of those disciplined. They aim to wire dispositions into bodies that become "second nature".

In each of the areas we have reviewed there is room for arbitrary (in the relevant sense, above, Sect. 2) and tacit (in the second of the two senses distinguished at the beginning of this section) agreements (in the generic sense; above, Sect. 2).[31] I shall call these entities "pre-conventions". The term "pre-conventions" is not used to suggest that these are things that precede, or in some way come before, conventions. Rather, it should be understood in the sense of "conventions that are first" (or "come before"): conventions that are mostly in the background of our activities and thoughts, and that, passing usually unnoticed, delimit their spaces.[32]

[28] Bourdieu (1977), p. 78.

[29] Bourdieu (1977), p. 78.

[30] Foucault (1975), part III.

[31] It is true that these two senses have not been defined, but merely illustrated (at the beginning of the present section). But, as I said, the problem—which is an hard one, and that I am unable to resolve—of satisfactorily defining them does not specifically concern the phenomena that we are discussing; it affects, rather, the whole domain of intentional phenomena. I hope that a simple illustration is enough.

[32] I wish to clarify, once and for all, that there is nothing inherently nice, or good, or just, or holy, in pre-conventions. A pre-convention may well be abhorrent. The fact that a pre-convention is normative does not entail, or in any way imply, that it conforms to justice. It does entail, presumably, that it somehow expresses one or more values. But the connection might be a distorted, a perverted, or a paradoxical one. Or, in any case, it may well be that, in the circumstances, its value is very low, or close to irrelevant.

5 Arguments (I): Induction, Salience and Projection

I now turn to a summary presentation (it is, in fact, the evocation of arguments that I assume to be, more or less, already known to the reader) of some arguments that support the view that there exist pre-conventions—more specifically, these arguments show that there is room for the existence of pre-conventions (they "leave room", or "open up space", for the latter), and that it is very probable—in fact, obviously true—that this space is not empty. These arguments are different in their content, in their conclusions, and in their consequences. But they turn out to have similar implications from the point of view that concerns as here.

The first argument is drawn from Lewis' theory of conventions. According to Lewis' account, conventions are solutions to recurring coordination problems: strategic interaction problems, that is, that are characterized by a coincidence (not necessarily complete coincidence) of interests between the parties, and by the availability of a plurality of equilibria, with respect to which the parties are relatively indifferent. Given a recurring coordination problem, a Lewis-convention is a regularity of conduct *R* such that each of the individuals involved prefers to conform to *R*, provided that the others conform to *R* (and, furthermore, each prefers that all the others comply, if the others—including himself—do, too), and this is common knowledge among them. For this reason, all conform to *R* each time the opportunity presents itself: expectations of conformity bring about conformity, and, in turn, conformity brings about expectations of conformity.

Lewis' theory has been amply and fruitfully debated. An overall assessment of its strengths or weaknesses does not concern us here, however. The important point for our purposes is, as we shall see in a moment, a different one (also identified by Lewis himself, and by some of those who discussed his ideas).

The main idea of Lewis' account of convention is captured by what I have elsewhere called the "dependency condition"[33]: when there is a convention (in this specific sense), each of the individuals involved does *A* (an action of a certain kind) in *S* (a recurring situation) because the others do it, because the others do it, because the others do it … (and so on). So, for example, a purely conventional (in this sense) fact is the fact that a given social venue is trendy: each one goes there because she expects to meet the others there, because she expects each one of the others to expect to meet the others there; and each one of them, for this reason, goes there—thus confirming, the others' expectations of meeting the others there. In this sense, we go to this place because we go to this place because we go to this place …

This is, however, only the pure case. Lewis' approach can be used to mold a plurality of concepts of convention. The dependency clause ("everyone does it because everyone else does") can be understood in several different ways, thus generating a plurality of definitions that capture different phenomena.[34]

[33] Celano (1995), pp. 35–87 and Celano (2014), pp. 597–667.

[34] Celano (1995), pp. 35–87; for a detailed exploration of the main possibilities, see Celano (2014), pp. 597–667.

It is not necessary to develop this line of inquiry here. The relevant point for our present purposes is this. Definitions *à la* Lewis begin with the clause: "A certain kind of behavior (performing action *A*) in a recurring situation *S* –i.e., a regularity of conduct *R*– is a convention among the members of the social group *G* if and only if …" (as I said, one can proceed in several ways, ending up with different concepts). The relevant problem here is the problem of the identity conditions of *A* and *S* (i.e., *R*); in particular, the conditions for the identification, by the members of *G*, of *A* as a certain *type* of behavior (how can one say that a_1 is a case, an instance, of *A*?), and *S* as the *same* situation that recurs (how can one say that s_1 is a case of *S*?). In virtue of what, that is, do members of *G* recognize a_1, a_2, … a_n as instances of the same type of behavior, and recognize s_1, s_2, … s_n as instances of the same type of situation? In short, how do they identify *R*, i.e. how do they determine what counts, now, as doing the same thing they did in the past?[35]

The existence of a Lewis-convention (and generally of a "convention" in one of the senses defined following this approach) presupposes that the members of *G* have the ability of doing this. What does it consist of?

The problem is, at bottom, how it is possible to *learn* a convention (in particular, a Lewis-convention): "learning by experience", through pattern recognition.[36] It is, generally, the problem of projection from past experience to the present case: what does it mean, here and now, to follow a precedent? What identifies a set of past cases as a set of *precedents*? In short: *which precedent*?[37] And here is Lewis' response:

> [O]f course, we could never be given exactly the same problem twice /…/ We cannot do exactly what we did before. Nothing we could do this time is exactly like what we did before –like it in every respect– because the situations are not exactly alike /…/ Guided by whatever analogy we notice, we tend to follow precedent /…/ There might be alternative analogies. If so, there is room for ambiguity about what would be following precedent and doing what we did before /…/ In fact, there are always innumerable alternative analogies. *Were it not that we happen uniformly to notice some analogies and ignore others /…/ precedents would always be completely ambiguous and worthless.*[38]

Lewis' answer to the question of what justifies one in considering certain behaviors and not others as the proper continuation of *R*—i.e., what counts as "following suit" with R—is thus: as a matter of fact, we notice the same analogies; and that is what fixes the identity of *R*, disambiguating past cases, and thus enabling us to proceed—to follow precedents. Certain options, and not others, appear to us as "doing, now, what we have done in the past". Sugden comments: for Lewis, "all that matters /…/ is that people have concepts"—roughly the same ones for the members of a

[35] The problem is formulated very clearly, concerning language, in Millikan (2008), pp. 87–99 who follows Lewis. See also Canale (2008), pp. 109–136 and the definition of the problem in Schauer (2007), pp. 23–26. Schauer calls this difficulty "Wittgenstein's problem" in the interpretation of custom. The reason for this reference to Wittgenstein will be clear in what follows. The fact that both Canale and Schauer discuss the problem when dealing with customs, and not conventions, is explained by the usual ambiguity (see above, Sect. 3) between the two notions.

[36] Sugden (1998), p. 379.

[37] Sugden (1998), pp. 396–397.

[38] Lewis (1969), pp. 37–38. Italics are mine.

certain group—"of 'natural' or 'obvious' *patterns*, which allow the concept of 'repeating successful actions' to make sense *to them*".[39]

This fact—the fortunate fact that, for the most part (there is no guarantee for this to happen, and there is no conceptual necessity involved), certain analogies, and not others, appear obvious to us—is not, therefore, a mere regularity: it is also what fixes the identity of *R*, disambiguating past cases, and thus determining what is the *correct* way to behave.[40] It is, in short, a normative fact.

This claim opens up a large space for the possibility of conventions—not, of course, Lewis-conventions (what we are talking about are precisely the facts that make the existence of a Lewis-convention possible), but *pre*-(Lewis-)conventions.

To realize this, we only need to ask a simple question. What fixes the identity of *R*—disambiguating, thus, past cases–, it is said, is the fact that, for the most part, "we" grasp the same analogies: certain analogies, and not others, appear to "us" as obvious. But who is the "we"? Who does the "us"—or the first person plural—refer to?

Most likely, the fact that "we" happen to notice the same analogies will depend, in many cases, on traits characteristic of human beings in general: "we", as members of the human species (features of the species' cognitive apparatus). In other cases, however, we shall be dealing with local regularities: "we", the members of this or that tribe. (For this to happen, it suffices that the patterns that are recognized as obvious be roughly the same for all members of the group, not necessarily for all human beings.) And this is precisely the space that can be occupied by, more or less arbitrary, agreements (in the generic sense indicated above, Sect. 2), which are neither mere rules nor mere regularities, but which partake of both—they guide action, fixing the *correct* way to proceed: pre-conventions.

Lewis' solution can be reformulated (Lewis himself does so) by resorting to the notion of *salience*.[41] The identity of *R* is fixed by the fact that, luckily (if and when that happens; as it has been said, nothing guarantees that it will happen), the same traits—roughly—appear salient to "us" (who? See above); and this makes it the case that they *are* salient (they are salient precisely because they appear to be so to all of "us").[42] In this way, it is the same analogies—between present and past cases—that strike us. And this allows "us" to understand, here and now, what counts as the precedent to be followed.

The problem of learning and practicing (i.e., the activity of complying with) a Lewis-convention—determining what counts as doing the same thing in the same

---

[39] Sugden (1998), p. 387.

[40] It is worth emphasizing a point that, in light of what I have said so far, should be rather obvious. Here, the question is not whether we should or shouldn't follow *R*, and why (this depends on whether the further conditions specified by a Lewis-type definition are met or not; here, we are assuming that they are). The question is, rather, what counts, each time, as complying with *R*: which action would be following the precedent (doing *the same* thing that we did in the past).

[41] See Schelling (1960) and Sugden (1998), p. 404.

[42] If two individuals take as salient different traits, then neither of them is right (this simply follows from the definition of the relevant concept of salience).

(the same type of) situation—is a special case of the "new" problem (or "riddle") of induction.[43]

The so-called "old" problem of induction was raised by Hume: the possibility of inferring a prediction on the basis of past experience is based on the assumption that, in the future, things will continue to go as they did in the past. What grounds this assumption? It cannot be an empirical thesis—this would simply beg the question—but neither can it be a logical truth, since it is, by definition, contingent.

The "new" problem of induction is this: why, among the infinite traits of past experience that we could project onto future experience, we select some (e.g., "blue", "green"), while we exclude others without much thought (e.g., "bleen")?[44] What—if anything—justifies the fact that predictive inferences in which certain predicates occur appear—more or less—plausible, while inferences in which other predicates occur are useless, even though the latter predicates are equally well formed, and the inferences in which they occur have the same form as the plausible ones?

The answer to this question seems to be the following: it is nothing more than a brute matter of fact that certain traits are projectible while others are not; and, therefore, that—even if formally identical—certain inductive inferences are (more or less) good, while others are worthless.

This is a generalized version, covering the entire field of inductive inferences, of the answer that Lewis gives to the problem of the identity conditions of a conventional regularity of conduct.[45] Some predicates appear salient to "us", and therefore *are* projectible—that is, can *legitimately* be projected. "Projectibility is no more than a kind of salience".[46] What fixes the correct way to build "our" vision of what will probably happen—the right way to proceed in drawing inferences, based on past experience, about future experience (Lewis: following the precedent, "doing the same thing")—is a set of matters of fact: "we" project, or have projected, some traits and not others.

Two observations. (1) This argument, in the same way as Lewis' one, leaves room, opens up space, for the existence of pre-conventions. "We" project some traits and not others; some traits and not others appear salient to "us". Who are "we"? Once again, which traits are salient—and, therefore, which inferences are legitimate—probably depends, in most cases, on features characteristic of human beings in general ("we" as members of the human species: features proper of the human species' cognitive apparatus). In other cases, however, we shall be dealing with local regularities; with, specifically, more or less arbitrary agreements among particular groups of people ("we" the members of this tribe): pre-conventions.

(2) The fact that Lewis' solution—which specifically regards regularities of conduct in recurrent strategic problems that have a certain structure (namely, coordination problems)—applies, in general, to the entire field of inductive inferences,

[43] This is noticed and explained in Sugden (1998), pp. 386–387.

[44] Goodman (1983).

[45] The order is not chronological. Chronologically, Goodman's argument comes first.

[46] Sugden (1998), p. 404.

means that a very large portion of the predicates that we habitually use—i.e., a very significant part of our ("our" must always be understood in light of what has been said above) concepts—are subject to the regimen indicated by Lewis. That is, the identity conditions, and the conditions of use—of understanding and application–, of a very large part of our concepts (those of the objects which are the subject matter of inductive inferences, and their properties), have the same structure as the identity conditions of a regularity of conduct which is a Lewis-convention. In short, our mastery of concepts, or at least a very large and significant proportion of it, has, according to the argument under examination, this structure. And that, *prima facie*, implies a remarkable expansion of the space that could be occupied by pre-conventions. Our conceptual competence—this is the hypothesis—is interwoven (also) with pre-conventions.

With this, however, we have now reached Wittgenstein.

6 Arguments (II): To Follow a Rule

Ludwig Wittgenstein famously asks what it is to follow a rule. The core of Wittgenstein's considerations on this issue appears in §§185–242 of *Philosophical Investigations* (1953). §§198–202 contain the climax of the argument.

These pages have been the subject of fierce exegetical controversy, and this is not the place to take an articulated stand on them.[47] I will present the bare bones of what I believe to be Wittgenstein's main conclusions relating to the matter at hand.

A preliminary point. When he speaks of "following a rule", in these pages, Wittgenstein is actually talking about the use—the understanding and application—of concepts generally. His arguments and conclusions concern the mastery of concepts as such. His main problem is: what are the identity conditions of a concept? That is, under what conditions, when we say (or think) something about something, are we doing the same thing that we have done in the past—attributing, now, to this thing here, the same property that, in the past, we have attributed to other things?

A concept is, therefore, a rule: the problem is that of its *correct* application. (Or, if we got it *right*). The correct use consists of the application of *the same* concept. The question is thus: under which conditions a set of cases of alleged application of the same concept can be said to correspond to a rule—that is, to be constituted by a set of cases which are, in fact, cases of *correct* application of that concept? Under what conditions a number of cases is a regularity i.e., the application of a rule? What fixes the identity of a—potentially infinite—series of cases of correct application of a concept?

And Wittgenstein's answer is: a finite set of cases, which we were shown during our training in the use of that concept—in the case of many concepts, when we were

[47] I follow J. McDowell's interpretation of these passages of Wittgenstein's. See especially McDowell (1979), p. 60 ff, and McDowell (1984), pp. 238–254.

children, often in school—and the practice, "use" (Germ. *Gebrauch*), and "habit" (Germ. *Gepflogenheit*) (§§198, 199) which, living together, we have developed.

Now, it is essential to understand that this concept of "practice", "use" or "habit", designates something very peculiar. Not a rule, of course. It designates a set of facts. But it designates a set of facts that fixes the identity of a rule. A set of facts, that is, which is a regularity—or a set of cases that corresponds to a rule (in the relevant sense here, stated above: a concept)—by virtue of itself: literally, a normative fact.

And this set of facts is produced in the course of the growth and upbringing of a person, thanks to the fact that this person *does* many things together with other people. It is only by living together with others, and doing things with them, that this practice is formed—this is the only way we learn to follow the rule "table", "ice cream", "walk", "+ 2", and so on and so forth. This is what Wittgenstein calls a "form of life". (There is nothing idyllic in sharing a form of life; there is nothing edifying in the fact that the basis of our mastery of—the ability to properly use—concepts is the sharing of a form of life. A form of life may include, to be sure, repugnant or unpleasant things.)

Despite the usual oracular style of the author, two quotations from *On Certainty* clarify what has been said so far:

> 139. Not only rules, but also examples [Germ. *Beispiele*] are needed for establishing a practice [Germ. *Praxis*]. Our rules leave loop-holes [Germ. *Hintertüren*] open, and the practice has to speak for itself [Germ. *für sich selbst sprechen*].[48]

Here, the term "Praxis" means what, above, we called a "practice": a regularity that "speaks for itself", and on which depends the identity of the rule of which it is the application.

> 204. Giving grounds, however, justifying the evidence, comes to an end; –but the end is not certain propositions' striking us immediately as true, i.e. it is not a kind of *seeing* on our part; it is our *acting*, which lies at the bottom of the language-game.[49]

Here, "language game" means, first of all, correctly (well enough, that is) using—understanding and applying—some concepts.

Two predictable observations. (1) In this case as well (above, Sect. 5), "we" ("our", the first person plural) can have both universal and local scope. All, or almost everyone, of the members of the human species may share certain practices, and, thus, certain concepts. (It may be the case that the mastery of concepts is, or certain aspects of the mastery of concepts are, common to all, because, at some level of abstraction—as a function of common biological, psychological or ethological traits–, all human beings share a certain form of life.) Or it may be practices, and therefore concepts, of our tribe: the particular form of life, which is peculiar to a particular group of human beings, not shared by others. The distinction, which in the abstract is neat, can be, in particular cases, nuanced.

(2) The argument opens up a large space for the possibility of pre-conventions. If the ability humans have to identify, understand and apply concepts has this structure,

---

[48] Wittgenstein (1969).

[49] Wittgenstein (1969).

then it is possible that what fixes the identity of some concepts—especially, local concepts—are arbitrary agreements (in the generic sense indicated above, Sect. 2). The use of at least some concepts would be, in the sense which is relevant here, a "second nature".[50]

Starting from Wittgenstein's reflections, quite a natural step is to hypothesize that the concepts in our minds are schematic representations of individuals, which fix the paradigmatic traits of the thing (the thing which they are the concept of). These may be either fictitious individuals which display traits from different experiences ("prototypes"), or real individuals, which constitute the paradigm of that thing for us ("The setter that my aunt had is, for me, *the* dog"; "exemplars"). This is the path that cognitive psychology has in fact taken.[51] The hypothesis is that it is these representations of individual instances that establish what counts as a correct application of the concept to new cases, following the analogies that appear salient to "us" (above, Sect. 5). When we think, we follow precedents. The concept—the rule—is the *ratio decidendi* which is buried in past cases.

7 Arguments (III): The Background of Intentionality

John Searle, following Wittgenstein,[52] elaborates the "thesis of the Background":

> Intentional phenomena such as meanings, understandings, interpretations, beliefs, desires, and experiences only function within a set of Background capacities that are not themselves intentional /…/ all representations, whether in language, thought, or experience, only succeeds in representing given a set of nonrepresentational capacities.[53]

Or, in other terms, "[i]ntentional states function the way they do only given a presupposed set of Background capacities", a "pre-intentional" Background,[54] which consists in a "set of capacities, abilities, tendencies, habits, dispositions, taken-for-granted presuppositions, and "know-how" generally".[55] And the Background of intentionality is a territory, which is inhabited by, among other

[50] On the mastery of concepts (the ability to use them correctly) as a "second nature" see McDowell (1996), pp. 123–124.

[51] Rosch (1973, 1975). Usually, people relate the theory of prototypes to Wittgenstein's idea that the identity conditions and the conditions of the use of concepts, or at least of many concepts, are not sets of necessary and sufficient conditions, but depend on family resemblances. The convergence of this idea and the conclusions stemming from the rule-following argument are apparent.

[52] Searle (1992), p. 177.

[53] Searle (1992), p. 175. Searle puts forward various arguments and considerations in favor of this claim in Searle (1983, ch. 5 and 1992, ch. 8); here, I cannot discuss them.

[54] Searle (1999), p. 109.

[55] Searle (1999), pp. 107–108. On *know-how* in the Background, see Searle (1983, p. 143; 1992, p. 194; and 2010, p. 155). Remember that "know-how" is one of the territories that can host pre-conventions, that I have indicated above, at 4.

things, more or less arbitrary agreements (agreements—in the generic sense indicated above, Sect. 2—that are embodied), or pre-conventions:

> Part of the Background is common to all cultures. For example, we all walk upright and eat by putting food in our mouths. Such universal phenomena I call the "deep Background", but many other Background presuppositions vary from culture to culture. For example, in my culture we eat pigs and cows but not worms and grasshoppers, and we eat at certain times of day and not others. On such matters cultures vary, and I call such features of the Background "local cultural practices."[56]

In *The Construction of Social Reality* (1995) Searle provided an extensive discussion of the Background in relation to social rules (specifically, in relation to the problem of the nature and role of the rules which are constitutive of institutional facts),[57] the topic we are interested in here. Let me report the essentials of Searle's account, with some comments.

Institutional facts and activities, Searle argues, depend for their existence and structure on sets of rules. But what is, in causal terms, the explanatory value of these rules? The problem arises out of three considerations.

(1) Normally, the creation of institutional facts is not the result of a set of conscious and deliberate, intentional acts, but occurs unintentionally.[58]
(2) Even in cases in which the creation of institutional entities takes place, originally, by means of a complex of conscious, deliberate, intentional acts directed at this purpose (such as, e.g., in the case of the entity "President of the Italian Republic"), "the subsequent use of the entities in question need not contain the intentionality" by virtue of which they were originally created.[59]
(3) The rules of an institution, for the most part, are not coded. Even when they are, "most of us are unaware of these codifications". And finally, even if we are aware, "the codifications are not self-interpreting. We have to know how to interpret or apply the codified rules"[60] (this is a special case of the initial move in Wittgenstein's argument, above, Sect. 6: it cannot be a rule, of course, that satisfies this need, as this would produce an infinite regress).

These considerations allow Searle to conclude that, even though the logical structure of institutions is made out of (systems of) rules, those who participate in institutional activities, usually, do not follow these rules, either consciously or

[56] Searle (1999, p. 109). See also Searle (1983, pp. 143–144; and 1992, p. 194). In Searle (2010, pp. 155–160), Searle shows that within the Background (but the notion is used here in a wider sense than in the text) one can find elements, which may vary from one community to the other, that impose "normative constraints", or that in general establish the way in which, in situations of a certain kind, people "should" behave.

[57] For a critical presentation of Searle's theory on institutional facts, see Celano (1997).

[58] Searle (1995), pp. 125–126.

[59] Searle (1995), p. 126.

[60] Searle (1995), p. 128, and pp. 142–143.

unconsciously.[61] Rules, moreover, are not by themselves sufficient to determine what counts as participation in a given institutional activity.[62]

But, given this conclusion, what causal role can be attributed to the rules of an institution in the explanation of the actual behavior of the participants to the institutional activity? It is in order to answer this question that Searle introduces, here, the notion of the Background.

According to Searle, as we know, intentional states only work against a Background of unintentional skills, dispositions, tendencies, whose work is a particular form of "neuropsychological causation".[63] This is true, Searle claims, also in the case of the participation in institutional activities. Participants develop tendencies, dispositions, skills that, while not intentional, are "sensitive to specific structures of intentionality"; e.g., to systems of rules. In the case of institutional activities, these skills, dispositions, tendencies are "functionally equivalent" to the systems of constitutive rules of the institutions in question, while not containing any representation of them.[64]

This is the crucial step. Here, once again, entities intermediate between rules and regularities, embodied norms (or, if you will, the pineal gland), emerge. Tendencies, dispositions, skills that are in the Background are not intentional in character: they are bodily elements. At the same time, however, they are "sensitive to /.../ structures of intentionality", such as the constitutive rules of an institutional activity; they are "functionally equivalent" to them—which can only mean that they guide conduct, fixing the distinction between *correct* and *incorrect* behavior (i.e., they perform the role of norms).

Thus, Searle concludes,[65] rather than saying, about the participants in an institutional activity, that e.g. "Tom acts so and so because he is following the rules of the institution", we should usually say: "Tom behaves so and so because he has a structure that predisposes him to behave in this way", and "Tom is predisposed to behave in this way because this is the way that *conforms* with the rules of the institution" (the term in italics indicates that what is at issue, here, is not a mere *de facto* regularity: the relevant bodily structure is "functionally equivalent" to the rule: it fixes what counts as *correct* behavior). In an explanation of this kind, the idea of a Background of unintentional skills, tendencies, and dispositions, makes it possible to account, in causal terms, for the explanatory value of the rules of an institution, even when we assume that the participants in the institution are not following rules (either consciously, or unconsciously).[66] *The body takes over.*

---

[61] If we restrict our view to a naïve, pre-Wittgensteinian, picture of what it is to follow a rule, of course.

[62] Searle (1995), pp. 127–128 and p. 137.

[63] Searle (1995), p. 129.

[64] Searle (1995), pp. 141–142.

[65] Searle (1995), p. 144.

[66] In this paragraph too, "rule-following" should be understood in a naïve, pre-Wittgensteinian, way. As we have seen, Searle's argument is aimed precisely at demonstrating that rule-following in fact requires, just as Wittgenstein himself claimed (*supra*, 6), "practice", "habits" (among these, possibly, the entities that I called "pre-conventions"); that is, it requires sharing a "form of life".

8 Conclusion: Nature and Convention

I conclude with some general remarks. These will be somewhat imprecise and not very strict considerations, because I will make intuitive use of the concept of nature, without specifying its content; and, of course, "nature" is a term that has multiple meanings, and so we should distinguish.[67] My only aim in this section is to make explicit the connections between the ideas presented so far—in particular, the claim that there are pre-conventions—and some habitual moves in philosophical conversation.

The antithesis "nature" *v.* "convention" is one of the topoi of Western philosophy, beginning with the Sophists. (The antithesis "nature" *v.* "culture" is its modern guise. The two antitheses do not overlap perfectly, but it is not important here to try and single out the differences.) Whether a certain thing—language, justice, the political community, logic or arithmetic, and so on—is what it is either "by nature" (*physei*) or "by convention" (*nomo, kata syntheken*) is one of the typical questions in Western philosophical inquiries. Conflicting traditions (e.g., at least according to some simplistic characterizations, natural law and legal positivism in legal theory, or the Aristotelian tradition and the modern one in political theory) are identified according to which of the alternatives they favor.

The antithesis is, however, a bit too naive. Not because there is nothing that is unmistakably so by nature (fire burns) or unmistakably so by convention (the fact that the yellow traffic light has a certain meaning; art. 138 of the Italian Constitution; the Treaty of Maastricht). But because the two terms are not mutually exclusive: there are phenomena of great importance for human life which do not fall exclusively in one or the other category, while participating in both.

The entities I have called pre-conventions—embodied conventions that have become "second nature"—are of this kind. If and when we glimpse at them, against the background of the things which we habitually direct our attention to, we land behind the scenes of the antithesis "nature" *v.* "convention" (or "nature" *v.* "culture").

I did not argue, and it does not seem likely at all to me, that pre-conventions are the only inhabitants of this territory. This is why I said that the arguments which I reviewed "leave room", or "open up space", for pre-conventions. The geography of this area, beyond the naive antithesis, is certainly very complex and varied. Pre-conventions are but a fragment of the Background. But it is here that we may find the conditions allowing us to frame one phenomenon as purely natural, or purely conventional (or cultural).

---

[67] Aristotle (1980, 1957), V, 4.

References

Aristotle (1980, 1957) Metaphysica. In: Jaeger W (ed) 2nd edn. Clarendon Press, Oxford
Bourdieu P (1977) Outline of a theory of practice. Cambridge University Press, Cambridge
Bourdieu P (1979) La distinction. Critique sociale du jugement. Engl. transl. Distinction. A Social Critique of the Judgment of Taste (1984). Harvard University Press, Cambridge
Canale D (2008) Paradossi della consuetudine giuridica. In: Zorzetto S (ed) La consuetudine giuridica. Teoria, storia, ambiti disciplinari. ETS, Pisa, pp 109–136
Casey E (1998) The ghost of embodiment: on bodily habitudes and schemata. In: Welton D (ed) Body and flesh. A philosophical reader. Blackwell, Oxford, pp 207–225
Celano B (1994) Dialettica della giustificazione pratica. Saggio sulla Legge di Hume. Giappichelli, Torino
Celano B (1995) Consuetudini, convenzioni. In: Comanducci P, Guastini R (eds) Analisi e diritto. Ricerche di giurisprudenza analitica. Giappichelli, Torino, pp 35–87. Now also in Celano (2010), pp 173–231
Celano B (1997) Fatti istituzionali: la teoria di J.R. Searle. In: Comanducci P, Guastini R (eds) Analisi e diritto. Ricerche di giurisprudenza analitica. Giappichelli, Torino, pp 19–54. Now also in Celano B (2010) Fatti istituzionali, consuetudini, convenzioni. Aracne, Roma, pp 15–61
Celano B (2014) Consuetudine: un'analisi concettuale. Diritto & questioni pubbliche 14:597–667
Fantl J (2012) Knowledge how. In: Zalta EN (ed) The Stanford Encyclopedia of Philosophy. URL = http://plato.stanford.edu/archives/win2012/entries/knowledge-how/
Foucault M (2002) (1975): Surveiller et punir. Naissance de la prison. Gallimard, Paris
Gauthier D (1979) David Hume, Contractarian. Philos Rev 88:3–38
Goodman N (1983) Fact, fiction, and forecast, 4th edn. Harvard University Press, Cambridge
Hume D (1976) (1740) A treatise of human nature. In: Selby-Brigge LA (ed) 3rd edn. Rev. by Nidditch P H. Clarendon Press, Oxford
Hume D (1975) (1777) Enquiries concerning human understanding and concerning the principles of morals. In: Selby-Brigge LA (ed) 3rd edn. Rev. by Nidditch P H. Clarendon Press, Oxford
Kahneman D (2011) Thinking, fast and slow. Penguin, London
Lewis D (1969) Convention. A philosophical study. Blackwell, Oxford
Lycan W (1986) Tacit belief. In: Bogdan R (ed) Belief, form, content, and function. Clarendon Press, Oxford, pp 61–82
Marmor A (2009) Social conventions. From language to law. Princeton University Press, Princeton
McDowell J (1979) Virtue and reason. The Monist 62(3):331–350. In: McDowell J (1998) Mind, value, and reality. Harvard University Press, Cambridge, pp 50–75
McDowell J (1984) Wittgenstein on following a rule. Synthese 58(3):325–363. In: McDowell J (1998) Mind, value, and reality. Harvard University Press, Cambridge, pp 221–262
McDowell J (1996) Mind and world, 2nd edn. Harvard University Press, Cambridge
Millikan R (2008) A difference of some consequence between conventions and rules. Topoi 27:87–99
Murphy JB (2007) Habit and convention at the foundation of custom. In: Perreau-Saussine A, Murphy JB (eds) (2007) The nature of customary law: Philosophical, historical and legal perspectives. Cambridge University Press, Cambridge, pp 53–78
Rosch E (1973) Natural categories. Cogn Psychol 4:328–350
Rosch E (1975) Cognitive representation of semantic categories. J Exp Psychol 104(3):192–233
Ryle G (1949) The concept of mind. The University of Chicago Press, Chicago
Schauer F (2007) Pitfalls in the interpretation of customary law. In: Perreau-Saussine A, Murphy JB (eds) (2007) The nature of customary law: philosophical, historical and legal perspectives. Cambridge University Press, Cambridge, pp 13–34
Schelling T (1960) The strategy of conflict, 2nd edn. Harvard University Press, Cambridge
Searle J (1983) Intentionality. An essay in the philosophy of mind. Cambridge University Press, Cambridge
Searle J (1992) The rediscovery of the mind. The MIT Press, Cambridge

Searle J (1995) The construction of social reality. Penguin, Harmondsworth
Searle J (1999) Mind, language and society. Philosophy in the real world. Phoenix, London
Searle J (2010) Making the social world. The structure of human civilization. Oxford University Press, Oxford
Sugden R (1998) The role of inductive reasoning in the evolution of conventions. Law Philos 17:377–410
Wallis C (2008) Consciousness, context, and know-how. Synthese 160:123–153
Wittgenstein L (1953) Philosophische Untersuchungen. Re-published in: Tractatus logico-philosophicus. Tagebücher 1914–1916. Philosophische Untersuchungen (1984). Suhrkamp, Frankfurt am Main. English transl. by Anscombe G E M; Hacker P M S and Schulte J. Philosophical Investigations. Rev. 4th edn. (2009). Wiley-Blackwell, Oxford
Wittgenstein L (1969) Über Gewiβheit. In: Anscombe GEM, von Wright GH (eds) Suhrkamp, Frankfurt am Main. English transl. On certainty. Basil Blackwell, Oxford

Re-examining Deep Conventions: Practical Reason and Forward-Looking Agency

Verónica Rodríguez-Blanco

Abstract According to Rodríguez-Blanco, there are many key distinctions that play an important role in mapping out plausible ways of thinking about law construed as a social practice. Among the varied dichotomies the one that has probably been most influential is the distinction between a description of an action and the normative characterisation of an action. The former aims to explain the action without resorting to the values or principles of the agent; the latter aims to show how actions are part of the normative landscape where values, principles and other normative standards play a key role. The focus might be on the values, principles and standards of the agent or on values, principles and standards that are objective. In previous work, Rodríguez-Blanco has defended the view that the primary conception of intentional action is normative all the way through. There is no "brute fact" or "pure facts" about actions and therefore actions cannot primarily be grasped by descriptors of the world either mental, physical or of a similar sort. She has argued that in order to make intentional actions intelligible we need to resort to the values or principles or good-making characteristics that the agent aims to bring about in the world and we need to understand that the values, principles or good-making characteristics of the action provide a unity and intelligibility to the various bodily movements of the agent. This is a complex and occasionally difficult understanding of agency but it is one that, in her view, is sound. The core elements of this account of agency are that (a) there is a parallel between practical reason or deliberative reasoning and intentional action; (b) practical reasoning involves practical knowledge which is non-observational; (c) the error of an action stems not from what the world looks like but from the performance of the agent; and (d) intentional action is primarily from the first person or deliberative point of view and therefore it is forward-looking. In this paper, Rodríguez-Blanco focuses only on (d) and argues that this feature provides the key premise for the conclusion that a characterisation of actions in social practices, including law, cannot be carried out on the basis of descriptions. She first shows that (d) is true and she then advances the best account of actions in terms of descriptions provided by legal philosophers in recent years, which is the

V. Rodríguez-Blanco (✉)
University of Surrey, Centre for Law and Philosophy, Guildford, UK
e-mail: v.rodriguez-blanco@surrey.ac.uk

L. Ramírez-Ludeña, J. M. Vilajosana (eds.), *Legal Conventionalism*, Law and Philosophy Library 126, https://doi.org/10.1007/978-3-030-03571-6_3

idea that actions and the resulting social practices can correctly be grasped as "deep conventions". Finally, Rodríguez-Blanco shows that conventions sensu stricto and deep conventions require (d) to be intelligible.

1 Introduction

There are many key distinctions that play an important role in mapping out plausible ways of thinking about law construed as a social practice. Among the varied dichotomies the one that has probably been most influential is the distinction between a description of an action and the normative characterization of an action. The former aims to explain the action without resorting to the values or principles of the agent; the latter aims to show how actions are part of the normative landscape where values, principles and other normative standards play a key role. The focus might be on the values, principles and standards of the agent or on values, principles and standards that are objective.[1] In previous work[2] I have defended the view that the primary conception of intentional action is normative all the way through. There is no "brute fact" or "pure facts" about actions and therefore actions cannot primarily be grasped by descriptors of the world either mental, physical or of a similar sort. I have argued that in order to make intentional actions intelligible we need to resort to the values or principles or good-making characteristics that the agent aims to bring about in the world and we need to understand that the values, principles or good-making characteristics of the action provide a unity and intelligibility to the various bodily movements of the agent. This is a complex and occasionally difficult understanding of agency but it is one that, in my view, is sound. The core elements of this account of agency are that (a) there is a parallel between practical reason or deliberative reasoning and intentional action; (b) practical reasoning involves practical knowledge which is non-observational; (c) the error of an action stems not from what the world looks like but from the performance of the agent; and (d) intentional action is primarily from the first person or deliberative point of view and therefore it is forward-looking.

I will not provide a full defence of features (a), (b) or (c) in this chapter; rather I will focus only on (d) and will argue that this feature provides the key premise for the conclusion that a characterization of actions in social practices, including law, cannot be carried out on the basis of descriptions. I will first show that (d) is true and I will then advance the best account of actions in terms of descriptions provided by legal philosophers in recent years, which is the idea that actions and the resulting social practices can correctly be grasped as "deep conventions". Finally, I will show that conventions *sensu stricto* and deep conventions require (d) to be intelligible.

---

[1] I am referring here to all the possible kinds of objectivity.

[2] See Rodriguez-Blanco (2014).

2 Intentional Action Is Primarily Forward-Looking

Imagine the following two examples:

Neighbour
You see your neighbour coming out of the supermarket and a few minutes later you see his well-known enemy (Mr Enemy) driving his vehicle and running into him. Your neighbour is killed.

Omelette
You are a cook and instruct a group of people who are attending your cooking workshop on how to make a good omelette.

In **neighbour** you can provide a description of the action in terms of mental states, i.e. the beliefs/desire pair that cause the bodily movements. The effect of this is to rationalise the action and make its description intelligible. You can, thus, say that Mr Enemy had the desire to kill his enemy *and* the belief that driving his vehicle over him would kill him.

Neighbour is a description of the action as a mental event and a consequential effect, which includes the bodily movements of Mr Enemy, e.g. his pressing the pedal, controlling the wheel, and the *further* effect of killing the neighbour. However, this account faces the difficulty encountered by some counterexamples which is that there is no connection between the mental state and the bodily movements. In other words, the agent has the appropriate mental state and the *further* effect has been obtained, nevertheless there is no intentional action. The description fails as a correct description of the action. Let us imagine the following alternative scenario:

Swerving the Wheel
You see your neighbour coming out of the supermarket and few minutes later you see his well-known enemy (Mr Enemy) driving his vehicle and running into him. Your neighbour is killed.

Swerving the wheel is exactly like **neighbour** but there is one key difference. What really happens is that Mr Enemy has the relevant beliefs and desires, i.e. the desire to kill your neighbour and he believes that driving his vehicle into him will enable him to kill him, but he suffers an involuntary spasm that makes him swerve the vehicle towards your neighbour and kill him non-intentionally. All the elements of an intentional action as mental events are present, i.e. the relevant desire and belief, nevertheless there is no intentional action. Consequently, the model of belief/

desire as a mental event causing the action does not really explain the action in **swerving the wheel**. The key problem is that the model cannot ensure the causal connection between the mental event and the *further* effect.[3]

In **omelette** the cook is not telling the participants his beliefs and desires so that they can act upon them. It would be absurd and unintelligible if he were to say, "I desire to instruct you to make an omelette because I can charge a fee for this and I believe that giving you these instructions will enable you to make an omelette and pay me a fee". What about if the desire/belief pair is present in every single instruction on how to make an omelette? In the example, the cook would have to say, "I desire the eggs to be stirred and I believe that putting them in this bowl and moving the fork in this way will enable the eggs to be stirred". The participants will probably look perplexed. It does not say anything about *how to make an omelette*. Worse, it does not say anything about the next steps in the omelette making process or about the *know how* required to follow these steps. It would presuppose an absurd sequence of randomly connected mental states (the pair belief/desire). There would be no answer to the questions, "Why should we *not* put the stirred eggs in the frying pan prior to the butter? Why shouldn't we begin the process with putting the frying pan on the heat, then taking the fork and stirring the eggs, then washing the frying pan, and finally pouring the eggs on the wet and unoiled frying pan?".

By contrast, in order to ensure success in his instructions the cook needs to tell the participants the chain of reasons that are required to correctly perform the action, i.e. the making of the omelette. His "know how" to make an omelette entails knowing the answers to the "Why?" questions involved in making an omelette, i.e. knowing why it is necessary to stir the eggs; knowing why there needs to be a knob of butter in the pan; knowing why the pan needs to be hot before you pour in the stirred eggs, and so on. He also needs to know "why" people make omelettes and the good-making characteristics of omelettes, i.e. that they are nutritious, delicious, and a quick and easy meal to make, etc. The cook presents the chain of reasons but the final end that unifies the series of actions is advanced by the agent who actually performs the action. It might be that the answer to the question "why?" is obvious in many circumstances due to the internal rationality of the activity or social practice, but perhaps in other circumstances it is required in order to explain "why" certain actions should follow others. The final end of "why" the participant aims to learn to make omelettes can be various, e.g. for nutritional reasons, for reasons of practicality or expense, but this final end provides unity to the action *when* the participant executes the set of actions in order to make an omelette. Let us imagine that the participant goes home and starts to make an omelette as instructed; he will "know how" because he knows "why" certain actions follow other actions. In response to the final question "Why are you making an omelette?" he might reply in

[3]This is called in the literature the deviant causation problem (see Chisholm 1976). Surprisingly, there are some philosophers who assert that this is a problem for every theory of action (see Enoch 2011a and also Enoch 2011b), p. 1. It is not a problem for accounts of action that do not rely on mental events. Furthermore, my diagnosis shows that something else is happening and that the idea that we can provide a pure description of actions is mistaken.

different ways, but always providing the end as a good-making characteristic, e.g. "because it is practical and easy", "because it is nutritious", "because it is delicious". If he responds "I do not know" we will probably suspect that his action is not intentional. I am not asserting that he constantly reminds himself of "why" he is making an omelette, but if the action is intentional he certainly knows "why" he is making it. In order to succeed in his action he is *only* looking forward; thinking about the next step in the series of actions and "knowing how" to make it and "why" there is a series of actions x, y and z.

The diagnosis of **swerving the wheel** is that action is conceived in its secondary conception, namely as a description of events, i.e. mental states, bodily movements and further effects that happen in the world. But the primary conception of an action is the model of **omelette**. If we ask Mr Enemy "why" he deliberately moved the wheel in the direction of your neighbour, he will respond that "he did not" and then understand that his action was not intentional.

The difficulty is that any correct description of an action and therefore of social practices must grasp the model of **omelette**. In other words, it needs to grasp the deliberative mode of the agent and this is only possible if we begin and finish with the answers to the question "Why?". The correct interpretation is not that we "effectively" ask the agent "why" he did this and not that. It is rather that it is implicit because we ourselves are "knowers" of the "know how" of the practice and tap into the good-making characteristics, values and principles of the intentional actions and resultant practices. We are all practical reasoners, we have acquired know how and exercise this capacity. Therefore we can perceive this capacity in others.[4]

3 A Criticism of Deep Conventions: Deep Conventions Are Always Forward-Looking and Therefore Presuppose Practical Reason

From this feature of forward-looking many paradoxes arise and the most significant one is that the responsibility for and evaluation of an action is backward-looking. Therefore, when making judgments about responsibility we cannot grasp the forward-looking feature if we are located in the backward-looking perspective. One solution to understanding how the forward-looking perspective can be grasped from the backward-looking view is to focus on capacities and how they work. Unfortunately, this piece of work is beyond the remit of this chapter. Another puzzling matter is the related intuition that collective social practices, such as rule-following, are better explained by conventions and not necessarily by the forward-looking approach. Furthermore, recent legal philosophers, for example

[4]This point requires a deeper analysis of perception and practical knowledge. This is, however, an under-researched area. The Aristotelian notion of "perception" is widely explored in ancient philosophy of history, but its connection to practical knowledge is almost absent in the secondary literature.

Andrei Marmor, have introduced the idea of deep conventions to show that descriptions can have a normativity, i.e. a force that is imposed on the subjects. The resulting thesis is what I will call the "Eliminatist Strategy", which can be formulated as follows:

Eliminatist Strategy *If* collective rule-following can be explained by deep conventions, then an explanation of rule-following exemplified by the model of **omelette** (i.e. the forward-looking approach,) can be **ruled out**.

The Eliminatist Strategy is puzzling, however, since it presupposes that there are *two different kinds* of practical rationality, one that determines "what we do when we act with others" and another that determines "what we do when we act individually".

The Eliminatist Strategy unjustifiably multiples rationalities. Why should there be two different practical rationalities, namely one when I act collectively and one when I act individually? I will attempt to challenge the Eliminatist Strategy by showing that *nothing* seems to justify two different kinds of practical rationality. I will show that deep conventions and conventions in general are only intelligible because "when we act with others" we are actually acting primarily under the model of **omelette** (the forward-looking approach). Therefore, there is no distinction in terms of our practical reasoning between "what we do when we act with others" and "what we do when we act individually". Let us first analyse the idea of deep conventions and conventions in general.

Marmor identifies three key features of what he calls "conventionality" (**conv**). They are:

(1) **Sociability**: conventions are social rules. This means that there is a group of people that normally follow a rule R in circumstances C.[5]
(2) **Rationality**: there is a primary reason "a" for members to follow the rule R in specific circumstances or members of the community P widely believe that there is such a reason.
(3) **Arbitrariness**: there is at least one potential rule S that if members of P had followed it in the specific circumstances, then reason "a" would have been a sufficient reason for members of P to follow S instead of R. Additionally, one cannot comply with rules S and R at the same time.

Concerning the requirement of Rationality, Marmor asserts that reasons are facts that count in favour of the action and that therefore reasons track values or good-making characteristics.[6] However, Marmor asserts that, "it is not part of this condition of conventionality that members of P must be aware of the reason, A, to follow R or, indeed, that they are aware of the fact that there is any such reason". This is puzzling since we follow the rules because of reasons and it is therefore mysterious how this reason can remain *opaque* to us. On this account there is no connection

[5] See Marmor (2007), pp. 586–610.

[6] Marmor (2007), p. 588.

between the reason for the action and the agent who moves his body and performs certain actions *because of a reason*.

According to Marmor, Arbitrariness is not fulfilled and therefore the rule is not a convention if a rule does not have an alternative rule that could have been followed without a significant loss of the purpose or function of the rule.

Marmor tells us that deep conventions (**deep-conv**) require conventionality (**conv**) plus five further conditions which are:

(1) **Social and psychological responsiveness**: deep conventions emerge as responses to basic social and psychological needs.
(2) **Instantiation**: deep conventions emerge as a result of surface conventions. This entails a practice and a "know how".
(3) **Practice through instantiation**: deep conventions are practised through instantiation in surface conventions.
(4) **Durable**: when comparing surface and deep conventions the latter are more durable and less amenable to change.
(5) **Resist codification**: deep conventions typically resist codification.

Marmor's typical example of deep conventions are games. For example, the game of chess is constituted by rules but these rules are performed under a shared normative background of deep conventions, "determining the concept of games and the essential point of engaging in such a practice".[7] Games of chess are a particular instantiation of the activity we call "playing a competitive game".

Marmor tells us that there is a difference between ethical and moral rules and **deep-conv**. Some features might overlap between these two different kinds of rules, but they remain different. In this section of the chapter I will challenge Marmor's demarcation between **deep-conv** and ethical and moral rules and show that this demarcation is problematic.

Let us begin with the ethical rule of "being respectful towards friends". It requires a "know how". It is not sufficient to "believe" that if I do not gossip and speak inappropriately about a friend then I have acted respectfully towards that friend. It is also necessary to act accordingly and this action should be performed with prudence and wisdom considering the circumstances of the occasion. This means that in order to be respectful to a friend I need to engage in a practice that becomes actual through a set of superficial conventions; for example, remaining silent when a friend feels embarrassed. Thus, the ethical rule of "being respectful towards friends" determines the practice of the superficial convention of "remaining in silence when a friend suffers an embarrassing moment". In this way the conditions of Instantiation and Practice Through Instantiation are fulfilled in the example. The ethical rule of being respectful towards friends is, arguably, a Response to Social and Psychological Needs, i.e. the establishment and ensuring of permanent bonds with other human beings. Finally, we could assert that the rule of "being respectful towards friends" is Durable and not susceptible to Codification.

[7] Marmor (2007), p. 594.

Let us think about another example, in this case the moral rule of "treating others with dignity". The rule is not a mere belief but entails the practice of and engagement with the "know how" of the content of the moral rule, e.g. acting in a non-discriminatory way. Such behaviour requires a special appreciation of the circumstances of the case and involves treating others with consideration, kindness and humanity. The action or set of actions require "knowing how" to be considerate and kind. This moral rule is also instantiated through superficial conventions, e.g. treating others with courtesy and acting appropriately according to the occasion. The moral rule determines the content of the superficial conventions. Similarly, one could also assert that the moral rule of treating others with dignity is a response to social and psychological needs, for example, evolutionary theories of morality aim to show that moral rules have emerged as a response to our psychological and social make-ups. Finally, one could also assert that this moral rule is not susceptible to being codified but remains more or less unchanged.

The argument that I have outlined above will be called the "no-differentiation argument". It shows that there seems to be no clear demarcation between **deep-conv** and ethical and moral rules. How then shall we proceed to undermine "the no-differentiation argument" and to show that there is a distinction between **deep-conv** and ethical and moral rules? How can we carve the space that Marmor is so eager to make for **deep-conv**? Arguably, the key feature that would enable us to distinguish **deep-conv** and moral or ethical rules is Arbitrariness. Thus, as stated above, a rule is arbitrary if there is a potential alternative rule that fulfils the same purpose or function as the original rule and participants follow the rule for the same reason "a". Let us examine whether Arbitrariness can undermine the "no-differentiation argument".

One hurdle that needs to be overcome in order to show that Arbitrariness is the key feature that differentiates between **deep-conv** and moral and ethical rules is that Arbitrariness is fulfilled by both deep and superficial conventions. Deep conventions are, however, also conventions *sensu stricto* and therefore they need to fulfil the set of characteristics for conventions (it is an abuse of the language to call them "conventions" otherwise). Furthermore, deep conventions only become intelligible when they come to the surface through conventions *sensu stricto*. Therefore, Arbitrariness will not enable us to distinguish between **deep-conv** and mere conventions. But perhaps Arbitrariness does enable us to distinguish between general conventions and ethical and moral rules. Let us explore this point by supposing the following example:

Friendship
Amanda has just discovered that the boyfriend of her best friend Sophia has been unfaithful on many occasions. Sofia knows nothing about the infidelities of her boyfriend. Amanda knows well how Sophia has sacrificed her career, friends and family to be with her boyfriend. Sophia rings Amanda to tell her that her boyfriend has proposed to her, that she has said "yes" and that they both want to start a family straight after the wedding. Amanda always aims to "be respectful towards her friends".

How should we understand this ethical rule in this context? It is not like the rules of chess which are clear and transparent to the players. In **friendship** Amanda must choose between keeping her silence regarding the infidelity of Sophia's boyfriend or have the courage to tell Sophia the truth. The purpose of the rule "being respectful towards friends" is to cultivate bonds of deep friendship where honesty, dignity, mutual respect and concern for the friend's interests are the predominant virtues. The purpose of the rule might be fulfilled with either the action of having the courage to tell Sophia the truth or the action of keeping quiet regarding the infidelities of her boyfriend. As pointed out by both Lewis[8] and Marmor, Arbitrariness does not require indifference, it only requires that there is an alternative rule or action whose reason for following it also applies to the original rule and there is no significant loss if the agent decides to act according to the alternative rule. Therefore, as the example shows, Arbitrariness is equally fulfilled in ethical rules.

Marmor advances the example of a moral rule such as "you should not kill" in order to show that there is a genuine distinction between conventions and moral rules. There is, Marmor tells us, no Arbitrariness in moral prohibitions and therefore moral rules are different from conventions. However, I argue that in the case of all prohibitions, there is no Arbitrariness and this is so because you have *been* asked not to act therefore there cannot be an arbitrary alternative action or rule-following. For example, let us imagine that the rules of chess were formulated as prohibitions, e.g. "You must not move the knight diagonally" or "You must not move the castle diagonally". If this is the case, of course, there is no alternative rule that satisfies Arbitrariness. The purpose of the prohibitions is to ensure that only one piece, i.e. the bishop, moves diagonally. It is, therefore, the structure of "prohibition" in all respects that determines that there are no arbitrary alternative rules rather than a substantive distinction between moral rules and conventional rules.

One might raise the following objections to my proposal.

(1) One could object that in **friendship** there is only one rule and there are no alternative rules. The rule is "one always ought to act with respect towards friends". Truly, one can say that there is no alternative rule, for example "one ought to treat friends with contempt". The objector could argue that this is precisely what distinguishes conventions and ethical rules. Therefore, the condition of Arbitrariness is not fulfilled in **friendship** and this condition enables us to draw the demarcation between conventions and ethical rules. However, one could argue that it is almost impossible to imagine ethical and legal rules with such a degree of concreteness as in, for example, the game of chess. Consequently, it is the feature of "concreteness" that makes the illusion or appearance of Arbitrariness. If we reach a certain level of concreteness for ethical rules we see that Arbitrariness is also fulfilled for ethical rules. Thus, for example, and following Marmor's view, in chess the rule that "the bishop should move diagonally" could find an arbitrarily alternative rule such as "the bishop should only move vertically". The primary reason to follow the rules is because the "game is entertaining", and this reason applies equally to the original and alternative rule. Nevertheless, the level of concreteness is such that Arbitrariness

[8] Lewis (1969).

is fulfilled *trivially*. In the case of ethical rules we can also create this level of concreteness, for example in **friendship**, and thereby show that Arbitrariness is fulfilled *trivially*. Let us suppose that in **friendship** Amanda adopts the rule "I ought to tell Sophia the truth by phone". The primary reason to follow the rule is "to cultivate honest relationships". One could create the following alternative rule: "Amanda ought to tell Sophia everything by letter". Arbitrariness is fulfilled in both rules since the primary reason, which is to cultivate honest relationships, applies to both rules. Therefore, we must conclude that what determines whether Arbitrariness is fulfilled or not is the level of concreteness rather than an intrinsic or substantive difference between ethical and conventional rules.

(2) One could also object that morality and ethics are not a matter of rules but rather of principles, which require interpretation. **Friendship** explores whether Arbitrariness could distinguish between conventional and non-conventional rules, but **friendship** is really about principles.

But this is not an objection to our proposal. Marmor's view relies on the mistaken assumption that one can reduce moral or ethical actions to moral or ethical rules and then in a second argumentative strategy he aims to show that there is a distinction between conventional, and ethical and moral rules. One could assert that this presents morality in a distorted way since in morality we are dealing with principles whose scope is widely interpreted and the sound interpretation gets us closer to the required action according to the circumstances of the case.

4 An Alternative Diagnosis

Is there any way to save the distinction between conventional and non-conventional rules?

Marmor has ignored what has traditionally been the key feature that enables us to distinguish between conventional and non-conventional rules. The distinction is often grounded in the idea that one follows the rule because others do so. This is called a "conventional reason" (**conv-rea**). However, **conv-rea** clearly contradicts Marmor's condition of Rationality established in the characterisation of "conventionality". If **conv-rea** operates then one could assert that there is no primary reason to follow the rule independently of the fact that others are following the rule.

It seems, however, that **conv-rea** is the key condition to draw a demarcation between conventional and non-conventional rules. On the other hand, **conv-rea** does not apply to the example of chess which, intuitively, is the best example that illustrates conventional rules. Let us imagine a dialogue between a chess player and an observer of the game of chess:

Observer:	Why do you move the knight in this way?
Player:	In order to block the king from moving.
Observer:	Why do you want to block the king from moving?
Player:	In order to put him in checkmate.

Observer: Why do you want to put the king in checkmate?
Player: In order to win.
Observer: Why do you want to win?
Player: To entertain myself.

It would be absurd to think that the player will say that he follows the rules of chess, e.g. moving the bishop diagonally to put the king in checkmate, because others do the same. Marmor himself admits that the primary reason for the player to play chess is because "it is entertaining".[9]

Marmor introduces another example of conventions, i.e. the artistic genre. He asserts that medieval Christian art searched for a representation of God in order for the faithful to know the Holy Scriptures and be close to the divine. In Islamic art, Marmor tells us, we find more or less the same end of art. However, in Islamic art, the artist does not represent figuratively but rather advances an abstract representation. According to Marmor, the representation is arbitrary since the end is fulfilled in both instances. However, if **conv-rea** is applied then the primary reason for an artist at the time to engage in either medieval Christian art or Islamic art cannot be "to know the Holy Scripture and be close to the divine". It should be, rather, that the members of the group follow the convention. Let us imagine the following dialogue between the artist El Greco and a spectator of the painter's work:

Spectator: Why are you painting Christ crucified?
Greco: In order to represent the sacrifice of Jesus.
Spectator: Why do you want to represent the sacrifice of Jesus?
Greco: Because all artists do so.

But this latter answer seems absurd and unintelligible: it does not throw any credible light on the actions of El Greco. Let us imagine that the dialogue continues as follows:

Spectator: Why are you doing what other artists are doing, namely representing the sacrifice of Jesus?
Greco: Because this is the best way to know God.
Spectator: Why do you aim to know God?

It would be absurd to assert that El Greco would return to a similar reasoning as **conv-rea**, namely "because everyone does". It is therefore necessary to introduce a primary reason to make intelligible the action of the artist. We should, therefore, conclude that there is something suspicious about the idea of conventions as standing independently of the reasons for actions that we have in certain circumstances.

[9] Marmor (2007), p. 594.

5 Conclusion: Forward-Looking and Primary Reasons for Actions

In the previous sections I have argued that forward-looking reasoning (see **omelette**) is the primary model of practical reasoning. Considering that law is a social practice and presupposing that social practices are somehow composed of intentional actions, then forward-looking reasoning should be the primary model to understand key aspects of law. The idea of "conventions" and especially deep conventions as advanced by Marmor are the most notable candidates to provide normative depth to descriptions of social practices like law. However, in this chapter I have shown that a clear demarcation between conventional and non-conventional rules is lacking or, at least, I have shown that this distinction is more problematic than is currently thought. I have indirectly argued that ethical, moral and conventional rules presuppose the **omelette** model of practical reasoning, i.e. a first person or deliberative stance that is forward-looking to be intelligible. The common thread between all kinds of rule-following is the capacity to engage from the first-person perspective which entails a forward-looking dimension and consequently conventional rules do not stand outside the phenomenology of the forward-looking perspective. Therefore, we have shown that the Eliminatist Strategy cannot stand scrutiny.

Hume published *An Enquiry Concerning Human Understanding* in 1748 and since then the idea of conventions has become prominent in Western philosophy; however, its precise characterisation is elusive. Contemporary philosophers like David Lewis and Andrei Marmor, among many others, have attempted to provide a precise demarcation between ethical and conventional rules, but have also searched for normative depth in conventional rules avoiding a collapse with ethical and moral rules. I have shown that Marmor's defence of an autonomous domain for conventional rules and the normativity of conventional rules is not fully satisfactory. By contrast, I have defended the view that there is a continuum between ethical, moral and conventional rules because the primary mode of action is normative all the way through. **Omelette** as the primary model of practical reasoning seems to rule both "what we do when we act with others" and "what we do when we act individually".

Acknowledgements I am grateful to Andrés Botero, Ken Ehrenberg, Sandra Gomora-Juárez, Jasminka Hasanbegovic, Maciej Juzaszek, Andrej Kristan, Dimitrios Kyritsis, Jose Juan Moreso, Dennis Patterson, Lorena Ramírez, Josefa Ruiz-Resa, Pablo Sánchez-Ostiz, Paolo Sandro, Helga Varden, Caridad Velarde and Pilar Zambrano for their comments on earlier drafts of this chapter.

References

Chisholm R (1976) Freedom and action. In: Lehrer K (ed) Freedom and determinism. Random House, New York

Enoch D (2011a) Reason-giving and the law. In: Green L, Leiter B (eds) Oxford studies in philosophy of law. Oxford University Press, Oxford
Enoch D (2011b) Giving practical reasons. Philos Imprint 11:1
Hume D (1999) In: Beauchamp TL (ed) An enquiry concerning human understanding. Oxford University Press, Oxford
Lewis D (1969) Convention. Harvard University Press, Cambridge
Marmor A (2007) Deep conventions. Philos Phenomenol Res 74(3):586
Rodriguez-Blanco V (2014) Law and authority under the guise of the good. Hart, Oxford, Paperback edition 2016

Part II
Conventions and the Rule of Recognition

Conventions, Reasons and the Law

Andrei Marmor

Abstract According to Marmor, many critics thought that Hart had not given any good reason to think that the rules of recognition are conventions, and in any case, no conventional understanding of such rules is plausible. Others, including Marmor himself, defended this conventionalism about the rules of recognition, albeit, on different grounds. His main aim in this essay is to clarify his position and provide some further arguments in support of the view that constitutive conventions are at the foundation of law. In particular, he tries to show, in the face of the criticisms that its proposal has received from Postema, that it is still necessary to postulate the constitutive character of the rule of recognition. Indeed, Postema has argued that it was sufficient to extend the notion of coordination employed by Lewis and himself at some earlier time (he now prefers to speak in terms of "cooperation") to argue that it is not necessary to take Marmor's step. In contrast, Marmor argues that there are innumerable conventional practices, which it would be wrong to describe as solutions to preexisting coordination problems. In his view, insisting on coordination belittles the talent and inventiveness of human beings. Our sophisticated social practices are not limited to solving the problems with which we find ourselves. People create practices that they consider valuable to undertake. And one of them is the legal practice.

1 Introduction

In the first edition of *The Concept of Law*, Hart famously argued that the idea of legality is grounded in social rules. In every society with a legal system in force, there are some social rules that determine what counts as a legally valid source of law, and how those sources relate to each other. These are the *rules of recognition*. Many years later, in the posthumously published postscript to *The Concept of* Law (2nd ed) Hart indicated that he understood the social rules of recognition to be

A. Marmor (✉)
Law School, Cornell University, Ithaca, NY, USA
e-mail: am2773@cornell.edu

L. Ramírez-Ludeña, J. M. Vilajosana (eds.), *Legal Conventionalism*, Law and Philosophy Library 126, https://doi.org/10.1007/978-3-030-03571-6_4

conventional in nature. This conventional characterization of the rules of recognition engendered a considerable amount of controversy. Many critics thought that Hart had not given any good reason to think that the rules of recognition are conventions, and in any case, no conventional understanding of such rules is plausible. Others, including myself, defended this conventionalism about the rules of recognition, albeit, on different grounds. My main aim in this essay is to clarify my position and provide some further arguments in support of the view that constitutive conventions are at the foundation of law.

2 The Emergence of Legal Conventionalism

Before we get to the details of any conventionalist account of the rules or recognition, the first order of business must be to clarify why would this controversy matter at all. We can begin to see the answer by observing two main problems with Hart's original characterization of social rules.[1] Hart thought that it is absolutely crucial to see the difference between a mere regularity of conduct and following a rule. Rule following has an essential normative aspect that is not necessarily present in any given instance of a regularity of behavior. We may exhibit a great deal of regularity of behavior in a certain context, simply because the relevant reasons (real or perceived) for action occur in some regular fashion. (Think about eating dinner, for example: we do it quite regularly, but not as an instance of following a rule.) Following a rule involves the idea that people regard the existence of the rule itself as a reason for action. They regard the rule as binding, in some sense, and point to the existence of the rule itself for justifying their own conduct and exerting pressure on others to comply. Well, this seems quite right, but what is it for a rule to exist? And why would the existence of a rule give anyone a reason to comply with it, that is, regard the rule itself as binding, over and above any reasons there might be to act in accordance with the rule's content?

The first problem is closely connected to an air of circularity about Hart's characterization of social rules. Somewhat crudely put, the problem seems to be that in order to explain what a social rule is, we need to rely on certain kinds of beliefs and attitudes widely shared in the relevant population; but those beliefs turn out to be beliefs in the existence of a rule.[2] If the aim is to define what rules are, this does not seem like a helpful definition. But that is not what Hart sought to offer here. What he purported to do is to offer an account of *social* rules, or a social practice, if you

---

[1] Hart's theory of social rules is scattered around several places, but most of it is in Hart (1961), pp. 82–86. For a more detailed explanation, see Marmor (2011a), pp. 51–59.

[2] I am aware of the fact that most philosophers these days refer to beliefs as one kind of attitude, and thus the expression "beliefs and attitudes" may seem odd. Perhaps, but I don't see a reason not to single out belief from other kinds of mental attitudes like positive or negative dispositions toward something, likes or dislikes, etc. That's what I mean but attitudes, and of course it may include beliefs and other epistemic attitudes.

will, in terms that are fully reducible to actual conduct, beliefs and attitudes of individuals. Thus, we can say that according to Hart a social rule exists in a given population if it is practiced in a certain way; that is, if it is believed by most members to exist, and believed to give them reasons for action, and reasons to demand conformity by others, etc.

But this brings the second and main worry into sharper focus: In *The Concept of Law* Hart has deliberately refrained from telling us anything about the rationality of the beliefs and attitudes that constitute what he calls the "acceptance" of a social rule. We have a social rule in a given population, Hart argued, when most members of the population *regard* the rule as normative or binding, that is, as giving them reasons for action. But what kind of reasons those might be? What makes it rational to regard the existence of a social rule as a reason for action? Think about it this way: suppose a rule R requires people, among them A, to φ in C. Now either there are reasons for A to φ in C, or not. If there are reasons for A to φ in C, the rule would seem to make no difference; and if there are no such reasons, then we need to explain how the existence of R, whatever it means, could give A a reason to φ in C. Hart's characterization of social rules, however, does not seem to give us even the beginning of an answer to what reasons people might have for following a social rule, as such. It does not tell us anything about the kind of reasons we might have for "accepting" a social rule, in the normative, reason giving sense, Hart had in mind. And of course, the same problem applies to the rules of recognition: Hart clearly assumed that judges and other officials, whose rules the rules of recognition are, as it were, regard the rules as binding, in the normative sense he identified. But then he gave us no account of what makes the rules binding, and what makes it rational for the relevant population to regard the rules of recognition as normative.[3]

It might be worth keeping in mind the broader philosophical context of this problem. Hart shared Kelsen's insight that the only way to account for the idea of legality, or legal validity, is by pointing to some norms that grant certain types of actions and events in the world the legal significance that we ascribe to them. There must be some normative framework in place identifying or establishing ways in which law is created and modified in a given community. Contra Kelsen, however, Hart sought to provide a fully reductionist account of law, an account that enables us to explain the legal phenomena by reducing the main elements of it to facts of a non-normative kind, that is, to facts about peoples' actual conduct, beliefs, and attitudes. In line with this reductionist project, Hart argued that the normative framework that grants actions and events in the world the kind of legal significance we attribute to them is not some kind of a theoretical presupposition, as Kelsen maintained; there is a social reality to it, in the form of an actual social practice, which is exactly what the rules of recognitions are meant to capture.[4] But now, as we see, the problem is that Hart's reductionism seems strikingly incomplete: while aiming to explain the normative

[3]As I explain in Marmor (2011a), pp. 57–59, Hart had some reasons to refrain from giving us an account of the reasons for following social rules, aiming to keep an account of the normativity of law separate from moral questions about law's merit or legitimacy.

[4]See Hart (1961), p. 105.

framework that renders the idea of legality intelligible, it actually seems to lack an explanation of what makes this framework normative at all.

Above I presented the problem in a crude way, but it may help us to see the solution that emerged for Hart and others sympathetic to his project. Let us consider again a social rule R requiring A to φ in C. As I said, if A has a reason to φ in C, the rule seems to be normatively redundant; and if A has no reason to φ in C, then it's not clear how the fact that there is a social rule would create a reason for A to φ in C. So what difference to reasons for action social rules can make? The answer that comes to mind is the Humean conception of conventions: in numerous cases, our reasons for action depend on what others do; A's reason to φ in C may depend on the fact that others also φ in C.[5] Hence social rules are not normatively redundant; they function as reinforcements of mutual expectations about each others' conduct. A would have a reason to φ in C if B, and C, *et al*, also φ in C, but not otherwise. The rule simply galvanizes these mutual expectations to a socially/publicly recognized requirement, enabling people to rely on others' conformity. So it seems that in this Humean view of conventions we have the completion of a reductionist account of the rules of recognition: rules need not be more than widely shared beliefs and attitudes. When the reasons for action in a given set of circumstances depend on general compliance, the widely shared beliefs and attitudes that constitute the rule function as an assurance about others' likely conduct in the relevant circumstance. In short, we need social rules when we need to coordinate our actions with others; rules function as coordination mechanisms, and it is in this coordinative function that their normativity resides.

Hart seems to have endorsed this Humean solution in the postscript. In fact, Hart suggested that he had always thought of the rules of recognition as "resting on a conventional form of judicial consensus".[6] But this is far from clear. The conditions that Hart originally identified as constituting the existence of a social rule do not secure the conventionality of the rules in question. Widely shared and practiced moral norms, for example, might qualify as social rules according to Hart's original definition. The Humean view, more recently developed by David Lewis in his influential analysis of conventions,[7] rests on the idea that a rule is conventional only if the reasons for action that apply in the relevant circumstances depend on others' conduct; the relevant reasons for action must be compliance-dependent. The idea that emerges in Hart's postscript, therefore, is a significant addition to the characterization deployed in the first edition of *The Concept of Law*, namely, that the reasons judges and other officials have for regarding the rules of recognition as binding are compliance-dependent reasons.

Is it really the case that judges' and other legal official' reason for accepting the rules of recognition are compliance-dependent? Obviously, if the main function of the rules of recognition is to solve a coordination problem for the parties concerned, then the answer is yes. In a few cryptic remarks in the postscript, Hart indicated that

---

[5] See Hume (2000), p. 320.

[6] Hart (1994), p. 256.

[7] Lewis (1969).

he came to the view that the rules of recognition are coordination conventions. No doubt, this view must have been influenced by David Lewis's theory of conventions as solutions that emerge to solve large-scale recurrent coordination problems, and several legal philosophers' suggestion to see the rules of recognition as Lewis-type social conventions.[8] It is not clear how much of the details of Lewis's theory Hart was willing to endorse, but clearly enough, he accepted the idea that the rules of recognition have a major coordinative function for those who follow it.[9] The philosophical attraction of this idea is considerable, but so are the problems that it engenders. Let me briefly recount the pros and cons.

The main advantage of the view under consideration here, namely, that the rules of recognition are coordination conventions (*a la* Lewis, more or less) is that it would constitute a very good explanation of the normativity of the rules of recognition while retaining Hart's main insight that they are social rules. According to Lewis, conventions are social norms that emerge as solutions to large-scale coordination problems that tend to recur under a set circumstances. As long as members of the relevant population have reasons to solve the recurrent coordination problem in question, and the existence of the convention solves the problem, individuals would have reasons to regard the convention as normative, precisely in the sense Hart has had in mind, namely, as giving them reasons to comply with the norm, and reasons to put pressure on others to comply, etc. Remember that the main challenge for Hart's practice theory of the rules of recognition was to explain the normativity of the rules; how can social rules constitute reasons for action? According to the coordination rationale, the answer becomes clear enough, and quite in line with Hart's original theory: if the judges and other officials, whose conduct, beliefs and attitudes constitute the rules of recognition, face a recurrent coordination problem in identifying and applying the sources of law in their jurisdiction, then their pertinent reasons are compliance dependent; and then the function of the rules is to provide information on what other officials are likely to do, and thus determine what each one of them needs to do in order to coordinate their conduct with others.

Some legal philosophers raised doubts about this explanation of the normativity of the rules of recognition. Leslie Green thought that the coordinative rationale of the rules of recognition cannot explain why would judges have to regard the rules as binding. Green argued that Lewis type conventionality does not sit comfortably with the obligatory nature of the rules of recognition; conventions do not seem to be the kind of norms we tend to regard as obligatory.[10] Admittedly, if one adheres to Lewis's formulation of conventionality, given in terms of subjective preferences of the agents involved, then there is a gap in the explanation. In line with game-theoretical framework Lewis adopted from economists, he defined the structure of a coordination problem purely in terms of the agents' subjective preferences. Thus, a coordination problem exists when two or more agents have a dominant preference

---

[8] As far as I know, the first to suggest a coordination rationale for the rules of recognition was Postema (1982), p. 165.

[9] Julie Dickson raised some doubts about this standard interpretation. See Dickson (2007), p. 373.

[10] Green (1996), p. 1687.

to act in concert with the other relevant parties, which is stronger than their preference for any one of the relevant alternatives for action available. But one would be right to complain that subjective preferences, per se, are not reasons for action. There is a great deal of coordination, in Lewis's sense, that a gang of bank-robbers would need in order to rob the bank successfully. But a solution to their coordination problem is not binding or obligatory, morally or otherwise.

Clearly enough, if we want to use Lewis's coordinative rationale to explain the normativity of the rules of recognition, or any other convention for that matter, we must shift from talk about preferences to talk about reasons. But that is not difficult to do. My own definition of conventionality, to which I will get shortly, has always been given in terms of reasons for action, not preferences. And the definition clearly applies to Lewis type coordination problems as well. In short, it is not difficult to give a Lewis-type account of conventions that defines the structure of coordination problems in terms of reasons for action, not subjective preferences.

But that does not seem to be Green's main worry. His worry is that conventions, qua solutions to coordination problems, are not obligatory, they do not seem to be binding in the sense in which we would want to account for the normativity of the rules of recognition. I remain unconvinced that there is any serious worry here. It is true, of course, that many coordination problems we face are rather trivial and often not very important to solve. However, there are also many large-scale recurrent coordination problems that we have an obligation to solve, even a serious moral obligation. If a convention exists that solves such problems, then there in obligation to comply with the convention. Generally speaking, when we have a moral obligation to solve a collective action problem and there is a salient solution to it, available for all to comply with, then we have a moral obligation to comply. In sum, whether a coordination based explanation of the rules or recognition can successfully explain the appropriate normative character of the rules, entirely depends on the kind of coordination problem the rules respond to and the reasons judges have for solving them.

In responding to Green's concern here I do not mean to suggest that I agree with the coordination rationale of the rules of recognition, of course, nor does it mean that I am willing to assume, without argument, that judges and other officials have an obligation to comply with the relevant rules of recognition. Whether there is such an obligation, and what kind of obligation it is, remains to be seen.

For now, the main question is whether it makes sense to account for the rules of recognition as norms that respond to coordination problems. And that partly depends, of course, on how we define what a coordination problem is. My objection to the idea that rules of recognition are coordination conventions rests on the narrow, technical definition of what a coordination problem is that Lewis relied on. A number of critics have argued, however, that this is a mistake, and a much broader and relaxed notion of what constitutes a coordination problem would be immune to the kind of objections I raised.[11] This is a very complex issue that I need to address

[11] See, for example, Kopcke-Tinture (2011), p. 183; Giudice (2010) and Postema (2011), pp. 529–533.

in stages. First, let me try to explain why Lewis himself uses a narrow definition of coordination problems, and why I think that it makes no sense to regard the rules of recognition as coordination conventions on the basis of Lewis's account. In the next section I will address the broader question of how to understand conventionality and what makes the rules of recognition plausibly understood in terms of constitutive conventions.

First, then, we need to understand why Lewis himself was drawn to the narrow, technical sense of a coordination problem that he used in his definition of conventionality. Lewis explicitly developed his theory of conventions in response to a specific challenge posed by Quine. Quine argued that no significant aspect of language can be deemed conventional because conventions must evolve from agreements, and it would be implausible to assume that we have ever agreed on conventions of language. Besides, we would need at least some rudimentary form of language to be able to agree on anything. Lewis wanted to respond to this argument by showing that conventions can evolve without any need for an agreement.[12] Conventions, on Lewis's account, evolve as social-normative solutions to large-scale recurrent coordination problems as an alternative to agreements, precisely because agreements are extremely difficult to come by (normally due to the large number of agents involved). The important point to bear in mind here, however, is that Lewis saw the challenge in genealogical terms; to answer Quine's objection to the conventionality of (some aspects of) language, we need an account of the ways in which conventional norms can emerge and evolve, over time, without assuming any kind of agreement between the parties concerned. How can it actually come about that a convention evolves without an agreement?

The coordination rationale provides Lewis with the answer, but only because it adheres to the narrow, game-theoretical sense of a coordination problem. The unique feature of a coordination "game" is that the dominant preference of all parties concerned is the preference for concerted action.[13] In such coordination "games", parties do not have any particular incentive to defect from cooperative action. Acting in concert with others is their dominant preference. Hence, what the parties need in order to solve the problem is information; each party needs to know what the other will do. Therefore, any particular option that somehow emerges is likely to be followed. Since there is no serious conflict of interests between the relevant agents, information about others' conduct is sufficient to solve the coordination problem. This, of course, makes it much easier to explain how large-scale normative solutions can organically evolve and remain stable for some time. On the other hand, when you think of a collective action problem that involves something like a "prisoners dilemma" situation, or any other similar "game" where parties have a strong incentive to defect, information is not sufficient. Solution to prisoners dilemma situations

[12] See Lewis (1969).

[13] Technically, it comprises two types of "games"—pure/perfect coordination, where the relevant agents are indifferent with respect to the alternative courses of action available, and imperfect coordination problems, e.g. "battle of the sexes" games, where the agents do have a preference for one of the options, but their dominant preference is to act on the choice that the others act on.

requires changing the pay-off scheme, usually by means of some external pressure or sanction. And this makes it much more challenging to explain how a social norm can spontaneously evolve, as it were, without some deliberate external intervention. When the structure of a collective action problem is such that it is dominated by an incentive to defect, a social norm is rather unlikely to emerge as a solution. Not impossible, but unlikely.

At least, then, we can see that Lewis had good reasons to adhere to a narrow, technical, sense of what constitutes a coordination problem. Furthermore, I hope it is also clear why I have assumed that it only makes sense to characterize a norm as a Lewis-type coordination convention just in case we can identify the specific coordination problem that had existed before the convention emerged, and then show how the convention functions a solution to that problem. This is a crucial premise in one of my main concerns about the scope of Lewis's account.[14] The argument was that it makes no sense to suggest that the rules of chess, for example, are coordination conventions because it makes no sense to assume that there was some coordination problem that had existed prior to the game, that the game of chess then evolved to solve. And this underscores one of the main concerns about the plausibility of the thesis that the rules of recognition are coordination conventions; to show that they are, we would need to assume that prior to the emergence of the rules of recognition in a given society, judges and other officials had faced some coordination problems that then got to be solved by the rules of recognition they follow. This seems to me even less plausible than the suggestion that the rules of chess are coordination conventions. For judges to have a coordination problem in the identification of what counts as law in the community, they must first be able to see themselves as judges, acting within and on behalf of an institutional setting that is already in place. But as Hart himself famously argued,[15] there is a great deal of law that has to be in place, and grasped as such, for any individual to count as a judge, or as a legislator, or any other type of legal official, acting in his or her official capacity. If the rules of recognition are to be at the foundation of law, they cannot be coordination conventions of judges; first there has to be law that establishes the office of a judge and other legal institutions.

Gerald Postema claims that my argument here "rests on a confusion about the Humean theory. The Humean account assumes the existence of a cooperation problem, of course, but this is a logical, not a temporal 'pre-existence'".[16] I find this objection a bit perplexing. A problem is always logically prior to its solution, in some sense, but for a solution to be logical, the problem has to be a logical one to begin with. Solving a coordination problem is not an exercise in logic, it is a practical problem that emerges only under some specific practical circumstances, concerning peoples' reasons for action (or preferences, if you want to stick to Lewis's account) relative to their actual alternatives of conduct. A coordination convention is not a logical solution to a coordination problem but a practical one. And such a

[14] See Marmor (2009), pp. 22–25.

[15] See Hart (1961, p. 133); see also Marmor (2009), pp. 162–163.

[16] Postema (2011), p. 531.

solution is called for only if the relevant parties have a practical problem to begin with.

It is quite right that we can keep two aspects of Lewis's theory separate, namely, we can keep separate his genealogical account about how conventions evolved to solve large scale recurrent coordination problems, and his functional explanation of the rationale of conventions as solutions to coordination problems. If Postema's point here is to suggest that we can have the functional explanation without the genealogical one, I certainly agree. We can see Lewis's theory as providing a functional explanation of social conventions, namely, as the kind of explanation that tells us what is the main function or rationale of a certain type of social norms; when the main function of a given social norm is coordinative, then it is a social convention. But this doesn't prove Postema's point. For any given norm (or any other means, for that matter) to function as a solution to a coordination problem, the problem, as such, has to be there first. The time sequence is also part of the functional explanation, not only the genealogical one. Norms can only function to solve a practical problem if there is a problem to be solved. And this means that the problem has to present, quite literally, before its normative solution comes into play.

To preempt a possible objection, let me emphasize that it is not part of the time-sequence argument that prior to the normative solution that emerges to a coordination problem, the relevant population must exhibit any particular awareness of the problem and/or its coordinative nature. A coordination problem may well exist even if the relevant agents are not quite aware of it.[17]

Still, a number of critics, including Postema, argued that the narrow-technical sense of what counts as a coordination problem, that is assumed both by Lewis and my own argument, is not necessary. A broader, and more relaxed conception of what counts as a coordination problem can be used to expand the scope of Lewis's definition of conventionality, showing that there is no need to come up with another type of social conventions I called constitutive conventions. In order to answer this objection, we need some background.

3 Constitutive Conventions

We have not yet said much about what conventions are, and why does it matter, philosophically speaking, whether a norm is conventional or not. I think that the answers to these questions have to be such that they explain their interdependence.

[17] I explained this in greater detail in Marmor (2009), pp. 5–7. Del Mar (2010) raised some perplexing objections to this idea, claiming that it is just not possible for a social norm to have an alternative in the relevant sense unless the population who follows the norm is aware of the alternative. As he puts it: "arbitrariness is an experience that depends on when and who experiences it". Clearly this is not the relevant notion of arbitrariness that we employ in this debate. Del Mar's assertion that "our nature, and the nature of our social world, is not one that can be determined as one way or the other", and others like it, make me suspect that there are much more profound issues, such as the very nature of analytical philosophy and respect for careful arguments, that we would have to disagree about.

Whatever it is that makes conventional norms unique or clearly identifiable is worth exploring only if there is some philosophical interest in the answer, that is, only if we can show why it matters. Since conventions are rules or norms purporting to guide human conduct, it is natural to assume that the answers to these questions reside in the domain of practical reasons.[18] More specifically, my intuition is that any account of conventionality must explain how norms relate to reasons for action. And from this perspective, two main features of conventional norms seem intuitively salient: arbitrariness and compliance-dependence. There is a clear sense in which we regard norms as conventions when the norm is partly-arbitrary, that is, when we have clear sense that the same purposes the norm is there to achieve, or functions it is there to serve, could have been achieved by some other alternative norm that the relevant population could have followed instead. And, relatedly of course, there is a clear sense in which reasons for following a conventional norm crucially depend on the fact that others in the relevant community follow that same norm as well.

The arbitrary nature of conventions stems from the idea that conventions are norms underdetermined by their underlying reasons. In countless areas of our lives, there are some reasons for having social norms that regulate our conduct in a given context, but the reasons are such that they do not fully determine the content of the desirable norm. Different, alternative, norms could instantiate those reasons just as well. Examples are abundant; there are reasons, for example, to have certain norms regulating how we should express our respect for others in various social interactions, but those reasons do not determine the particular ways in which respect needs to be outwardly manifested; various ways of manifesting respect in a given context might do just as well. And we can clearly see that by observing variations in the relevant social norms that prevail in different societies; different conventions seem to serve one and the same social function and none is necessarily superior to the other. As Postema rightly noted, however, it is not the case that a norm's underdetermination by its underlying reasons *entails* that the norm is a convention: "Underdetermination means only that the value can be realized, respected, or served in a number of different ways; however, only when the value is compliance-dependent [...] is the determining activity a convention".[19]

I largely agree with that. But in order to state the position more precisely, I need to reiterate the definition of conventionality that I suggested elsewhere.[20] A precise definition would show, I hope, that compliance-dependence is part of the definition of the arbitrariness condition itself. In other words, I agree with Postema that underdetermination by reasons of a norm or social practice, by itself, does not entail that the norm/practice is conventional, because it does not entail that the norm is arbitrary in the requisite sense. Let me provide the formal definitions and explain.

[18] This does not mean that understanding the nature of conventions is necessarily exhausted by the ways in which they relate to reasons for action. Conventions may serve other social functions that are not directly instantiated by reasons for actions.

[19] Postema (2011), p. 529.

[20] Marmor (2009), chapter 1.

A rule, R, is *conventional*, if and only if all the following conditions obtain:

1. There is a group of people, a population, P, that normally follow R in circumstances C.
2. There is a reason, or a combination of reasons, call it A, for members of P to follow R in circumstances C.
3. There is at least one other potential rule, S, that if members of P had actually followed in circumstances C, then A would have been a sufficient reason for members of P to follow S instead of R in circumstances C, and at least partly because S is the rule generally followed instead of R.

The rules R and S are such that it is impossible (or pointless) to comply with both of them concomitantly in circumstances C.

A reason for following a rule R, is *compliance dependent* if and only if, for a population P in circumstances C

(a) there is a reason for having R, which is also a reason for having at lease one other alternative rule, S, *and*,
(b) part of the reason to follow R instead of S (in circumstances C) consists in the fact that R is the rule actually followed by most members of P in circumstances C. In other words, there is a reason for following R if R is generally complied with, and the same reason is a reason for an alternative rule if that alternative is the rule generally complied with.

As we can see, conventionality is defined here in terms of relation to reasons.[21] Given that A is a reason for R, if R is generally complied with, and A would have been a sufficient reason for an alternative rule if that alternative is generally complied with, then R is conventional relative to A. Note that R need not be conventional altogether as there may be some other reasons to comply with R that are not arbitrary, and hence compliance-dependent type reasons. A norm would be purely conventional, however, if there are no such other reasons.

As we can see from condition (3) of conventionality, which is the condition that aims to capture the idea of arbitrariness, it already incorporates the compliance-dependence condition. The relevant distinction here is between reasons for having a norm and reasons for complying with it. When the reasons for having a given norm are such that they underdetermine the content of the norm, then it is possible, but not necessary, that reasons for complying with the norm are compliance dependent reasons. Again, I agree with Postema that underdetermination, by itself, does not entail compliance dependent reasons, but that is so, because it does not entail arbitrariness either. And vice versa, not all cases of compliance dependence entail arbitrariness. Let me explain.

Postema's intuition, I take it, is that it is possible for values or reasons for action to be realized in practice in various ways, none necessarily superior to another,

[21] Some critics were puzzled by my insistence that the reasons in play here are actual reasons for action and not merely perceived or motivating reasons. See Lestas (2013), p. 1 and Smith (2011), p. 451. My response is in Marmor (2011b), p. 497.

without it being the case that one has any particular reason to realize the value just as others happen to do. Consider, for example, the practice of bringing a bottle of wine to the host of a dinner party. Presumably, the value instantiated by this practice is the value of expressing a token of appreciation to the host for the dinner. But one can express this kind of appreciation in a number of other ways, besides bringing a bottle of wine. The fact that most invitees bring wine to dinner does not give you any particular reason to do the same. You can bring flowers, or desert, or something else. But this may well show us that not every social practice, even one that is underdetermined by its underlying reasons, is necessarily a social convention. Underdetermination by reasons is a necessary condition of conventionality, not a sufficient one.

Compliance-dependence of reasons is a bit trickier. There are two ways in which reasons for action can be compliance-dependent, and only one of them is relevant to the conventionality of a rule. Let me call them ex ante and ex post compliance-dependence: A reason for action is ex ante compliance-dependent when the facts that constitute the reason for action initially include facts about others expected conduct in the relevant circumstances. A paradigmatic example is a coordination problem, of course. Suppose two agents, A and B, would like to meet for a discussion or something, and hence need to coordinate a meeting place, so they agree on a place, say X. When the time comes, A's reason to go to X incudes the fact that she expects B to go to X as well; and the same applies to B, of course, his reason to go to X includes the expectation that A will go there too.

A reason for action is ex post compliance dependent when the facts that constitute the reason for action do not initially include facts about other's conduct, but they can be *defeated* by widespread non-compliance with the required conduct. Consider, for example, cases of pollution; suppose there is a lovely natural pond in our neighborhood. The residents would have a reason not to pollute the pond. The facts that constitute this reason concern facts about the natural and aesthetic value of the pond, and thus, each person has a reason to refrain from polluting the pond irrespective of others. However, if this reason is not generally complied with and the pond gets hopelessly polluted, the reason not to pollute may be defeated; it is no longer an operative reason. The distinction may seem a bit too subtle but it is important. Many kinds of reasons for action are not ex ante compliance dependent, but general non-compliance with the conduct required by the reasons may well defeat (though not under-cut) the reasons. I hope that my definition above shows clearly enough that the kind of compliance dependence of reasons that is relevant to the conventionality of rules is the ex ante kind.

Let us take some stock. The circumstances that give rise to the emergence of a social convention consist of two main facts: first, the fact that there are some reasons for a normative regulation of conduct in a given area (call these the *underlying reasons*), but those reasons under-determine the content of the normative regulation that is called for. Second, the fact that people's reasons for complying with the normative solution in question are ex ante compliance-dependent reasons; the facts that constitute the underlying reasons include facts about expected conduct of others similarly situated (in the relevant population). Clearly enough, both of these conditions obtain in standard (narrowly defined) recurrent coordination problems of the kind Lewis had in mind. And then we can say that if a social norm evolves to solve the problem, the social norm is conventional. But I have argued that the solution to coordination problems is not the only type of cases where the two conditions obtain. Many types of social activities are created by conventional norms, but not as a response to any pre-existing recurrent coordination problem.[22] In many cases the underlying reasons have nothing to do with the need to solve a recurrent coordination problem that is somehow already in place, before conventions emerged in response to it. The underlying reasons are sometimes reasons to create new types of activities that people may find valuable to engage in for a variety of reasons. Of course once we have the activity in place, its practice may engender some coordination problems in it, that may need to be solved by some additional rules or conventions. But the essential point is that we have countless conventional practices, such as playing structured games, sport tournaments, structured artistic genres, etc., that would be ill described as solutions to some pre-existing coordination problems. Insisting on the coordination rationale of all social conventions seriously underestimates the resourcefulness and inventiveness of human nature. Our elaborate social practices are not limited to solving problems we encounter. People invent activities and practices that they find valuable to engage in. Numerous structured activities have been invented or emerged over the centuries that enable new forms of social interactions to evolve and new values to emerge in the pursuit of those activities.

In response, Postema argues that my understanding of the coordinative rationale of conventions confuses means with ends; the solution of the relevant coordination problem is always a means to and end, not the end itself: "conventional practices need not be and rarely are solely, or even primarily, concerned with solving cooperation problems. They are concerned with achieving, realizing, respecting or promoting certain values.... Solving a coordination problem is the (or an important) *means* for doing so".[23] Of course I agree with Postema that it is rarely, if ever, the case that coordination is an aim in itself. If Jerry and I want to have coffee and chat, our aim is to have coffee and chat, together; that's exactly why we care more about agreeing on a place to meet than we care about the exact location. Fixing the location is a problem we have to solve in order to achieve something else, that is, having coffee together. And that is usually how coordination problems figure in our practical reasoning; we want or need to do something that requires coordination with others; coordination is not, by itself, the aim we seek to achieve, only a means to achieving something else. I don't think that anyone was really confused about this. Still, the question remains whether social conventions evolve in order to solve the relevant coordination problem or not. My argument is that sometimes they do, and sometimes they don't. And, crucially, that they do only if there is a coordination problem first, and then a norm that evolves in order to solve that problem.

In other words, the underlying reasons for having conventions are sometimes reasons to create new types of social activities, that may realize some recognized

---

[22] See Marmor (2009), chapter 2.

[23] Postema (2011), p. 531.

values and, often, create new ones. Consider, for example, American football, a game created (mostly be coaches in US colleges) around the late nineteenth to early twentieth centuries. The creation of this new game was not called for by coordination problems in soccer or rugby that American football is based on; nobody thought that there is a coordination problem in soccer (or rugby) that needs to be solved by some new or additional rules. The idea was to create a new game, one that would instantiate somewhat different skill sets and different types of athletic achievements. The function of rules in this game, as in most others, is constitutive, not coordinative; it is to constitute a new form of activity, something that people would find valuable to engage in.

To take another example, consider the emergence of several revolutionary genres of painting and sculpture during the first decades of the twentieth century, such as abstract painting, cubism, Dada, surrealism, etc. These new, and at the time revolutionary, genres emerged from intentional and creative effort of the artists involved, experimenting with new ideas, promoting various agendas, and sometimes, though not always, coordinating their artistic endeavors with fellow artists. As a consequence, new artistic genres emerged, with new conventions and practices, followed by many other artists for decades. Gradually, conventions galvanized about what counts as a cubist or an abstract painting or sculpture, what makes them different from Dada or Surrealism, etc. I think that it would border the ridiculous to suggest that these constitutive conventions are, actually, coordination conventions that emerged as solutions to some kind of a large-scale recurrent coordination problem that artists had faced and needed to solve by following some rules. Impressionist art had not faced a coordination problem that needed to be solved by the invention of cubism and abstract art; impressionism was fine, for what it aimed to accomplish; cubism emerged from it as an innovation, expanding the horizon of artistic genres and creating new forms of aesthetic and artistic appraisal. Cubism was not a solution to a coordination problem, or to any other problem, for that matter; it was an invention that expanded the frontiers of what art can accomplish and what can be appreciated about it.

As I mentioned earlier, some critics have charged that my conception of what counts as a coordination problem is too narrow; if we are a bit less uptight about it, critics claimed, we may not need to distinguish constitutive conventions from the Lewis-type coordination conventions.[24] None of the critics I am aware of, however, suggested any particular details about how to relax the conditions of what constitutes a coordination problem, which makes it a bit difficult to respond to this objection. But perhaps the idea is that anything we do *together*, any activity that is jointly done by a group of individuals, and perceived by the participants as some kind of a joint activity, is a form of coordination.[25] And then of course, any practiced convention would be coordinative, by definition. Which is precisely what makes the suggestion unhelpful. In other words, we can certainly say that whenever people engage

[24] See note 11 above.

[25] I do not mean to refer here off-handedly to Margaret Gilbert's account of conventions as jointly accepted principles of action. My critique of her specific view is in Marmor (2009), pp. 25–30.

in some activity together, they act in concert with each other and therefore or, in this sense, they coordinate their conduct. But this loose use of the word "coordination", no doubt linguistically legitimate, would be too loose to be philosophically helpful. It would make, for example, every aspect of language use a matter of coordination, including those aspects which are clearly not conventional, even on Lewis's account. There are many things we do together, and in ways that may matter to us that we do them together, that are not conventional in any sense, even if they occur with some regularity.

Most importantly, however, this loose idea of coordination, as just about anything we do together, would be totally unhelpful in solving the problem about the normativity of the rules of recognition that we started with. Remember that the challenge for Hart was to explain what makes the rules of recognition normative, what makes them binding, in some sense, on those who need to follow the rules. If the answer is that just about anything we do together is a matter of coordination, then we really do not have even the beginning of an explanation of what makes doing things together normatively binding, or even rational. Many things we do together, are such that we have no reason to do or no reason to do together. Togetherness is normatively significant only when the relevant reasons for action are ex ante compliance dependent. But once we see this, we are quickly back to square one: we would need an explanation of what makes reasons in various contexts ex ante compliance dependent. A coordination problem, in the narrow technical sense, is clearly one such answer. If coordination is expanded to include other cases, we would need a different kind of explanation of what makes the relevant reasons for action, in those other cases, ex ante compliance dependent.

The idea that many conventions are constitutive of certain structured types of human activities is meant to be such an alternative explanation. It is meant to explain the rationale of compliance dependent reasons by way of articulating the function of the conventions in constituting activities that people find worth engaging in, as the kind of activities they are. The details of this account I gave in my book, and I will not repeat them here.[26] If somebody wants to say that constitutive conventions are also, in some sense, coordinative, I would have no reason to object. As long as it is conceded, of course, that they are not coordinative in the narrow, technical sense of coordination problems. Which means that the rules are not there to solve a pre-existing coordination problem, which is really what matters. In other words, the real debate here is not about the question of whether all conventions are necessarily coordinative; in some sense, they are. The debate is about the question of whether all conventions are responses to pre-exiting coordination problems. I have not seen any suggestions to convince me that they are. The suggestion that everything we need to do in a group, together somehow, is a coordination problem, and therefore every convention is there to solve such problems, seems to me utterly vacuous. It amounts to no more than saying that social conventions are social, they involve people doing stuff together.

---

[26] Marmor (2009), mostly chapter 2.

Here is one main difference about the reasons for action involved in the two types of conventions, coordination and constitutive: if the social norm in question is a solution to a large scale coordination problem, then the reasons for following the rule on each particular occasion is exactly the same reason for having the convention in the first place, namely, to solve the relevant coordination problem. To take a familiar example, if the rule about which side of the road to drive is there to solve a large-scale coordination problem of how to avoid collisions, as it is, then on every occasion of driving on the road, people's reason to follow the rule are exactly the same as the reason for having the rule, namely, to coordinate driving in order to avoid collisions. But this is not necessarily the case with constitutive conventions. The reasons for having a certain type of conventional activity or practice do not necessarily transmit to reasons for complying with the conventions on every occasion of its application. And this is attested by the fact that people can have very different views about what makes a certain practice valuable and worth having, yet comply with its constitutive rules in actually engaging in the activity in question and willingly participating in the practice. And this is clearly manifest in the legal case as well. There are many reasons for having law and legal institutions in our society; what those reasons are, and how to weigh the various competing considerations about them, are highly contentious matters. People, judges included, can have very different views about the need to have law and various legal institutions. But despite the differences about the underlying reasons in play here, we can follow the same constitutive conventions; we can participate in a conventional practice even if we have very different views about the main point of the practice and the reasons for having it. If you think that a set of rules is there only to solve some coordination problems, the distinction between reasons for having a rule and reasons for complying with it would be impossible to explain.

This brings me to the last point I want to make here, concerning the question of whether the rules of recognition should be seen as obligatory or not. As we noted earlier, critics of legal conventionalism have stressed that a conventional account of the rules of recognition would not be sufficient to explain their obligatory nature. The underlying assumption of this critique is that judges and other legal officials have an obligation to comply with the rules of recognition, and this obligation is difficult to explain if we regard the rules as constitutive conventions. Let me reiterate my response to this objection because it is also relevant to the previous point.[27] The answer is that the objection confuses the legal-institutional obligation of judges to comply with the rules of recognition, an obligation they certainly have, with the different and independent question of whether they would also have a moral obligation to do so. Constitutive conventions can easily explain the former. Judges would have an obligation to comply with the rules of recognition because the rules constitute the game they are playing, so to speak; complying with the rules of recognition just is what makes an act judicial in the relevant institutional sense. The rules determine what the practice is. The legal obligation to follow the rules of recognition is exactly like the chess-player's obligation to follow the rules about, e.g. how to move

[27] See my *Philosophy of Law* (Marmor 2011b), pp. 167–168.

the bishop on the board. Complying with such rules just is what playing the game is. Whether anyone has a reason to play the game, is a separate question entirely. And the same applies to judges; whether they have any moral or other reasons to play the game is not something that can possibly follow from the rules of the game. The rules of recognition cannot constitute a reason, not to say an obligation, to engage in the legal game, so to speak. Whether judges, or anyone else for that matter, have a moral obligation to comply with the rules of recognition is always on open question, one that can only be answered on moral grounds.

References

Del Mar M (2010) Marmor's social conventions: the limits of practical reason. Philos Soc Sci 41:420–445
Dickson J (2007) Is the rule of recognition really a conventional rule? Oxf J Legal Stud 27:373–402
Giudice M (2010) Review of Andrei Marmor "Social Conventions". The Notre Dame Philosophical Reviews, 1
Green L (1996) The concept of law revisited. Michigan Law Rev 94:1687–1717
Hart HLA (1961) The concept of law. Oxford Clarendon Press, Oxford
Hart HLA (1994) The concept of law. Postcript, 2nd edn. Oxford Clarendon Press, Oxford
Hume D (2000) A treatise of human nature. Oxford University Press, Oxford
Kopcke-Tinture M (2011) Positive law's moral purposes: towards a new consensus? Am J Juris 56(1):183–214
Lestas G (2013) The DNA of conventions. Law Philos:1–37
Lewis D (1969) Convention: a philosophical study. Blackwell, Oxford
Marmor A (2009) Social conventions: from language to law. Princeton University Press, Princeton
Marmor A (2011a) Philosophy of law. Princeton University Press, Princeton
Marmor A (2011b) The dilemma of authority. Jurisprudence 2(1):121–141
Postema G (1982) Coordination and convention at the foundation of law. J Legal Stud 11:165–203
Postema G (2011) Legal philosophy in the twentieth century. Springer, Holland
Smith D (2011) The role of conventions in law. Jurisprudence 2:451–461

The Rule of Recognition as a Constitutive Convention

Jorge L. Rodríguez

Abstract In his contribution, Jorge L. Rodríguez criticizes the position that Marmor has defended in previous works. Basically the criticism is that, according to Rodríguez, it cannot be the case that a convention is constitutive, and therefore the rule of recognition cannot be of this type. According to this author, the concept of convention employed by Marmor is too weak: it leads to consider a rule as conventional even though all the members of a community follow it because they consider that it is correct, and a rule may not be considered as conventional even though everyone is following it just because others follow it. Moreover, it seems to be pointless to speak of constitutional conventions inasmuch as, according to Rodríguez, the arbitrary character of conventions is incompatible with the constitutive character of a rule. As a consequence, Marmor's view would be affected by an internal inconsistency because, following his own definitions, the constitutive character of the rule of recognition is incompatible with its conventional character.

1 Introduction

In the "Postscript" to the second edition of *The Concept of Law*, H.L.A. Hart accepted a criticism of his original characterization of social rules led by Ronald Dworkin.[1] Dworkin pointed out that Hart ignored the difference between *conventional social practices*, where the general agreement of the members of the group is part of the reason each has for following them, and *concurrent practices*, that each member of the group follows by independent convictions. However, Hart held that

[1]According to the practice theory of rules, their existence depends upon a form of social practice comprising both patterns of conduct regularly followed by the majority of the members of the group, and a distinctive normative attitude towards such patterns of behavior (acceptance). The latter consists in a disposition of the members of the group to take such patterns of behavior as guides for their future conduct and as standards of criticism of the behavior of others that can legitimize claims and various forms of pressure for conformity, see Hart (1994), p. 254.

J. L. Rodríguez (✉)
Law Department, University of Mar del Plata, Mar del Plata, Argentina
e-mail: jorge.rodriguez@pjba.gov.ar

L. Ramírez-Ludeña, J. M. Vilajosana (eds.), *Legal Conventionalism*, Law and Philosophy Library 126, https://doi.org/10.1007/978-3-030-03571-6_5

his characterization of social rules would still apply to a special type of rules: *conventional rules*, and, more specifically, that his *rule of recognition* would be a conventional rule in that sense.[2]

Despite Hart's own words, the genuine scope of Hart's commitment to a conventionalist interpretation of the rule of recognition has been a matter of controversy.[3] In fact, by the time Hart wrote the "Postscript", David Lewis' study on conventions had already been published and become a classic, and it is difficult to claim that the rule of recognition constitutes a convention in Lewis' sense. It is important to recall that, according to Lewis, conventions are characterized as follows: a regularity R in the behaviour of members of a population P, as agents in a recurrent situation S, is a convention if and only if it is true that, and is common knowledge in P that, in almost any instance of S among members of P:

1. Almost everyone conforms to R.
2. Almost everyone expects almost everyone else to conform to R.
3. Almost everyone has approximately the same preferences regarding all possible combinations of actions.
4. Almost everyone prefers that anyone conform to R, on the condition that almost everyone conform to R.
5. Almost everyone would prefer that any one more conform to R', on the condition that almost everyone conform to R', where R' is a possible regularity in the behaviour of the members of P in S such that almost anyone in almost any instance of S among the members of P could conform to both R' and R.[4]

It does not appear easy to justify that the rule of recognition of a legal system necessarily constitutes a solution to a recurrent problem of coordination, as in the case of Lewis-conventions.[5] Some specific legal rules may aim to solve problems of coordination, but this cannot be defended as true for legal rules in general, and even less so for the rule of recognition in particular.[6] This is not only so because of the empirically controversial question of whether judges and other officials of any political community use the rule of recognition to solve a difficulty of the singular structure of a problem of coordination, but because it is not even clear what problem of coordination there might be prior to the existence of a rule of recognition in a certain legal system.

Moreover, if—as most interpreters have understood—the rule of recognition is prescriptive in nature and imposes on judges and other officials the duty to apply certain rules, and not others, to justify their decisions, such a trait is not easy to reconcile with Lewis-conventions. This is so because the latter are reconstructed in

[2] See Hart (1994), pp. 255–257.

[3] See, for instance, Dickson (2007), pp. 373–402.

[4] See Lewis (1969), p. 78.

[5] See Marmor (2001), pp. 12–13; Marmor (2011), p. 76; Coleman (2001c), pp. 94–95.

[6] See Green (1999), pp. 35–52; Marmor (2001), pp. 9–10; Marmor (2009), pp. 165–166; Celano (2003), p. 350.

purely descriptive terms, and so it is impossible to derive from them any obligation whatsoever without additional premises.[7]

Finally, a characteristic feature of conventions is their *arbitrariness*, i.e. the fact that when facing a conventional practice, it must be possible to specify an alternative to that which is in force so that if this latter alternative had been followed, it would have been preferred to the former (Clause 5). This idea of arbitrariness is not apparent in the rule of recognition. Although it is certainly possible to conceive of alternative criteria to identify the law with respect to those actually followed in any legal domain, the selection of certain criteria does not seem to be arbitrary, but rather dependent upon complex and very significant political and ideological considerations.[8]

Andrei Marmor has attempted to evade such objections by offering a reinterpretation of the Hartian rule of recognition as a conventional rule in way that closely resembles that of Lewis, but with the singular characteristic of being a *constitutive convention*.[9] In general terms, his contribution seems highly valuable for several reasons. Among them is the manner in which Marmor highlights the conventional character of the criteria of identification of the law in order to offer a defence of a positivistic conception of legal systems, an idea that I personally share. Secondly, Marmor emphasizes the constitutive nature of the rule of recognition, departing from the majoritarian interpretation that views it as a regulative rule, an interpretation that is subject to several objections and does not capture the fundamental goal that inspires the Hartian construction.

These reasons justify a careful analysis of Marmor's ideas, as we will see in the following sections. However, this analysis will show that Marmor's interpretation cannot ultimately be accepted because of the unsurmountable tension between its two basic features, understood in the way Marmor proposes: the *constitutive* character and the *conventional* character of the rule of recognition.

2 Conventions and Reasons

In his characterization of conventions, Marmor takes as a basis Lewis' classical analysis, which he even defends against a number of critical voices. Yet he introduces some variants in it, mainly with the aim of extending the scope of conventional phenomena to comprise situations that are excluded from the realm of Lewis-conventions. According to Marmor's own characterization, a rule R is conventional if, and only if, the following conditions are satisfied:

---

[7] See Green (1988), pp. 117–121; Marmor (2001), pp. 28–29; Celano (2003), p. 350.

[8] See Marmor (1998), pp. 201–202; Celano (2003), p. 351.

[9] See Marmor (1998), pp. 509–531; Marmor (2001, 2009, 2011).

1. There is a group of people, a population P, that normally follow R in circumstances C.
2. There is a reason, or combination of reasons, A, for members of P to follow R in circumstances C.
3. There is at least another potential rule R' that if members of P had actually followed R' in circumstances C, A would have been a sufficient reason for members of P to follow R' instead of R in circumstances C, and at least partly because R' is the rule generally followed instead of R. Rules R and R' are such that it is impossible (or pointless) to comply with both of them concomitantly in circumstances C.[10]

The most prominent similarities between the two characterizations are highlighted by Marmor, who points out that the two salient features of Lewis-conventions, which his own characterization would equally capture, are (1) that conventional rules are, as anticipated, *arbitrary*: if a rule is a convention we should be able to point to an alternative rule that could have been followed to achieve basically the same goal and (2) that the reasons to follow a conventional rule are closely related to the fact that others (in the relevant community) also follow them.[11]

There are, however, important differences between these two ways of conceiving conventions. First, according to Lewis conventions are facts. He claims that his definition of conventions does not contain normative terms, nor is "convention" in his analysis a normative notion. However, conventions can be regularities to which we believe we ought to conform, since there will be certain probable consequences implied by the fact that an action conforms to a convention, giving presumptive reasons, according to our shared opinion, why such an action ought to be carried out.[12] For Marmor, in contrast, conventions are "*a species of norms: they are rules that regulate human conduct*".[13]

I do not think it sufficiently justified to assume this strong conceptual commitment, according to which no convention that i*s* not a rule may exist. In any case, it will not be necessary to dispute this point for the purposes of this paper.

Second, and in obvious connection with the former, while the analysis of Lewis is presented in terms of *expectations* and *preferences* of members of the relevant community, in Marmor's characterization these notions are replaced by the reference to *reasons for action*. Concerning the requirement that there must be a reason or combination of reasons for members of the relevant community to follow the conventional rule in the given circumstances, Marmor explains that a reason for following a rule involves the assumption that this is valuable, functional to a purpose or point, or good in some respect (not necessarily moral),[14] adding that

[10] See Marmor (2009), p. 2; Marmor (2011), p. 77.

[11] See Marmor (2009), p. 1.

[12] See Lewis (1969), p. 97.

[13] Marmor (2009), p. x.

[14] See Marmor (2009), p. 5.

> This formulation assumes that there is a fact of the matter about reasons for action, as about some matters of value [...]. This objective assumption is not necessary for the rest of the argument in this book. Expressivists can follow the argument on their own terms.[15]

Moreover, Marmor considers that this condition for the conventionality of a rule does not require that members of the relevant community be conscious of the reason to follow the rule, and he underlines that people can follow conventional rules for the wrong reasons or for no reason whatsoever.[16] In other words, in Marmor's view, the reasons for following conventional rules are not only objective but can be entirely opaque.[17]

Marmor's substitution of expectations and preferences of members of the relevant community for objective reasons for action in his characterization of conventional rules may be explained by the fact that, in his view—following Raz—the basic function of rules is to replace in practical deliberation (at least part of) the applicable first-order reasons.[18] This is of course a controversial theoretical commitment, but one I will not discuss here. What I wish to point out is that the objectivity of reasons to comply with conventional rules, together with their possible lack of transparency, are not easy to reconcile with the idea that such reasons are in part dependent upon the fact that others also follow them (*compliant-dependent* reasons).[19] There is a strong tension between these ideas: Marmor is claiming, on one hand, that a distinctive characteristic of conventional rules is that the reason for following them depends upon others following them ("[...] *I have a reason to do P (and not Q or R) if, and only if, I have reason to assume that others will do P as well (and not Q or R)*"),[20] which strongly suggests that the relevant reasons to assess the conventionality of a rule are subjective reasons. On the other hand, he states that the conventionality of a rule "[...] *does not depend on the subjective conception of the reasons for following the rule by those who follow it*".[21]

The third clause of Marmor's characterization of conventional rules contains a twofold requirement. It implies that there must be an alternative rule that could have been followed in the circumstances supported by the same reason that justifies the one actually followed. But it also implies the aforementioned idea that the reasons to follow a conventional rule are dependent upon the fact that others follow it too.[22]

Regarding the former requirement, i.e. the arbitrariness of conventional rules, it does not seem problematic to claim, as Marmor does, that there must be a conceivable alternative that is supported by the same reasons and fulfils the same functions

---

[15] Marmor (2009), p. 5, note 4.

[16] See Marmor (2009), p. 5.

[17] See Marmor (2009), p. 6.

[18] See Marmor (2009), p. 13; Raz (1994), p. 214.

[19] See Marmor (2009), p. 11.

[20] Marmor (2009), p. 21.

[21] See Marmor (2009), p. 5.

[22] See Marmor (2009), p. 10.

of the original rule for the relevant population.[23] Nevertheless, Marmor adds to that tenet that arbitrariness is not to be understood here as equivalent to indifference. A rule is arbitrary in the requisite sense, even if people have reasons to prefer one over the other, as long as the reason to prefer one of the alternatives is not stronger than the reason to follow the rule that is actually followed.[24] This latter claim is perfectly sound if we understand conventions in Lewis' style, i.e. as solutions to recurrent coordination problems. But if we view the scope of conventions as wider than, and not restricted to, solutions of coordination problems, as we will see in the next section Marmor does, it is difficult to see why each member of the relevant population will have a stronger reason to follow the rule that others actually follow than to follow the rule he believes ought to be followed.

In Marmor's analysis, moreover, the assertion that a rule is a genuine alternative to that which is actually followed is relative to the relevant (objective) reasons:

> Given that A is a reason for R, if R is generally complied with, and A would have been a sufficient reason for an alternative rule if that alternative is generally complied with, then R is conventional relative to A.[25]

This implies that a rule may be conventional with respect to certain reasons and not with respect to other reasons, something that appears counterintuitive, to say the least.

Regarding the latter requirement, i.e. the compliance-dependent character of the reasons to follow conventional rules, it is rather surprising that this idea is only captured in the third clause of Marmor's reconstruction and not in the second, which is precisely concerned with the reasons to follow conventional rules. In contradistinction, when Marmor explains the conditions that should be met for a reason to be compliance-dependent, he states the following:

1. there is a reason for having R, which is also a reason for having at least one other alternative rule, S, and,
2. part of the reason to follow R instead of S (in circumstances C) consists in the fact that R is the rule actually followed by most members of P in circumstances C. In other words, there is a reason for following R if R is generally complied with, and the same reason is a reason for an alternative rule if that alternative is the rule generally complied with.[26]

These conditions are not explicitly incorporated into Marmor's reconstruction of conventional rules with respect to the reason, or set of reasons, to follow them, but only indirectly through its third clause, which has a merely counterfactual character. Notice that Marmor's reconstruction does not require that the reason A to follow the conventional rule R depends in part upon R being actually followed by others. It only requires that A is such that, were the relevant population to follow R' instead

[23] See Marmor (2009), p. 10.

[24] See Marmor (2009), p. 8.

[25] Marmor (2009), p. 12.

[26] Marmor (2009), p. 11.

of R, A would be a sufficient reason to follow R' and not R, at least in part because R' is actually followed. The result of this is an important weakening of the idea that the reason to follow conventional rules are compliance-dependent.

Consider the following example. Let P be a vegetarian community. It happens that members of P normally follow rule R, stating that no meat should be eaten, and thus Marmor's Clause 1 is satisfied. Let us also assume that there is an objective reason A for members of P to follow that rule, that reason being that it is more efficient from an economic perspective for members of P to have homogeneous alimentary preferences. This satisfies, in turn, Marmor's Clause 2. Now, regarding reason A, we can conceive of an alternative rule R' to the effect that meat should be eaten at every meal, and R' is such that if members of P had actually followed R', A would have been a sufficient reason for following R' and not R, at least partly because R' would have been the rule generally followed by members of P, where R' and R are incompatible.

In this case, all three conditions for the existence of a conventional rule that Marmor imposes appear to be met. However, what is in fact the case is that each and every member of P follows rule R with complete independence from reasons of economic efficiency. Every one of them does so exclusively by virtue of moral reasons. Can we say that R is a conventional rule after all?

This example resembles one offered by Marmor himself (inspired by Burge)[27] according to which an orthodox Jewish community believes that Hebrew is a holy language descended directly from God. Marmor claims that despite that belief, Hebrew would remain conventional even when spoken by these orthodox Jews since the fact that they are wrong about the reasons for following the rules would not disprove that they are conventional.[28] Nonetheless, it is one thing to say that a rule may be conventional even though its followers are not entirely conscious of that fact, and quite another to say that conventional rules may be compliance-dependent, even though the reasons for following them are objective and lack transparency for those who follow them.[29]

To sum up, Marmor offers a weak reconstruction of conventions. The fact that the reason justifying a convention depends in part upon the fact that others follow it is not expressly formulated in Clause 2 of Marmor's characterization, but appears only in Clause 3, which has a counterfactual character. The major problem with Marmor's proposal is that conventions understood in this way are entirely independent from people's beliefs and preferences. A rule may be conventional in Marmor's sense, even though everyone in the relevant community follows it because they believe that one ought to act as the rule indicates, and may be unconventional, even though everyone in the respective community follows it only because others follow it too.

---

[27] See Burge (1975), pp. 249–255.

[28] See Marmor (2009), pp. 5–6.

[29] See Marmor (2009), p. 11.

3 Constitutive Conventions?

Although the weakening of Marmor's characterization of conventions goes perhaps further than the author wishes, it should be noted that it is intentional since it responds to Marmor's decision to assign a conventional character to phenomena that would be beyond the reach of Lewis-conventions, especially that what Marmor calls *constitutive conventions*.

The idea of a constitutive convention is delineated by Marmor based on Searle's distinction between regulative and constitutive rules.[30] Though Marmor recognizes that the criterion of distinction between these two types of rules proposed by Searle has certain difficulties, he argues that constitutive rules such as those determining how to play chess satisfy all the conditions of conventionality that he outlines.[31]

However, in the first place, it is debatable whether being actually practiced is a necessary condition for a rule to be a constitutive rule, i.e. that it must necessarily satisfy Clause 1 in Marmor's characterization. The reason to include Clause 1 in an explanation of conventions is intimately connected with the compliance-dependent nature of conventions. If an important part of the reason that justifies following a convention is that others follow it too, then conventions should be practiced for being conventions. But the compliance-dependent character of the reason to follow a convention is justified, in turn, if conventions are understood as solutions to coordination problems. When facing a coordination problem, each member of the relevant community has a stronger preference for coordinating her behaviour with that of others than the preferences she may have among the different alternatives of action. Thus, it makes perfect sense to maintain that there is a reason to follow the course of action that others follow. But in situations where this coordination goal is not present, why should we require that a constitutive rule be practiced for being a constitutive rule? Someone can invent a game, with a set of constitutive rules that define how to play it, and the existence of these rules will be absolutely independent from their being followed by anyone. Unless with "existence" of a rule we want to refer precisely to the fact that it is actually followed, in which case Clause 1 would be trivially verified, purely by definition, by any "existing" rule in this sense.

Marmor uses a curious argument to justify his position on this point:

> Conventional rules can constitute a social practice only if the rules are actually followed. Conventions, unlike moral rules for example, do not exist in the abstract: 'it ought to be the case that it ought to be the case that *p*' normally entails that 'it ought to be the case that *p*', whereas 'it ought to be the case that it is a convention that *p*' does *not* entail 'it is a convention that *p*'. Only practised conventions are conventions.[32]

Of course, if a convention is constitutive of a social practice, this presupposes the existence of such social practice. The relevant question here, however, is whether a

[30] See Searle (1969), pp. 33–35; Searle (1995), Chapter 2.

[31] For a critical view on Searle's distinction between regulative and constitutive rules, see for example Schauer (1991), pp. 6–7; Raz (1975), pp. 108–111.

[32] Marmor (2001), p. 18.

constitutive rule must be followed to be a constitutive rule. Can constitutive rules exist 'in the abstract'? I cannot see why not, unless, as I said, 'existence' is interpreted here as a kind of factual or social existence, i.e. the existence of a rule is equated with its being followed.

It is also correct to argue that "*it ought to be the case that it is a convention that p*" does not entail "*it is a convention that p*". This, however, is just a consequence of the fact that *Op* does not entail the truth of *p*, i.e. that from the duty to do *p*, it does not follow that *p* is in fact the case. To assert that it is a convention that *p* is to assert a fact, a fact that may not be verified even though we have very good reasons to argue that it *ought* to be verified. This is true even when we assume, as Marmor does, that conventions are rules, because *to assert the existence* of a rule is quite different from *formulating* a rule.[33] By contrast, if "*it ought to be the case that it ought to be the case that p*" seems to entail "*it ought to be the case that p*", this makes sense if "*it ought to be the case that p*" is not interpreted as the assertion of a fact—as in the case of the existence of a convention—but as the formulation of a rule.[34] From all this, of course, it does *not* follow that constitutive conventions cannot exist without being practiced but, at most, the platitude that constitutive conventions cannot constitute social practices without being practised.

Clause 2 in Marmor's characterization of conventions is so weak ("*there is a reason, or a combination of reasons, call it A, for members of P to follow R in circumstances C*") that it is difficult to even conceive of any rule not satisfying it, be it constitutive or regulative. In particular, if a rule satisfies Clause 1, i.e. if "*there is a group of people, a population P, that normally follow R in circumstances C*", the group will surely do so for some reason, so that once Clause 1 is satisfied, the satisfaction of Clause 2 is vacuous when the reasons in question are subjective reasons. If, as Marmor assumes, these reasons are understood as objective reasons, satisfaction of Clause 2 is no longer vacuous: people could actually follow a rule that has no objective reason to follow. However, it remains a very weak condition if those reasons, though objective, are not interpreted as conclusive.[35] However, if Clause 2 were to be replaced by a stronger clause, requiring members of P to follow R in C, at least in part because other members of P follow it too, it is dubious that constitutive rules would necessarily satisfy it. Constitutive rules, like those defining the movements in a game of chess, are compliance-dependent in the sense that we can say they exist insofar as they are practiced, but they are not based on compliance-dependent reasons in the sense that we follow them because others follow them too. If no one played chess, it would still make perfect sense for me to do so if I thought there were good reasons for it.

Regarding Clause 3 in Marmor's characterization, we could obviously say that constitutive rules like the rules of chess are arbitrary in the sense that the relevant

---

[33] The difference between asserting the existence of a rule and formulating a rule corresponds to von Wright's distinction between *norm-propositions* and *norms* (see von Wright 1963, p. 106).

[34] In deontic logic, the possibility of admitting iterated deontic operators is a contested issue (see, for instance, von Wright 1983, pp. 142–150).

[35] See Marmor (2009), pp. 7–8.

population might have followed in C other rules, but not in the sense that such population might have followed in C other rules *to play chess*. Marmor himself argues that "*the identity of a conventional practice crucially depends on its constitutive rules*",[36] and this is important because in that case no situation whatsoever could count as a genuine alternative in order to speak of the arbitrariness of a constitutive convention.

Marmor responds to this problem stating that if the rules of chess were significantly different, then the game would be a different one, but it is doubtful whether small changes in the rules would produce a different game. He asks us to consider the example of two communities of chess players, one playing with a rule that allows castling while the other plays without that rule. In such a case, Marmor believes that we would not say that these two communities are playing different games, but rather that both are playing chess, only somewhat differently. However, if this were so, the rule of castling, although obviously constitutive of the move of castling, could not be considered *a constitutive rule of chess*. The game of chess, defined by a set of rules not including the rule enabling castling, would present two variants depending on the admission or rejection of such a rule. By contrast, if the rule of castling is admitted among the constitutive rules of chess, a game similar to that of chess which does not accept the rule of castling would not count as a genuine alternative according to Marmor's own characterization of the condition of arbitrariness. In fact, I think it can be shown in general terms that the idea of a relevant alternative to be able to speak of arbitrariness is incompatible with the constitutive character of a rule.

We must recall that in Marmor's analysis, as indicated in the preceding section, a rule R' is an alternative to another rule R that is actually followed if the reason to follow R would justify following R', if R' were the rule actually followed. In other words, to say that rule R' is an alternative to another rule R, in the relevant sense to claim that R is arbitrary, is a relative statement regarding the reason that justifies following it. But there is something peculiar in constitutive rules:

> It is a typical feature of conventions constituting such practices as the game of chess, that they partly constitute the point or value of the activity itself, and it is in this sense that we can talk about autonomous practices: namely, that the point of engaging in them is not fully determined by any particular purpose or value which is external to the conventions constituting the practices.[37]

Faced with a set of constitutive rules like those of chess, one may take into account reasons to follow them that are *internal* to the practice of chess, i.e. constituted at least in part by the rules of chess itself, or reasons that are *external* to the rules that constitute this practice. As far as any reason or value that is internal to the practice itself, determined by its constitutive rules, there is no possible rule that can be taken as an alternative to the rules of chess because nothing other than the very rules of chess can instantiate an inherent value of the game. In relation to any rea-

[36] See Marmor (2009), p. 43. For a critical view on Marmor's thesis on the arbitrariness of constitutive conventions, see Arena (2011), pp. 441–506.

[37] Marmor (2001), p. 14.

son, purpose, or value that is external to the practice constituted by such rules, the requirement in Clause 3 of Marmor's characterization, according to which the reason to follow the rule actually followed would be a sufficient reason to follow an alternative rule if the latter were actually followed, would fail: "*There is, after all, an indefinite number of potential practices which could instantiate those same general human concerns which are instantiated by chess*".[38] To put it briefly, for any external reason regarding the practice of chess that could justify its rules, for instance, that chess be an entertaining or intellectually challenging game, there are many alternative practices that could be justified by those same reasons. That is to say, there are many other games that are entertaining and intellectually challenging, but none of them satisfies the condition that the reasons in question be sufficient to justify following an alternative practice to chess if the alternative were indeed followed.[39] If this is correct, for any constitutive rule, internal reasons do not allow alternative rules, and external reasons are insufficient to justify following alternative rules because they are being followed. Hence, no rule can be simultaneously constitutive and conventional in Marmor's sense.[40]

4 The Rule of Recognition as a Constitutive Convention

As was anticipated, Marmor characterizes the rule of recognition of a legal system as a constitutive convention. Assuming the previous objections to the conceptual category of a constitutive convention can be answered one way or another, let us briefly examine this idea. According to Marmor, Hart argues that in every community that has a legal system there is a special class of secondary rules, the rules of recognition, which identify certain types of actions and events that create the law. Rules of recognition are social rules followed by a community and which constitute what counts as sources of legally valid norms in that community.[41] Contrary to the presupposed character of Kelsen's basic norm, Marmor observes that the rule of recognition is a social rule effectively followed by a certain community.[42] In identifying the sources of law, judges and other officials follow certain rules, and therefore such rules do not need to be presupposed. Thus, Marmor concludes that the Hartian notion of the rule of recognition is essentially the same idea that Kelsen tries to grasp with his basic norm, though characterized reductively in terms of social facts.[43]

With his interpretation of the rule of recognition as a constitutive rule, Marmor offers a fairly sound answer to the problem of its normativity. On this topic, Marmor

[38] See Marmor (2001), p. 15.

[39] Additionally, in this kind of situation it is even difficult to think of incompatible alternatives.

[40] A similar objection was suggested in Celano (2003), p. 358.

[41] See Marmor (2011), p. 49.

[42] See Marmor (2011), p. 50.

[43] See Marmor (2011), p. 51.

distinguishes between the idea of obligation that would follow from the rule of recognition and the different question of whether judges and other officials have a moral or political duty to get involved in the practice that is constituted by such a rule. The rule of recognition, conceived as a constitutive rule, would determine the practice of law. The legal obligation that would follow from it would resemble the obligation of a chess player to move the bishop only diagonally. A constitutive rule could not prescribe the obligation to participate in the practice constituted by it. If such an obligation exists, that is a different matter that cannot be determined by the rule that constitutes the practice. The reasons for obeying the law should be assessed on moral or political grounds, not derived from the norms that determine what counts as law.[44]

As for its conventional character, Marmor argues that the rule of recognition satisfies all the previously outlined conditions for a rule to be conventional. He initially dismisses certain arguments that could be offered in order to show that the rule of recognition does not satisfy Clause 1, i.e. that it would not be a rule effectively followed in a certain community. He then concentrates on Clause 2, stating that "*it would be extremely unlikely*" that, concerning the rule of recognition, it would be false to say that there is a reason or combination of reasons to follow it,[45] and explores what those reasons might be.[46] Finally, with respect to Clause 3, i.e. the arbitrariness and compliance-dependent character of constitutive conventions, Marmor puts forward two arguments that would justify the conventionality of the rule of recognition, neither of which appears to him to be "*really controversial*": (a) different legal systems have different rules of recognition; and (b) the reasons judges and other officials have for following certain rules in the identification of the sources of law are closely tied to the fact that other officials follow those same rules.[47]

I will not discuss the truth of these last two statements here. My interest is to emphasize that even if both are true, they are insufficient to warrant the conventional character of the rule of recognition in the initial characterization made by Marmor. In other words, there is a different underlying notion of conventionality here, even weaker than the one needed for something to be a convention in Marmor's sense. Marmor himself seems to recognize this in certain passages:

> A given rule can be arbitrary, in the sense we have defined, even if it reflects moral or political convictions … The crucial question is not whether the rules of recognition reflect political convictions, but whether those same convictions provide sufficient reasons for acting in

---

[44] See Marmor (2011), pp. 81–82.

[45] See Marmor (2011), p. 78.

[46] See Marmor (2011), pp. 78–79. Marmor states that in his original account Hart argued that the rationale of the rule of recognition was the need for certainty in the identification of the law, and that in the "Postscript" Hart seemed to add a reason based on the need for coordination. And though Marmor considers that it is not open to discussion that the rule of recognition contributes to those goals, he claims they are insufficient to justify having a rule of recognition since the reasons to have rules of recognition would be, in his view, closely linked to the reasons for having law.

[47] See Marmor (2011), p. 81.

> accordance with the rule, even if the rule in question is not followed by others. By saying that the rule is conventional, we suggest a negative answer only to this last question.[48]

It is one thing to say that a rule R is conventional in the sense of being actually followed in a certain community, and that the reasons justifying it are such that, if in the relevant community another rule R' were actually followed instead of R, those reasons would be sufficient to follow R' instead of R precisely because R' is the rule actually followed. It would be quite another thing to say that a rule R is conventional in the sense that there are alternative rules that could have been followed, and that the reasons that justify following R are such that, if nobody followed R, it would not make sense to follow it. In this latter notion of conventionality, the condition of compliance-dependence has been entirely disassociated from that of arbitrariness, the result of this being an almost trivial notion of conventionality that could be perfectly satisfied by many moral rules. As Bruno Celano sharply points out, the obligation to keep promises, for instance, is such that it would not make sense if no one kept them.[49]

At the beginning of this paper I said that the way Marmor emphasized the constitutive character of the rule of recognition seemed valuable. To what extent is it possible to reconcile this idea with a non-trivial sense of conventionality? To examine the point, we must make some preliminary clarifications on the meaning in which the rule of recognition may be said to be a constitutive rule.

Hart's writings contain some ambiguities on the scope of the typologies of rules he distinguishes between. At times Hart seems to argue that the pair of primary rules and secondary rules, and the pair of duty-imposing rules and power-conferring rules, are coextensive: primary rules would be duty-imposing rules, whilst secondary rules would be power-conferring rules.[50] Though there is some consensus that the first of these assimilations is sustainable, this cannot be said of the second. In the first place, doubts have been raised on the power-conferring character of all secondary rules.[51] Nor is it clear in Hart's work what the normative status of secondary rules would be, and this has generated considerable debate, especially with respect to the rule of recognition.[52]

Many theorists understand the rule of recognition as a rule of conduct that imposes duties, i.e. as a regulative rule with a normative status similar to that of primary rules.[53] It has been argued that this is the only interpretation that is consistent

[48] Marmor (2001), p. 21.

[49] See Celano (2003), p. 353.

[50] See, for instance, Hart (1965), p. 358.

[51] This is what Raz, among others, argues. In his view, not all secondary rules confer powers; only rules of change and rules of adjudication do so. By contrast, the rule of recognition is the exception (see Raz 1971, pp. 794–795 and note 24). Ambiguities in the Hartian typology have also been pointed out by many, including Green (1996), pp. 1687–1717; MacCormick (1981), pp. 130–134; Waluchow (1994), p. 75.

[52] Thus, MacCormick claims that secondary rules are a sort of "*mixed bag*" (see MacCormick 1981, p. 133).

[53] For example, Alexander and Schauer (2009), Hacker (1977), pp. 1–25, Himma (2009), Perry (2009), Shapiro (2009, 2011).

with other aspects of Hartian theory, especially with Hart's distinction between duty-imposing rules and power-conferring rules, as well as with the practice theory of rules.[54] As a regulative rule of conduct, the rule of recognition would prescribe judges the duty to apply the legal norms identified by it.[55]

However, this interpretation, according to which the rule of recognition not only provides the criteria for identifying all norms in a legal system, but also imposes on judges the obligation to use and apply the norms thus identified, is highly controversial. In fact, a general legal rule prescribing judges to *comply* with each of the other legal rules would be entirely redundant since the content of such an obligation would already arise from those same rules.[56] Let us suppose norm N_1 imposes the duty to pay certain taxes. The enactment of a different norm N_2 imposing the duty to comply with N_1 would be completely pointless. On the other hand, if the rule of recognition implies an obligation to *apply* the norms identified by itself, that obligation would be redundant regarding the content of the rules of adjudication in the system. What is more, such an obligation would never be ultimate because it would make perfect sense to continue asking for the justification of the duty to comply with it. Meanwhile, if the question concerns whether there is a moral obligation to follow or apply the norms in a legal system, this type of justification could never be provided by a rule with the characteristics of the rule of recognition. In other words, to evaluate the duties imposed by legal rules, we need to have a previous set of conceptual criteria allowing us to identify them.[57]

If we take the norm that starts the chain of validity in a legal system as a rule of conduct that imposes on judges the obligation to apply other rules because they meet certain requirements that make them valid, with such requirements being set by that very same initial norm, this generates two problems. In the first place, it cannot be argued that the rule of recognition, understood as a rule of conduct, is a valid legal rule. Second, Hart would inevitably fall in circularity because in order to identify the rule of recognition, the practice of judges and officials should be examined, but at the same time, in order to identify judges and officials within the system, it would be necessary to resort to the rules of adjudication that are valid according to the rule of recognition.[58]

All these difficulties vanish if we abandon this prescriptive reading and admit that the rule of recognition restricts itself to fixing the criteria of identification of the law.[59] Therefore, the rule of recognition would be a purely conceptual rule imposing

---

[54] See, for example, Raz (1971), pp. 795–815; Ruiz Manero (1991), pp. 281–293; Shapiro (2009); Waluchow (1994).

[55] See MacCormick (1981), pp. 145–146; Raz (1971), pp. 795–815; Raz (1975), p. 146; Ruiz Manero (1990); Shapiro (2009, 2011).

[56] See Bulygin (1976), pp. 31–39; Bulygin (1991a), pp. 257–278; Bulygin (1991b), pp. 311–318.

[57] See Bulygin (1991a), p. 278.

[58] See Bulygin (1991b), p. 317.

[59] See Bulygin (1976), p. 387. In the same sense, Zipursky (2001), pp. 246–247.

no duty whatsoever.[60] This interpretation is not entirely alien to Hart's words, for he sometimes assimilates the rule of recognition to a simple test of validity or a set of criteria for identifying valid norms,[61] interpreting its primary function to be to eliminate the problem of uncertainty over which norms count as legally valid.[62] Moreover, it has the great virtue of clearly distinguishing between a descriptive notion of validity, understood as the membership of a norm in a legal system, and a prescriptive notion of validity, understood as the obligation to comply with a norm.[63] The rule of recognition interpreted as a conceptual rule that determines the criteria of identification of the norms that belong to a legal system would be exclusively linked with validity in the first sense, not in the second.

Marmor, following Searle, maintains that constitutive rules not only determine but also regulate conduct,[64] and, in particular, that the rule of recognition as a constitutive rule would not only determine what counts as law in a certain community, but also impose on judges and other officials the duty to follow the criteria set by itself for the identification of the law.[65] However, his emphasis on the constitutive rather than the purely regulative character of the rule of recognition, and his idea that the "obligation" that follows from it resembles the obligation of a chess player to move the bishop only diagonally—it would only establish how one must act if one decides to participate in the practice, but it cannot prescribe the duty to participate in the practice that it constitutes—are in line with the purely conceptual reading of the rule of recognition.

Still, a difficulty remains in this reconstruction. Following Kelsen, a given norm N is valid in the sense that it belongs to a legal system if its promulgation is authorized by another norm N_1, which for that reason is considered hierarchically superior to N. N_1, in turn, is valid if its promulgation was authorized by another norm N_2, and so this chain continues until we reach the first positive norm in the system, whose promulgation has not been authorized by any other positive norm. In Kelsen's view, its validity would derive from a presupposed *basic norm*, an idea that is highly controversial. But beyond that problem, Kelsen has made an important point in claiming that the way to identify whether a given norm belongs to a legal system is by reference to other positive norms of the system, with the only exception being the first historical constitution.

---

[60] Because of the difficulties offered by Searle's distinction between regulative and constitutive rules, I will use von Wright's less problematic distinction between prescriptions and (conceptual) rules when appropriate. See von Wright (1963), Chapter 1.

[61] See Hart (1961), pp. 103–104; Hart (1968), p. 338.

[62] See Hart (1961), pp. 94–95.

[63] These two senses of validity are usually confused. For ambiguity in the notion of validity in *Pure Theory of Law*, see Ross (1961), pp. 199–220; Raz (1971), pp. 795–815; Raz (1974), pp. 94–111; Bulygin (1990), pp. 29–45; Nino (1978), pp. 357–376; Nino (1985); Garzón Valdés (1977), pp. 41–68.

[64] See Marmor (2009), p. 32.

[65] See Marmor (2009), p. 167.

Unlike this recursive analysis, Hart seems to maintain that the rule of recognition contains the criteria of validity (understood as membership in a legal system) of *all* the rules of the system,[66] not only that of the first positive norm. Nevertheless, at the same time Hart asserts that the rule of recognition is an *ultimate* rule, explaining it as follows:

> The sense in which the rule of recognition is the *ultimate* rule of a system is best understood if we pursue a very familiar chain of legal reasoning. If the question is raised whether some suggested rule is legally valid, we must, in order to answer the question, use a criterion of validity provided by some other rule. Is this purported by-law of the Oxfordshire County Council valid? Yes: because it was made in exercise of the powers conferred, and in accordance with the procedure specified, by a statutory order made by the Minister of Health. At this first stage the statutory order provides the criteria in terms of which the validity of the by-law is assessed. There may be no practical need to go farther; but there is a standing possibility of doing so. We may query the validity of the statutory order and assess its validity in terms of the statute empowering the Minister to make such orders. Finally, when the validity of the statute has been queried and assessed by reference to the rule that what the Queen in Parliament enacts is law, we are brought to a stop in inquiries concerning validity: for we have reached a rule which, like the intermediate statutory order and statute, provides criteria for the assessment of the validity of other rules; but it is also unlike them in that there is no rule providing criteria for the assessment of its own legal validity.[67]

Here Hart seems to accept, like Kelsen, that the criteria of validity of all the rules in a legal system, with only one exception, are provided by other positive norms: those that confer the power to create them, i.e. the rules of change in Hartian terminology. The only exception would be a rule such as "*What the Queen in Parliament enacts is law*", and it would not make sense, according to Hart, to discuss its validity or invalidity because there is no rule to provide the criterion for the assessment of its own validity. In this sense, that ultimate rule would be equivalent to Kelsen's first historical constitution.

Hart recognizes that there is some overlap between the content of the rule of recognition and that of the rules of change, stating that

> Plainly, there will be a very close connection between the rules of change and the rules of recognition: for where the former exists the latter will necessarily incorporate a reference to legislation as an identifying feature of the rules, though it need not refer to all the details of procedure involved in legislation.[68]

However, the connection is narrower than Hart seems to be willing to recognize here. Wherever there are rules of change, the rule of recognition will necessarily have to incorporate a reference to *any mechanism* they contemplate to modify the

[66] Hart (1961), p. 135.

[67] Hart (1961), p. 107. Raz remarks, on the one hand, that there is no reason to think that the rule of recognition contains all the criteria of validity of the rules in a legal system, since many other rules (of change) would also set criteria of validity. Yet, he tries to save the Hartian idea arguing that there are criteria of validity that, though legally binding, are not legally valid and, consequently, must be stipulated by the rule of recognition (see Raz 1971, pp. 809–810). In this suggestion, however, there is a confusion between validity as membership (a descriptive notion) and validity as binding force (a prescriptive notion).

[68] Hart (1961), p. 96.

law. And these mechanisms will not be confined to the deliberate promulgation or derogation of rules by legislation but extend to procedures for the modification of the current constitution, the introduction or elimination of judicial precedents, and all others. In other words, the content of the rule of recognition would be completely absorbed by that of the rules of change. For any rule of the system, except for the ultimate rule, the rules of change are sufficient to identify their validity in the sense of membership in the legal system. In order to assess the validity of any rule derived from that ultimate rule, we would need nothing more than an examination of the conditions specified by the rules of change, and thus nothing like a rule of recognition would be required. But when we reach the ultimate rule (in Hart's example, "*What the Queen in Parliament enacts is law*"), Hart does not argue, as one would expect, that the rule of recognition is precisely what provides the criteria for assessing the validity of that ultimate rule, but rather appears to identify the ultimate positive rule (or first positive norm, depending on the point of view) with the rule of recognition.[69]

To summarize, the problem is not merely that of a partial overlapping of contents: there seems to be no possible function to assign to the rule of recognition that is not already satisfied by the rules of change. This observation is not new: Norberto Bobbio already warned that if the rules of change are the rules that provide the necessary and sufficient criteria to determine which rules are valid in a legal system, it is difficult to imagine what differentiating function the rule of recognition might have.[70] More recently, Waldron observes that although Hart seems to encourage us to think that specifying the criteria of validity in the rule of recognition is quite separate from, and more fundamental than, laying down a rule of change, the opposite is in fact true: the rule of recognition does nothing that the rules of change have not already done.[71]

5 Saving the Rule of Recognition as a Constitutive Rule

There are, in my opinion, only three alternatives to escape the objections presented in the preceding section. The first is to accept in all its terms what has been pointed out so far, namely that the function of providing criteria for identifying the valid rules in a legal system is exhausted by the rules of change, and yet retain the expression "rule of recognition" simply to refer—as Hart himself seems to do in certain passages—to the ultimate rule of change. Under this reading, the rule of recognition can be a conceptual or constitutive rule, but it will not specify *all* validity criteria in a legal system. Nor can we say under this interpretation that the rule of recognition is in fact followed in a certain community because, as Hart rightly points out, there

[69] See also Hart (1958), pp. 54–55; Hart (1994), p. 247.

[70] See Bobbio (1975), p. 241.

[71] See Waldron (2009), Sect. IX.

is a difference between the *ultimate* character and the *supreme* character of a rule.[72] As previously stated, the rule of recognition would be an ultimate rule since it would provide criteria for assessing the validity of the other rules in the system, but it would not itself be subject to evaluation as valid or invalid according to the criteria of validity set by other rules.[73] Hence, Hart contends that no question can arise as to the validity or invalidity of the rule of recognition itself since it can be neither valid nor invalid.[74] In contrast, a rule is supreme if there are several potentially conflicting ones, with a hierarchical order giving it relative primacy over the rest.[75]

The ultimate and supreme characters of a rule are not only conceptually distinct, but in fact they may not coincide, nor do they ordinarily coincide in the same rule. As Kelsen rightly explains, the constitution in force in a given legal order, as its supreme norm, may nonetheless derive its validity from a previous constitution which is no longer in force. This analysis will eventually lead to a first historical constitution,[76] which is ultimate in a Hartian sense. Therefore, though in any hierarchically structured legal system in force there will be a supreme rule or set of rules, its ultimate rule may well have been suppressed many years ago and not be followed by anyone today. Thus, in this sense the rule of recognition does not even satisfy Clause 1 in Marmor's characterization of conventional rules, i.e. that it is actually followed in the relevant community.

A second alternative is to bring together in a unique set all the criteria for identifying the rules of a legal system, and to call that set a "rule of recognition". In this sense, Eugenio Bulygin states that the rule of recognition of a legal system is a conceptual (not prescriptive) rule that specifies the criteria for the identification of all norms in a legal order O_i. Such criteria might be formulated as follows[77]:

1. The set of norms $[N_1, N_2, \ldots, N_3]$ is the original system (first constitution) of O_i.
2. If a norm N_j is valid in a system S_t that belongs to O_i, and N_j confers legal power to authority x to enact norm N_k, and x enacts at time t N_k, then N_k is valid in system S_{t+1} (i.e. the system corresponding to the moment following t) and S_{t+1} belongs to O_i.
3. If a norm N_j is valid in a system S_t that belongs to O_i, and N_j confers legal power to an authority x to derogate norm N_k that is valid in S_t, and x derogates N_k at time t, then N_k is not valid in system S_{t+1} (i.e. the system corresponding to the moment following t), which belongs to O_i.

[72] See Hart (1961), pp. 195–107.

[73] See Hart (1961), p. 107.

[74] See Hart (1961), p. 109. The only reason why Hart claims here that the rule of recognition can neither be valid nor invalid is because he is identifying validity with the *regular creation* of a norm according to the criteria set by other norm or norms. By contrast, if we understand "validity" as membership in a legal system, the rule of recognition will be a valid rule according to the interpretation analyzed in the text.

[75] See Hart (1961), p. 105.

[76] See Kelsen (1960), p. 200.

[77] See Bulygin (1991a), pp. 257–278.

4. All valid norms in a system S_t that belong to O_i that have not been derogated at time t are valid in a system S_{t+1} of O_i (corresponding to the moment following t).
5. All logical consequences of valid norms in system S_t that belongs to O_i are also valid in S_t.[78]

Rule 1 determines the membership of the set of original rules in the system, i.e. its first constitution, and identifies by extension all those original rules. Rules 2, 3, and 4 determine the dynamic nature of the legal order, establishing the conditions for the legality of normative changes, while Rule 5 assigns systematic structure to the various static sets of rules that belong to the dynamic sequence. These rules, according to Bulygin, would jointly constitute a definitional scheme of a legal order and provide a recursive definition of a "*valid norm in system* S_t *of the legal order* O_i".

Let us look more closely at this definitional scheme. Disregarding Rule 5, which constitutes a controvertible theoretical assumption and has no bearing in the present discussion,[79] it should be noted that Rules 2 to 4 are a generalization of the criteria for incorporation and elimination of legal norms already specified by the rules of change in the legal system. Note that Rules 2 and 3 have a conditional formulation whose antecedent mentions the existence of a rule of change, whereas Rule 4 presupposes the accomplishment of a valid act of normative modification in which legal powers conferred by the rules of change are exercised. The explicit formulation of these three rules makes it possible to see more clearly the results of the normative acts of enactment and derogation of legal norms on the dynamic level. Finally, Rule 1 is not in itself a positive norm, and should not be identified with the original rules in the system mentioned in it, but rather determines the membership of those original rules in the system.

In this interpretation, the rule of recognition will be constitutive of all that counts as valid law in a certain legal community. But again, it will not be a conventional rule in Marmor's sense; strictly speaking, we cannot even say that it is followed or practiced by judges and other officials in a legal community. This is because what judges and other officials use to identify valid law are *the rules of change*. The formulation in a single rule of the entire set of identification criteria in a legal system has undeniable value as a theoretical reconstruction, but the practical function of setting the (conceptual) criteria of admission and rejection of derived norms is exhausted by the rules of change in that system.

There is a one other possible interpretation of the rule of recognition as a constitutive rule. The rule of recognition may be understood as a conceptual rule that identifies as part of a legal system the ultimate rule of change (the first historical constitution in Kelsenian terminology), i.e. precisely as Rule 1 in the definitional schema presented above does.

Let us look at this interpretation in more detail. The attribution of competence is a complex normative phenomenon, which requires, on one hand, a stipulation of the

[78] Bulygin (1991a), pp. 263–264. The English translation is mine.

[79] For a critical analysis on this idea, see Ferrer Beltrán and Rodríguez (2011), pp. 116–133.

conditions that certain acts must satisfy to count as a valid instance of normative creation, criteria that must be set by certain definitional, conceptual, or constitutive rules. On the other hand, it is necessary to assign normative consequences to such acts, and this requires the enactment of rules of conduct or prescriptions. If we take the example of a contract, we need a set of conceptual rules specifying what requirements are to be met for something to count as a valid contract and, on the other hand, prescriptions indicating what consequences follow from the existence of a valid contract.[80] The competence or normative power to make contracts is determined by the first of these groups of rules, which are conceptual rules. But this legal power only makes sense if there are also certain prescriptions that specify the normative consequences that follow from the existence of a valid instance of contract and, in general terms, of any valid instance of normative production.

Thus, as Ross clearly explains, "valid contract" is nothing more than an expression used to link certain antecedent facts with certain normative consequences.[81] In more general terms, "validity" is a term that is ambiguously used both in conceptual rules that specify the conditions that must be satisfied for certain acts to count as the creation of a norm, and in prescriptive norms imposing the normative consequences that follow from it.

If this is correct, we may say that to be able to confer legal power for the enactment of a norm at level 1, we require the following at level 2:

(i) One or more conceptual rules that set the conditions for certain acts to count as the creation of a valid norm in level 1, and
(ii) One or more prescriptions imposing the duty to comply with the norms of level 1.

This will be iterated as many times as normative levels exist in each legal system, until we reach an ultimate level *n* (the first historical constitution), i.e. the set of original rules in the system. At this point, if someone were to ask what all the valid rules in the system are, in the sense of having been regularly created in accordance with other rules of the system, it seems clear that this can be determined by simply examining the power-conferring rules (conceptual rules) of a higher level, while the ultimate rules of change (the first historical constitution) will be neither valid nor invalid in the considered sense.

If we were asking why the first positive rule of a legal system must be obeyed (the prescription that justifies its validity as binding force), this would undoubtedly depend on an extralegal assessment; for simplicity, a moral assessment. But if we want to identify all valid rules in the system, in the sense of being members of such a system, the first historical constitution should also count as a valid norm. But a conceptual rule is still required to interpret the first act of prescription as the creation of a valid norm.[82] Such a rule does not exist as a rule positively enacted by

[80] This is basically the idea that inspires the institutional theory of law. See, for instance, MacCormick and Weinberger (1986).

[81] Ross (1957), pp. 23 ff.

[82] In an analogous sense, Ross states that "Since the series of authorities cannot be infinite, the

anyone. But should we not presuppose it in order to identify the first historical constitution as valid in the sense of membership in the legal system?

This interpretation seems to give reason to Kelsen, at least partially, since the presupposition of a conceptual rule is required to interpret the first positive norm (the ultimate rule of change) as a member in the legal system. This also seems to justify the claim that, in addition to the rules of change that assign legal powers to create norms, every legal system must also have a rule of recognition, identifying the ultimate rule of change as a rule that belongs to the legal system. Furthermore, it would explain the need for a rule such as Rule 1 in the definitional scheme of a legal order proposed by Bulygin: a conceptual rule identifying the first historical constitution as part of the system, a rule that has not been enacted by anyone but must be assumed to make it possible to interpret a certain set of rules as a legal system.

If the rule of recognition is understood in this way, it will be a constitutive rule. However, as in the two alternative readings above, it will not be conventional in Marmor's sense; like the Kelsenian basic norm, it will not be a rule that is presently followed or practiced, but rather a presupposed norm.

Of course, nothing of what have been stated here poses any objection to the possibility of calling the rule of recognition, in any of the three versions explored, *conventional* in some interesting sense that differs from that proposed by Marmor, or to the possibility of considering law in general to be conventional in the sense that its existence and content depend exclusively on complex social facts, and not on moral merits.[83]

References

Adler K, Himma E (eds) (2009) The rule of recognition and the U.S. Constitution. Oxford University Press, Oxford

Alexander L, Schauer F (2009) Social facts, constitutional interpretation and the rule of recognition. In: Adler K, Himma E (2009), chapter VII

Arena F (2011) Marmor on the arbitrariness of constitutive conventions. Jurisprudence 2(2):441–506

Bayón JC (2002) El contenido mínimo del positivismo jurídico. In: Zapatero V (ed) Horizontes de la filosofía del derecho. Homenaje a Luis García San Miguel. Publicaciones de la Universidad de Alcalá, Alcalá de Henares, pp 33–54

Bobbio N (1975) Per un lessico di teoria generale del diritto. In: Studi in memoria di Enrico Guicciardi. Cedam, Padova, pp 47–55. Cited by the version published under the title Norme secondary. In: Bobbio (1994), pp 233–244

Bobbio N (1994) Contributi ad un dizionario giuridico. Giappichelli, Torino

Bulygin E (1976) Sobre la regla de reconocimiento. In: Bacqué J (ed) Derecho, filosofía y lenguaje. Homenaje a Ambrosio L. Gioja. Astrea, Buenos Aires, pp 31–39

---

inevitable conclusion follows that in the final instance the highest norms of competence cannot be enacted –they must be presupposed" (Ross 1958, p. 80).

[83] See, for instance, Coleman (2001b), p. 114 ff.; Bayón (2002), pp. 33–54.

Bulygin E (1990) An antinomy in Kelsen's theory of law. Ratio Juris 3:29–45
Bulygin E (1991a) Algunas consideraciones sobre los sistemas jurídicos. Doxa 9:257–278
Bulygin E (1991b) Regla de reconocimiento: norma de obligación o criterio conceptual. Réplica a Juan Ruiz Manero. Doxa 9:311–318
Burge T (1975) On knowledge and convention. Philos Rev 84:249–255
Celano B (2003) La regola di riconoscimento è una convenzione. Ragion Pratica 21:347–360
Coleman J (ed) (2001a) Hart's postscript. Essays on the postscript to the concept of law. Oxford University Press, Oxford
Coleman J (2001b) Incorporationism, conventionality, and the practical difference thesis. In: Coleman (2001a), pp 97–147
Coleman J (2001c) The practice of principle. Oxford University Press, New York
Dickson J (2007) Is the rule of recognition really a conventional rule? Oxf J Leg Stud 27(3):373–402
Ferrer Beltrán J, Rodríguez J (2011) Jerarquías normativas y dinámica de los sistemas jurídicos. Marcial Pons, Madrid
Garzón Valdés E (1977) Algunos modelos de validez normativa. Revista Latinoamericana de Filosofía III(1):41–68. Cited by the version published in Garzón Valdés (1993), pp 73–105
Garzón Valdés E (1993) Derecho, ética y política. Centro de Estudios Constitucionales, Madrid
Green L (1988) The authority of the State. Oxford University Press, Oxford
Green L (1996) The concept of law revisited. Mich Law Rev 94:1687–1717
Green L (1999) Positivism and conventionalism. Can J Law Jurisprud 12:35–52
Hacker P (1977) Hart's philosophy of law. In: Hacker P, Raz J (1977), pp 1–25
Hacker P, Raz J (1977) Law, morality and society. Essays in honour of H.L. A. Hart. Clarendon Press, Oxford
Hart H (1958) Positivism and the separation of law and morals. Harv Law Rev 71:593–629. Cited by the version published in Hart (1983), pp 593–628
Hart H (1961) The concept of law. Oxford University Press, Oxford. Cited by the 1994 second edition
Hart H (1965) Lon L. Fuller: the morality of law. Harv Law Rev 78:1281–1296. Cited by the version published in Hart (1983), pp 341–364
Hart H (1968) Kelsen's doctrine of the unity of law. In: Kiefer H, Munitz M (eds) Ethics and social justice. State University of New York Press, Albany, pp 309–342. Cited by the version published in Hart (1983)
Hart H (1983) Essays in jurisprudence and philosophy. Oxford University Press, Oxford
Hart H (1994) Postscript to *The concept of Law*, 2nd edn. Oxford University Press, Oxford, pp 238–276
Himma K (2009) Four concepts of validity. Reflections on inclusive and exclusive positivism. In: Adler K, Himma E (2009), chapter V
Kelsen H (1960) Reine Rechtslehre. Franz Deuticke, Wien. Cited by the 1989 English version. Smith, Gloucester (Mass)
Lewis D (1969) Convention. Harvard University Press, Cambridge
MacCormick N (1981) H.L.A. Hart. Edward Arnold Publishers, London. Cited by the 2008 second edition. Stanford University Press, Stanford
MacCormick N, Weinberger O (1986) An institutional theory of law. New approaches to legal positivism. Reidel, Dordrecht
Marmor A (1998) Legal conventionalism. Leg Theory 4(4):509–531
Marmor A (2001) Positive law and objective values. Oxford University Press, Oxford
Marmor A (2009) Social conventions. From language to law. Princeton University Press, Princeton
Marmor A (2011) Philosophy of law. Princeton University Press, Princeton
Nino C (1978) Some confusions around Kelsen's concept of validity. Archiv für Rechts-und Sozialphilosphie 64:357–376. Cited by the version published in Paulson S, Litschewski B (1998), pp 253–262
Nino C (1985) La validez del derecho. Astrea, Buenos Aires

Paulson S, Litschewski B (eds) (1998) Normativity and norms. Critical perspectives on Kelsenian themes. Clarendon Press, Oxford
Perry S (2009) Where have all the powers gone? Hartian rules of recognition, noncognitivism, and the constitutional and jurisprudential foundations of law. In: Adler K, Himma E (2009), chapter XI
Raz J (1971) The identity of the legal systems. Calif Law Rev 59:795–815
Raz J (1974) Kelsen's theory of the basic norm. Am J Jurisprud 19:94–111
Raz J (1975) Practical reason and norms. Hutchinson, London. Cited by the 1990 second edition. Princeton University Press, Princeton
Raz J (1994) Ethics in the public domain: essays in the morality of law and politics. Clarendon Press, Oxford
Ross A (1957) Tû – Tû. Harv Law Rev 70:812–825
Ross A (1958) On law and justice. Stevens, London
Ross A (1961) Validity and the conflict between legal positivism and natural law. Academia. Revista sobre enseñanza del Derecho 12(2008):199–220. Cited by the version published in Paulson S, Litschewski B (1998)
Ruiz Manero J (1990) Jurisdicción y normas. Centro de Estudios Constitucionales, Madrid
Ruiz Manero J (1991) Normas independientes, criterios conceptuales y trucos verbales. Respuesta a Eugenio Bulygin. Doxa 9:281–293
Schauer F (1991) Playing by the rules. A philosophical examination of rule-based decision-making in law and in life. Clarendon Press, Oxford
Searle J (1969) Speech acts: an essay in the philosophy of language. Cambridge University Press, Cambridge
Searle J (1995) The construction of social reality. Simon & Shuster, New York
Shapiro S (2009) What is the rule of recognition (and does it exist)?. In: Adler K, Himma E (2009), chapter IX
Shapiro S (2011) Legality. Bellknap Press, Cambridge
Von Wright GH (1963) Norm and action. A logical inquiry. Routledge & Keagan Paul, London
Von Wright GH (1983) Practical reason. Philosophical papers, vol I. Basil Blackwell, Oxford
Waldron J (2009) Who needs rules of recognition?. In: Adler K, Himma E (2009), chapter XII
Waluchow W (1994) Inclusive legal positivism. Oxford University Press, Oxford
Zipursky B (2001) The model of social facts. In: Coleman (2001a), pp 219–270

Social Facts and Law: Why the Rule of Recognition is a Convention

Josep M. Vilajosana

Abstract The author shows that the existence of law in a given society requires the presence of a unitary practice of identification of rules (a rule of recognition). It is also argued that the best way of understanding this rule is to see it as a constitutive convention, which allows the autonomous identification of the law of a particular community. According to this author, just as the existence of money requires the belief that it exists, the existence of a legal system depends ultimately on a set of beliefs shared by the relevant persons. After developing this position, a series of recurrent criticisms of conventionalist positions is reviewed with the aim of rejecting them. These criticisms are: if the rule of recognition is understood as a convention then it cannot account for the normative nature of the convention, nor for the presence of principles in legal systems, nor for the disagreements between lawyers; finally, the problem of the arbitrariness of the rule of recognition and its alleged banality is addressed.

1 Introduction

To say that something is conventional in the most general way is to equate it with the artificial and oppose it to the natural. This concept of convention, however, is too broad to give an appropriate account of characteristic social phenomena, including the law, and all social phenomena would in this sense be considered conventional precisely because they are not natural. In legal theory, therefore, the conventions that are commonly dealt with are related to social facts combined with an additional feature.

Social facts are made up of a series of behaviours by the members of a society. All those who carry out these actions must consider the conduct of others. Conventionality arises when one can formulate, for each verbal and non-verbal behaviour of a participant, a meaningful counterfactual statement such as *if others*

J. M. Vilajosana (✉)
Law Department, Pompeu Fabra University, Barcelona, Spain
e-mail: josep.vilajosana@upf.edu

L. Ramírez-Ludeña, J. M. Vilajosana (eds.), *Legal Conventionalism*, Law and Philosophy Library 126, https://doi.org/10.1007/978-3-030-03571-6_6

did not say or do what they do, I would not say or do what I do. This already quite specific way of considering conventions does not focus on its artificial or social character. The contrast is no longer made between the social and the natural, but it is instead made between *convention* and *conviction*. One who takes action through conviction might say *even if no one says or does a thing before I do, I would say what I say or do what I do.*[1]

The current discussion on the conventional character of law has more to do with this specific view and begins with philosopher David Lewis, author of *On Convention*, who treated the concept of convention technically by linking it to the abundant literature on collective action and strategic decisions.[2] From there, this concept went on to the theory of law by making an interpretation of Hart's rule of recognition as a convention in the sense of Lewis. The history of this discussion continues through the pioneering works of Ullmann-Margalit (1977) and Postema (1982), pp. 165–203, although some significant differences exist between them, and recent authors.[3]

In this chapter, I show that the existence of law in any given society requires the unitary practice of identifying norms, that is to say, a rule of recognition. I argue that the best way to understand this rule is to see it as a constitutive convention, which allows for autonomous identification of the law in a community. In this way, I will outline an account of law as a social creation: just as the monetary system requires a belief in its existence, so too does the existence of a legal system depend, ultimately, on a set of beliefs shared by the relevant group of people. I will develop this position and its advantages in Sect. 2 before devoting the last section to examining and addressing possible objections to the present thesis.

2 The Conventionality of the Rule of Recognition

According to Hart, two conditions are needed for a legal system to exist: (1) a rule of recognition specifying the criteria of legal validity must be effectively accepted by its officials and (2) the rules identified with the rule of recognition must generally be followed by the majority of the population.[4] On this point, Hart in fact refers to the existence of *all* secondary rules, and not the rule of recognition alone. However, if we understand that the rules of adjudication and the rules of change are identified according to the rule of recognition, it ultimately suffices to refer to its conditions of existence in order to establish the conditions of a legal system.

---

[1] The formulation of these counterfactuals is taken from Narváez (2004), p. 280.

[2] Lewis (1969).

[3] See Lagerspetz (1995); Marmor (1996), pp. 349–371; Shapiro (2001), pp. 149–191; Coleman (1998), pp. 381–425; Coleman (2001); Bayón (2002), pp. 33–54; Narváez (2004); Vilajosana (2003), pp. 41–63; Vilajosana (2006), pp. 521–538; Vilajosana (2010a).

[4] Hart (1961), p. 147.

While the problems in (1) revolve around conditions for the rule of recognition to exist, requiring the presence of conventional facts, in (2) they refer to the "efficacy" of the rules, which can be explained by turning to social, non-conventional facts. This seems to be the position of Hart when he argues that, unlike what occurs in social rules (including the rule of recognition), determining the effectiveness of primary rules does not require the presence of an internal point of view. Be that as it may, I will deal primarily with the first condition. I understand this proposal to be applicable to any theory of law and not exclusively to positivist theories. Non-positivist authors will surely add other conditions of existence, but I hold that they cannot rule out taking these two conditions into account.

I propose that the first condition for the existence of a legal system be that for every legal system, a convention with a constitutive dimension be used to serve the function of autonomously identifying the positive law of a given community. Let us analyse the meaning and implications of the elements of this condition.

2.1 Convention

In some of Hart's statements, he maintains that the rule of recognition is a social rule and that it exists as a matter of fact. This may be interpreted as meaning that the existence of the rule of recognition as a social rule is a conventional fact. I must qualify that Hart initially considers his "practice theory of rules" to be a general theory to give an account of all social rules. However, after the criticism formulated by Raz and Dworkin, Hart reduces in the postscript to *The Concept of Law* the scope of this theory by limiting it to a subclass of social rules, which he calls "social conventions", that includes the rule of recognition.[5]

If this is so, the truth of the proposition expressed by the sentence "In society *S* there is the rule of recognition *R*" will depend on the existence of conventional facts. What are these conventional facts exactly?

As is well known, Hart understands that the rule of recognition exists as a normally coincidental practice of public officials and private individuals when identifying a particular society's law, the content of which is manifested by the use of certain identification criteria by these persons.[6] However, the use of shared identification criteria must be accompanied by a certain attitude that Hart calls the "internal point of view". The authorities of a particular society, and especially the judges among them, act in a way that is consistent with their respect for the rule that allows them to identify the valid law of that society. This is reflected in a set of normative commitments about this convergent behaviour, seeing it as justified, and condemn deviations. Hart calls this critical-reflexive attitude the internal point of view.

---

[5] See Hart (1994), p. 256.

[6] See Hart (1961), p. 134.

The internal point of view can be translated into terms of conventional fact. Thus, the statement "In society *S* there is the rule of recognition *R*" can be analysed as follows:

1. Most part of the legal community (officials, judges, attorneys and legal scholars) in society S use criteria *C1, C2 ... Cn* (which form the rule of recognition for S) each time they must identify the law of S
2. Most part of the legal community in S believe 1.
3. The belief that 1 is given as a reason to use those criteria in these circumstances.
4. The previous clauses are common knowledge to most part of the legal community.[7]

Regardless of how Hart's words are interpreted, what reason could justify the adoption of a conventionalist version of the first condition of existence of legal systems? I think there are at least two reasons. First, this approach is necessary to avoid a return to infinity, and second, it is the most appropriate way to break with a possible vicious circle. While the first problem was already consciously addressed by Hart, the second was not.

2.1.1 A Finite Return

It is commonly understood that in legal systems some rules authorise the creation of others, which bring forth yet more rules. This process, however, must have an endpoint or can go back to infinity. Proposals to address this have been developed, as is known. The solution of Kelsen, according to which the *Grundnorm* was a presupposed norm, is not adequate because it either generates a return to infinity of the presupposed norms or it introduces sociological elements, making the proposal "impure" according to the very same perspective of the author.[8]

Hart raised the issue most clearly and made the decisive step towards its resolution. Closure of the system requires a rule that confers validity to the rest of the rules, but "it can neither be valid nor invalid but is simply accepted as appropriate for use in this way".[9] This is the rule of recognition. Its existence is necessarily a question of fact since it cannot be derived from other norms in the system. Moreover, it is a conventional fact because of the necessary coordination that must be in place to identify the law of a certain society: without a coordinated practice of identification, the law would not exist as a social phenomenon. I will return to this question later.

---

[7] The latter is an application of the characterisation of the Lewis convention (1969). His different definition of "convention", which is even more sophisticated, can be found on p. 42, p. 56, and p. 78.

[8] See Kelsen (1960), p. 202.

[9] Hart (1961), p. 132.

2.1.2 A Virtuous Circle

The second problem involves a vicious circle. Determining the content of a legal system requires the concurrent identification of, minimally, the authorities of that system, but identifying the authorities of that system requires us to have identified the rules of change and adjudication through the rule of recognition. In other words, we cannot know who should be considered an authority without the prior presence of a rule of recognition, but the latter cannot exist without the conduct of the authorities.

This problem must be faced sooner or later because a good part of the answers to other questions depend on its elucidation. One such question was raised by Prieto Sanchís in relation to one of my previous works based on the analogical use I made of Searle's idea on the continued existence of money with respect to the continued existence of law[10]: in both cases, people would be required to "believe in" money or "believe in" the law and act accordingly. Prieto remarked on this by saying, "… the analogy with the example of Searle on money is well brought. However, would the sheet of paper each carries in his or her wallet (and which become scarcer each day) stop being money the day we all stop believing that it is money, or rather we would stop believing that it is money when it stops working as such? Does the law and its rule of recognition exist by virtue of a belief, so that, once this belief has disappeared, the legal order would collapse, or rather do we believe that it is law because it works as such (perhaps a question of will rather than belief) and we would only abandon that belief if it ceased to function and lost all effectiveness?"[11]

This example highlights how the concept of law that normally interests us is that which allows us to identify existing legal systems. There may be some reason to study non-existent (ideal) legal systems, but they are not usually the primary objects of study for legal scholars. On the other hand, the example shows how problematic it is to speak of authorities when they are permanently ineffective. In other words, there seems to be a *conceptual* link between the concept of authority most appropriate to its use by the legal community and the *effectiveness* of a legal system. Someone who is systematically disobeyed by members who are subject to the rules that form a given legal system (or who do not even take those rules into consideration) has not authority in that system. These observations can shed light on the approach I advocate here.

There are two ways to break this vicious circle. The first would be to do away with the circular character of the argument by holding that a legal authority is not rule-dependent. This is suggested by Nino, who instead of characterizing primary organs as the authority because they can determine *de facto* the exercise of the state monopoly of coercion in a particular case.[12] This option, which is also adopted by Prieto, presents problems of adaptation with respect to what is usually considered

---

[10] See Searle (1995).

[11] Prieto Sanchís (2008), p. 491 (free translation by the author). See my response in Vilajosana (2008), pp. 507–536.

[12] Nino (1982), p. 60.

"legal authority", and furthermore it does not allow a legal authority to be distinguished from any authority with a simple "*de facto*" power.[13]

The second solution would be to accept the circularity, but detach it from its vicious character. This would consist of understanding legal authority in terms of conventional facts.[14] Thus, a group of individuals would guide their behaviour by a certain rule; that is to say, they would use the rule as a good reason for action. If that rule is given (and the rules identified through it are followed by the majority of the population), a certain legal system exists. If a legal system exists, then the rule guiding the behaviour of our initial group of individuals is correctly described as the rule of recognition *in that legal system*. Therefore, the individuals who guide their behaviour by that rule are properly understood as "authorities". They are, in a sense, authorities by virtue of that rule (or, rather, by virtue of rules identified through that rule), but they are not authorities before that rule (neither in a factual nor a logical sense). Their behaviour makes the existence of the rule possible, but it is the rule that makes them authorities.[15] In this way, the introduction of reciprocal attitudes and beliefs eliminates the vicious character of the circle. These attitudes and beliefs are circular, but the theory is not.

This is where an analogy with the existence of money makes sense. In a given society, something (a physical object, say an accounting book) represents money (it is a store of value and is accepted as an medium of exchange) *only* if the majority of members of that society believe that it is money and act in agreement with this belief, that is, they accept it as a store of value and use it habitually as an medium of exchange. Note that the existence of shared beliefs and the corresponding behaviour is a *necessary* condition of the existence of money, but it is not necessarily *sufficient*. An additional condition may be established, for example, whereby money must be emitted by a bank or another official body. What must be emphasized here is that if the condition is not fulfilled, the money does not exist.

This is how I see, *mutatis mutandis*, the existence of law in a given society: the existence of a rule of recognition, interpreted in the way described above, is a necessary condition for the existence of a legal system in a society. It follows from there that if there is no convergence of beliefs, attitudes, and behaviours to determine the norms of that system through the same criteria, the legal system fails to exist. This is only one necessary condition, however, and at least one more is required: the effectiveness of the norms identified through the criteria that form that rule.

After this detour, we are in a position to address the interesting question, posed by Prieto, of whether beliefs are prior or subsequent to the effective functioning of the system. For this purpose, we must remember that the behaviours that are relevant to determining the existence of a legal system fall into two categories that either refer to the first condition (the existence of the rule of recognition) or the

---

[13] On this criticism, see Ruiz Manero (1990), pp. 130–132.

[14] For example, following the line argued by Lagerspetz (1995), p. 159 ff.

[15] As expressed by Coleman (2001), p. 101. See also, in similar terms, Shapiro (2001), pp. 149–191. I fear, however, that Shapiro would no longer agree with what I affirm in the text, taking into account what he maintains in Shapiro (2011).

second condition (the efficacy of the rules). It would be incomprehensible, at least in relation to the first condition, to understand behaviours as being separate from shared beliefs. For this reason, if what I am saying here is to be accepted, to raise the question in terms of whether the beliefs precede the behaviours, or vice versa, would be unintelligible. I will now explain why.

First, we find actions consistent with beliefs, and attitudes on identification criteria for the norms of the system commonly used by those who are professionally engaged in identifying the law. Specifically, we observe the invocation of certain rules by lawyers in the courts insofar as these are identified using certain criteria (we usually equate them to the sources of law), the use of these same criteria by administrative bodies and courts when issuing their decisions, and the use of these same identification criteria among the practitioners of legal science when systematizing and analysing the legal norms to be studied.

This first type of act has the peculiarity of been a conventional fact in the terminology I have used previously. The meaning of these behaviours cannot be apprehended without reference to the beliefs of those who carry them out. Moreover, such beliefs are not independent from each other but are related, as the concept of mutual knowledge shows. The concept of conventional fact attempts to capture this idea. Conventional fact may be a subtype of social fact that is characterised by the presence of certain already mentioned traits, with mutual knowledge standing out.

As with money, only that which certain agents identify as the law of a certain society is considered to be the law of that society. Is this not circular after all? Indeed it is, though there is an explanation: it shows the *constitutive* dimension of the rule of recognition. There is nothing strange about speaking about circular (reflexive) phenomena. For instance, scientists are continually talking about biconditional causal relations and feedback.

Just as pieces of paper can cease to be money in a society when users stop believing and act accordingly, by no longer giving them value or accepting them as an exchange tool due, for example, to hyperinflation, *even when the competent organ is circulating them and the state endorses them*, so too can the legal system as a whole cease to be the law of a given community if jurists generally stop believing in it and act accordingly, i.e. the cited clauses and consequent behaviours come to an end. This would be the case in Spain, for example, regardless of what is written in the civil code on the sources of law. I believe that this is what Hart suggests when he states that the existence of the rule of recognition is a matter of fact. If there is a discrepancy between a formal norm (if any) on the sources of law and the beliefs, attitudes, and behaviours that form the rule of recognition, the latter must be taken into account for the purposes of what interests us now, simply because such beliefs, attitudes, and behaviours (the conditions of existence for that rule of recognition) are *constitutive* of the law in the community in question.

Furthermore, in addition to the behaviours that constitute the conditions of existence of a rule of recognition, the existence of a legal system in a certain society requires the presence of other types of acts that account for the effectiveness of the rules. These may be acts of compliance with the norms of the system by its addressees and acts of the courts sanctioning non-compliance. As I said, these acts are obviously social facts, but they are not necessarily conventional.[16]

2.2 The Constitutive Dimension of Conventions

The central criticism made by Hart on the work of Austin is that it offers a distorted image of the law. The explanation of the legal phenomenon based exclusively on habits of behaviour leaves out the typical normative element of that phenomenon. The introduction of the rule of recognition as a convention aims to overcome the drawbacks of the Austinian position. The challenge, then, is to show how a social practice can "generate" norms without falling into natural law.

One promising way of approaching this question would be to start from the already mentioned work of David Lewis. According to this author, a typical problem of coordination occurs when several agents have a particular structure of preferences regarding their respective models of behaviour. This means that among the various alternatives presented to them in a given set of circumstances, each agent has a preference to act as other agents do that is stronger than his own preference for acting in a certain way. Most problems of coordination are easily solved through simple agreements among agents to act according to an arbitrarily chosen alternative, and thus ensure uniformity of action among them. However, when a coordination problem is recurrent and agreement is difficult to reach (for example, because the number of agents is considerably high), a convention is likely to arise.

We can highlight two of the advantages presented by this approach.[17] First, it rescues and clarifies the intuition that conventions, in some sense, are arbitrary: if a rule is a convention, there must be at least some alternative that agents might have chosen. Second, it offers an answer to the question on the normativity proper to conventions: the reasons to follow a rule that is a convention are strongly linked to the fact that others also follow it. It would not make sense to follow a conventional rule if it is not actually practiced by the relevant community, since it would not serve to solve the coordination problem at its base.

At this point, can it be said that the concept of convention of Lewis is simply transposable to the rule of recognition, the existence of which is a necessary condition for the existence of a legal system?[18] In this respect, one might wonder if the typical structure of the rule of recognition responds to the structure Lewis is thinking of.

On one hand, it would be too demanding to require that a set of preferences be structured *ex ante* in a certain way. That is, it seems unrealistic to think that each judge would have his own preference (when considering criteria for legal validity),

[16] About the role of efficacy, see Vilajosana (2010b), pp. 103–118.

[17] In the sense expressed by Andrei Marmor, who I follow on this point. See Marmor (2001a), p. 200.

[18] One of the first to attempt this was Postema (1982), pp. 165–203.

but all would have a dominant preference to act as they expect others to do.[19] This idea, then, can be abandoned without rejecting the role reserved for conventional facts, as I have treated them. On the other hand, it may be undemanding as a model for a particular normative practice such as the law. At this point, it may be useful to focus our attention on the constitutive dimension of conventions. Marmor has proposed what he calls "constitutive conventions" in opposition to "conventions of coordination" (the model of which would be that proposed by Lewis).[20] However, as I state in another work, these two concepts are not mutually exclusive, since constitutive conventions destined to solve problems of coordination could exist (as occurs in the case I develop here). Given that the proposal I defend differs therefore from the perspective of that author on this point, I prefer to speak about "the constitutive dimension of conventions" (which could be applied to coordination) rather than "constitutive conventions" in the meaning used by Marmor (which would imply that they exclude the problem of coordination).[21]

In legal theory, it is common to distinguish between two types of rules, regulative and constitutive. The latter have the virtue of contributing to the "creation" of social reality and obey the canonical formula "X counts as Y in context C". Although the problem of normativity in the rule of recognition is usually approached by considering the rule to be regulative,[22] it is not unreasonable to think that the rule of recognition is a constitutive convention in that sense. Just as money in a society is what its members believe money to be, what counts as law in a given society comes therefore from the use of certain identification criteria for the law of that society by the legal community and by the diverse beliefs and expectations generated.

If we proceed in this way, it becomes clearer where the factor of autonomy of law as a social phenomenon resides, and which is one of the meanings of its normativity. Both circumstances are related to the conventional nature of legal practices. Each judge can use the previously mentioned criteria for very different reasons (for example, moral or strategic reasons), but all must agree to use these and not others, because others also use these and not others. This point is important, and should therefore be clear. Of course, each rule of recognition reflects the concrete circumstances and political convictions of the society in question and the moment in question. However, this is not relevant in this context. What is relevant is the question of whether these same convictions provide, on their own, sufficient reasons to act in

[19] In the same sense, see Coleman (2001), p. 95. It should be noted that this author has changed his position on this point, given that in previous work he had aligned himself, together with Postema, with the more mimetic translation of the framework of Lewis in the problem that concerns us.

[20] See Marmor (1996), pp. 349–371.

[21] Vilajosana (2003), pp. 41–63. It seems that, in posterior writings, Marmor did also realise that this compatibility is possible. For the proposal of Marmor, see Tusset (2007), pp. 179–198.

[22] Hart himself gave cause for it by considering that the rule of recognition, despite being a secondary rule, imposes obligations. See, in this respect, the controversy that Ruiz Manero and Bulygin have maintained in the journal *Doxa*: Bulygin (1991), pp. 311–318; Ruiz Manero (1991), pp. 281–293.

accordance with the rule, even if the rule in question is not followed by others. I would answer no.[23]

3 Responses to Possible Objections

Conventional theories, particularly those that conceive the rule of recognition as a convention, have been subjected to various criticisms. Since these critiques, if found successful, could adversely affect the conventionalist view of the rule of recognition I have outlined here, I shall conclude by examining briefly those that seem to me to be the most outstanding in the hopes of showing that none achieve their goal.

3.1 The Normativity of the Rule of Recognition

With regard to the problem of normativity and the rule of recognition, we should start by making a distinction to avoid a number of misunderstandings. It is one thing to predicate normativity from the rule of recognition and it is quite another to question the normativity of the law as a whole or, indeed, the process of applying the law understood as a social practice. There is another way of viewing the normativity of the law that is often confused with the above. It involves the question of whether the law binds the judges. To be clear, I am only concerned in the present work with the normativity proper to the rule of recognition.

It is necessary to elucidate how, if possible, the *practice of identification* of the law in a given community may be considered compulsory for those who perform this task. What is at issue now is to focus on this specific task of identification: the shared use of certain criteria to identify the law of a particular society. We must not focus on other problems, such as the justification of the duty to obey the law or the justification of institutionalized sanctions. By understanding the problem of the rule of recognition this way, we can look for possible answers.

The discussion on the normativity of practices is often raised in a mutually exclusive and exhaustive way: there is no normativity, or normativity exists, and then it is moral. Hart's internal point of view has sometimes been interpreted using the latter and I will not deny that some of his texts may give rise to this exegesis.[24] But I believe that, although these options are obviously exclusive, they are not, on the other hand, exhaustive. It is possible to speak of normativity precisely in the same way the normativity of conventions is spoken about.[25] I do not affirm that this is the

[23] Recall the counterfactual that lies behind every convention I mention at the beginning of this work.

[24] This is what, for example, MacCormicck and Weinberg (1986), pp. 132–133; Garzón (1993), pp. 317–335, do.

[25] For criticisms on the attempts to establish the binding character of conventions, see Green (1988), pp. 117–121; Celano (1995), pp. 15–77; Marmor (2001b), pp. 28–29.

sense of normativity that the conventionalist authors have defended when speaking of the normative character of conventions. In fact, these authors are not clear when they maintain that the practices of identification of a legal system give rise to the *obligation* to identify the legal system in question in that way. What I hold is that the most plausible manner to consider that practice as normative (where "normative" simply means "to have a reason to act") is the one expressed in this text. Should anyone consider that this reason lacks normative character, I have no problem in recognizing that there is nothing normative in the practice of identifying the law of a particular community. This normative element, present in conventions, consists of one fact: to be involved in a conventional practice implies that certain action be carried out because others also do it.[26] This may sound strange if we confuse the problems that I have identified here and take this idea as an answer to the problem of justification of the law. Indeed, this answer would be an absurd response to the problem of the duty to obey the law since that problem inevitably requires a response from the moral sphere.[27] However, if we appropriately limit the question and ask ourselves why some subjects should use certain criteria and not others to identify the law of a society, it is not unreasonable to conclude that one reason is because others also use them. It is the same reason we use to follow any convention. To be clear, this need not be the *only* reason. But this reason must be present for the rule of recognition to exist as a convention, according to the third clause of the abovementioned scheme.

When that rule exists, and other rules identified through it are effective, a certain legal system may exist and have rules that will surely impose certain *legal* obligations on the judges. Obviously, without the existence of a legal system, there can be no legal obligations.

Once we reach this point, the last problem I mention, related to normativity and not to be confused with any previous ones, must be addressed. It is often formulated through this notoriously ambiguous question: are judges under the obligation to comply with legal norms? If so, what type of obligation is involved? As I stated above, this is a problem that can only be addressed once the conditions for the existence of a given legal system are defined. Only then will the system itself establish a mandatory standard or a constitutive rule from which a technical rule can be inferred, indicating the conditions for someone to be considered a judge in relation to that system. This may be the case in the Spanish legal system, for example, where the organic law on judicial power establishes that one of the conditions of access to the judiciary is to swear or promise to comply with and enforce the constitution and all other elements of the legal system. Logically, there are those who may not be satisfied with this answer and would prefer to continue to ask why promises should be kept. This question can only be moral for the simple reason that we usually define moral reasons as ultimate reasons. It is not surprising, then, that ultimate reasons are moral: in the way they are usually understood, if other reasons exist, either they are

[26] See Lewis (1969). If this element were not present, the problem of coordination at the source of each convention would not be resolved.

[27] See Vilajosana (2007), chapter IV.

not ultimate or they are moral. None of this, however, has anything to do with the conditions that make the existence of law possible.

3.2 Conventions and Principles

Dworkin believes that in judicial practice we can find several considerations that judges deem relevant to rule on the cases presented to them. This is why there is no rule of recognition to validate all the reasons, both moral and non-moral, that are relevant when making judicial decisions.[28]

Dworkin's thesis on this point could be summarized in the following way. The law of a particular country contains principles in addition to rules. Principles are identified not only by their origin, but also by their content. But the content of principles must have a moral component. Therefore, if we want to identify the law of a particular country, we must refer to moral issues, or at least refer to those needed to identify these principles. But what would the criterion for a legal principle to exist be if we cannot simply relate it to its origin with acts of creation? According to Dworkin, a *legal principle* exists if it follows from the best political and moral interpretation of past legislative and judicial decisions in the area in question. Legal principles, then, would occupy an intermediate space between legal rules and *moral* principles.

Legal rules are created by the relevant institutions and their validity is derived from their origin, that is, the source of law in question (e.g. legislation or custom). *Moral* principles are defined by their content, and their validity is also related exclusively to their content. Legal principles, on the other hand, take their validity from a *combination* of source-based and content-based considerations. This view is generalized by Dworkin, who calls it "law as integrity" and describes it as follows: "According to law as integrity, propositions of law are true if they figure in or follow from the principles of justice, fairness and procedural due process, which provide the best constructive interpretation of the community's legal practice".[29]

The validity of a legal principle is derived, therefore, from a combination of facts and moral considerations. Relevant facts are related to legal decisions (from both legislators and judges) carried out in the past within the corresponding scope. Moral and political considerations involve the ways in which such past decisions may be better justified by morally correct principles.

It should be remembered, however, that the rule of recognition, as a social rule, plays a decisive role not only in identifying the law but also in establishing its autonomy in relation to other normative orders in the same society, such as social-moral orders or social customs. It is difficult to make this distinction because these are all normative phenomena that originate in social practices. The concept of the rule of recognition attempts to provide this distinction by giving the conduct and

---

[28] For the criticism outlined in this section and in the following section, see Dworkin (1977, 1986).

[29] Dworkin (1986), p. 225.

intentions of a determined set of people a decisive role in the constitution of legal practice.

Dworkin's scheme relies ultimately on the legal practice of a particular society. But his approach takes the legal nature of that practice for granted. For law as integrity, legal statements are true and appear in or follow from principles of justice and equity and from procedural principles like due process, which offer the best constructive interpretation of the community's *legal* practice. But how does Dworkin identify those legal practices among all the social practices that occur in a given community? Two possibilities come to mind. In each case, we must start from an undeniable premise: if a practice is legal, then it will have some relationship with the law of that community. One possibility would be to apply the definition of law that Dworkin himself gives, but if we do this, the argument becomes circular: to know if a practice is legal, we must turn to the elements that allow us to identify the law of a certain society, but among these elements there is the reference to the legal practice that we had to identify. The other possibility would be to find independent criteria to determine when a practice is legal. This is precisely what the rule of recognition provides.

The shortcomings that I detect in the Dworkinian theses and the virtues of the scheme that I defend may be made clearer with an example. Imagine that someone wants to identify the content of Roman law in a certain historical period (for example, relative to the time of the emperor Augustus). The question is, which steps should be followed? Or better yet, which steps do *all* professors of Roman law follow? Do they reference a law that is similar to the best possible interpretation of Roman institutions, taking into account the principles of justice? I do not think so. What they do is try to identify through the relevant empirical procedures the criteria the users of the law during the period in question themselves used, making sure the system as a whole was effective. Therefore, faced with the dilemma of choosing between identifying the law by taking into account the identification criteria actually used by the officials, if not others, of a legal system and identifying it through the interpretation of *legal* institutions (without knowing that they are of a legal character), it seems more reasonable to do what all professors of Roman law do. If this is the case in the identification of Roman law, why should it be different for the identification of the law during any other historical period or at any latitude?

3.3 Convention and Disagreement

According to Dworkin, a great deal of controversy among lawyers and among judges on how certain cases should be decided *legally* would lead to the conclusion that the law cannot be based on an official consensus like that which seems to follow from the existence of a rule of recognition.

In this respect, we could ask ourselves two questions. Does this generalised controversy really exist? If so, is it the kind that makes it necessary to call into question the existence of a rule of recognition as a social rule? It would not be unreasonable to respond negatively to both questions.

With regard to the first question, there are undoubtedly disagreements among lawyers, in general, and among judges in particular, on how to decide judicial cases. The very fact that there are judicial proceedings in which at least two parties can make arguments in favour of their respective positions and reasonably invoke legal reasons for the ruling to be propitious to them is an indicator that this controversy is inseparable from the legal practice itself.

Exactly how far does this controversy go? Can it be said that the presence of these disputes with respect to judicial cases simply supposes that the law as a whole is controversial? What happens to the many legal decisions that are taken out-of-court, such as contracts that are unchallenged, laws that are enforced, and so forth? Surely, the cases that could be brought to court, but are not, are more frequent than those that are.

With regard to the second question, it must be remembered that not every dispute in court is relevant to questioning the existence of a rule of recognition. Many of these controversies concern the attribution of meaning in certain normative formulations and can be resolved by appealing to a more or less established consensus within the legal community (with arguments that do not necessarily allude to principles or have a moral component).

The only controversy relevant to the criticism I analyse here are those that affect the criteria of legal validity, which form a concrete rule of recognition. But does such deep controversy really occur in the practices of interpretation and application of the law that we know?

Let us take as an example a simplified formulation of the rule of recognition in the Spanish legal system. This rule could read as follows: "The constitution of 1978 and all the norms accepted by it or created in accordance with the procedures that it establishes, without having been repealed, shall be considered valid Spanish law." This idea, in the field of the application of law, would be specified in a series of hierarchically ordered criteria in what is known as sources of law. An example of sources of law would involve cases in which the constitution is applied first; in its absence, law in the broadest sense (with their own hierarchies of law in the technical sense, regulations, etc.) would be applied; in its absence, customary rules would apply; and when this application is not possible, the general principles of law shall apply.

We must ask ourselves, do judges apply customary rules over laws? Is there a discrepancy between the laws being subordinated to the constitution? Let us consider the question in a more general way. Is the normal (i.e. continuous and stable) functioning of a legal system compatible with a permanent, in-depth discussion of such criteria? If such a permanent and profound discussion of the criteria for legal validity were to take place, we would be faced with pathological legal systems (as Hart once called them), and they would not be precisely paradigmatic cases, something that would be required in order for Dworkin's criticism to be plausible. A system in which the criteria for legal validity were deeply and permanently questioned would simply be unsustainable.

Let us imagine that for a certain time in society *S*, judges generally apply the rules emanating from a democratically elected parliament. At a certain moment, a group of people take power and begin to issue norms directed at the entire population of *S* with the pretention that judges apply these norms. For a certain period of time, judges might be divided over whether to apply the norms emanating from that revolutionary committee. This would be the pathological case often accompanied by civil war. But after this convulsive stage, one of two possibilities may occur: judges will generally apply the norms that emanate from the parliament or they will apply those of the revolutionary committee. In the latter case, a change in the rule of recognition takes place in society *S*. But the truth is that it is counterintuitive to think that the situation I have described as pathological is normal, although Dworkin seems to describe it this way.

This does not mean that there can be no discrepancies about the scope of certain validity criteria that make up the rule of recognition. I merely hold that these discrepancies cannot be deep or widespread, something that Dworkin's argument would require in order for his conclusion to follow effectively from his premises. Nor does it mean that there can be no doubt as to whether a particular rule is part of a particular legal system or whether that rule is applicable or not. It would only be necessary to add a certain clarification about the existence of interpretative practices. According to what Anscombe[30] states in relation to another context, what is important is that so long as group members recognize and understand a given behaviour as subsumed under the relevant description, the practice of identifying legal norms, even if apparently transformed, remains the same.

3.4 The Arbitrary Character of a Conventional Rule of Recognition

A possible criticism of the conventionalist view of the rule of recognition is that in order to consider it a convention, we should admit that it is arbitrary, since the feature of arbitrariness is what defines convention. But if we did this, we would be oblivious to the importance of the rule of recognition from a social and political point of view.

Celano has expressed it in the following terms: "The idea that the rule of recognition is arbitrary seems hasty, almost derisory. The rule of recognition specifies the criteria for identifying what constitutes the valid law. This is not an issue comparable to the decision whether to drive on the right or on the left (a paradigm of the coordination problem). The rule of recognition is the result of political, institutional, ideological conflicts; of revolutions and *coups d'état* (…). That certain criteria of validity are actually accepted and used is a historical fact (…). It is a fact that

[30] Anscombe (1957), p. 84 ff. In the same sense, see Celano (1995), p. 54.

invokes conflicting values and principles. The hypothesis according to which (...) it is something arbitrary is not plausible".[31]

This attack seems very plausible at first sight. When identifying the law of a community, how can we define the decisions of their subjects as arbitrary when in that process such important questions of value are at stake? However, before succumbing to the apparent charm of this criticism, we ought to ask what is meant by "arbitrary" in conventionalist terms.[32]

It is important to remember that the arbitrariness of convention does not amount to indifference.[33] If a person has lived in London for 20 years and then moves to Barcelona, she is not indifferent to the side of the road she drives on. She has become accustomed to driving on the left and would prefer to continue to do so (therefore, the choice is not indifferent). However, it is precisely due to the problem of coordination and an already established convention in Barcelona to drive on the right that this person must conform, although she would clearly be more comfortable continuing with what she was accustomed to. Arbitrariness of convention, therefore, manifests itself not in the possible indifference of each participant toward relevant social practices, but in the fact that there is more than one option to solve the problem of coordination.

Beyond this, in this critical line which I comment, confusion exists between the *existence* of a legal system and its *identity*. It could be said that all the elements present in these words of Celano are important. However, they are not important for the existence of a legal system, they are in fact important for its identity. Using one of these elements would lead to the identification of different legal systems, but it would not affect their existence. The question of whether the set of identification criteria actually used by the relevant population is *A* (for example, defining a democratic political regime) or *B* (defining an authoritarian political regime) is relevant to the identity of the system, but does not affect its existence at all: democratic regimes are as "existent" as authoritarian ones, so long as the requisite conditions are met.[34] The only thing this situation shows is that different options are available. This fundamental element leads us to conclude that the trait of arbitrariness, in the sense that interests us here, is present. Of course, we would much prefer that the type of existing legal system belongs to *A* and not to *B*, and that is what makes us reluctant to call such a choice arbitrary. But the meaning of "arbitrary" that is relevant in relation to the existence of the rule of recognition (and therefore with the existence of legal systems) is related to the fact that those who dedicate themselves professionally to identifying the legal system use the *same* criteria, regardless of whether they belong to a democratic or an authoritarian regime, include precedents or not, establish one type of normative hierarchy or another, and so on.

---

[31] Celano (2003), p. 351 (free translation from Italian). In similar terms, see Shapiro (2011).

[32] For the concept of arbitrariness, see Marmor (2006), pp. 683–704.

[33] See Lewis (1969), pp. 76–80.

[34] For the identity of legal orders and precisely the relation with these questions of value, I refer to Vilajosana (1997).

3.5 The Supposed Banality of the Conventionalist Thesis

One last criticism that I want to comment on is the one that sustains the banal nature of the conventionalist thesis applied to the rule of recognition. This criticism refers in particular to the so-called dependency condition, which is understood in the following way: when a convention is in place, the fact that one conforms because others do is one of the reasons why each conforms. This is just one of the conditions that I emphasize when I speak of the existence of a rule of recognition as a conventional fact.

Bruno Celano, for example, affirms that the necessary character of this condition may be plausible, but it is banal: "It is an empirical thesis according to which, in the case of the rule of recognition, each of the officials (whatever the reasons why he is convinced that the rule should be followed, or why he follows it) thinks that it would not make much sense to stick to the rule, unless all (or almost all) others did. Which is plausible, but banal."[35]

I agree that the thesis is plausible and reasonable (that is why I defend it), but I am not sure about the negative element that would incorporate banality at this point. Celano himself gives a clue about what a banal thesis would be. It would be a thesis that is not informative, theoretically not interesting, and philosophically not very illuminating.[36] But does the conventionalist thesis have these features?

Let us focus first on the positive aspect of the thesis, which Celano admits. The thesis is plausible and reasonable. If this is so, how do we interpret the fact that many authors discuss it? Why, as we have seen, does Dworkin put a lot of effort into trying to show that a conventional rule of recognition is not possible? If it were a banal thesis, any reasonable person would admit it (and I will not be the one to say that Dworkin is not reasonable), although he or she would add that it does not bring anything new. I have already said what I think of the condition of dependence. If we focus on the concrete scope I have given to the rule of recognition, we must remember that its existence depends on the *practices of identification* in a given legal system carried out in a given society. It is the use of identification criteria for a certain legal system that is at stake (and not something else) when we speak of such practices. But such criteria should be the same if we intend to identify the *same* kind of legal system. Participants would therefore be required to consider the criteria used by others. This is, as I stated earlier, the problem of coordination that lies at the basis of the need for officials (at least) to use the same criteria to identify their legal system.

Perhaps the term *banal* refers in fact to the circular character of the phenomenon. However, as I stated earlier, far from being a source of worry, it gives us the clue to producing a philosophically attractive explanation of how social reality can be

[35] Celano (2003), p. 353.

[36] If we interpret, *a sensu contrario*, what is said in Celano (2003), p. 347.

generated through constitutive rules in terms that are comparable to the existence of money and, in my opinion, the existence of law.[37]

References

Anscombe GEM (1957) Intention. Blackwell, Oxford
Bayón JC (2002) El contenido mínimo del positivismo jurídico. In: Zapatero V (coord) Horizontes de la filosofía del derecho: homenaje a Luís García San Miguel, vol 2. pp 33–54
Bulygin E (1991) Regla de reconocimiento: ¿Norma de obligación o criterio conceptual? Réplica a Juan Ruiz Manero. Doxa 9:311–318
Celano B (1995) Consuetudini, convenzioni. In: Comanducci P, Guastini R (eds) Analisi e diritto. Giappichelli, Torino, pp 15–77. Spanish translation by Moreso J J, cited as: Costumbres, convenciones. In: Dos estudios sobre la costumbre. Fontamara, México 2000
Celano (2003) La regola di riconoscimento è una convenzione? Ragion Pratica 21:347–360
Coleman JL (1998) Incorporationism, conventionality, and the practical difference thesis. Leg Theory 4:381–425
Coleman JL (2001) The practice of principle: in defence of a pragmatism approach to legal theory. Oxford University Press, Oxford
Dworkin R (1977) Taking rights seriously. Duckworth, London
Dworkin R (1986) Law's empire. Harvard University Press, Cambridge
Garzón E (1993) Algo más acerca de la relación entre el derecho y la moral. In: Derecho, Ética y Política. C.E.C, Madrid, pp 317–335
Green L (1988) The authority of the State. Oxford University Press, Oxford
Hart HLA (1961) The concept of law. Oxford University Press, Oxford
Hart HLA (1994) In: Bulloch P, Raz J (eds) Postscript to the concept of law, 2nd edn. Oxford University Press, Oxford
Kelsen H (1960) Reine Rechtslehre, 2nd edn. Frans Deuticke, Wien
Lagerspetz E (1995) The opposite mirrors. An essay on the conventionalist theory of institutions. Kluwer, Dordrecht
Lewis D (1969) Convention. A philosophical study. Basil Blackwell, Oxford
MacCormicck N, Weinberg O (1986) An institutional theory of law. New approches to legal positivism. Reidel, Dordrecht
Marmor A (1996) On convention. Synthese 107:349–371
Marmor A (2001a) Legal conventionalism. In: Coleman J (ed) Hart's postcript. Essays on the postscript to the concept of law. Oxford University Press, Oxford, pp 193–217
Marmor A (2001b) Positive law and objective values. Clarendon Press, Oxford
Marmor A (2006) Legal positivism: still descriptive and morally neutral. Oxf J Leg Stud 26(4):683–704
Narváez M (2004) Wittgenstein y la teoría del derecho. Una senda para el convencionalismo jurídico. Marcial Pons, Madrid
Nino CS (1982) Introducción al análisis del derecho. Ariel, Barcelona
Postema GJ (1982) Coordination and convention at the foundations of law. J Leg Stud 11:165–203
Prieto Sanchís L (2008) Identificación y justificación del derecho. Anuario de Filosofía del derecho 25:487–506
Ruiz Manero J (1990) Jurisdicción y normas. C.E.C, Madrid
Ruiz Manero J (1991) Normas independientes, criterios conceptuales y trucos verbales; Respuesta a Eugenio Bulygin. Doxa 9:281–293

[37] Celano has himself admitted a non-vicious circularity in relation with his vision of customary norms as social rules. See Celano (1995), pp. 15–77.

Searle JR (1995) The construction of social reality. Simon and Schuster, New York
Shapiro SJ (2001) On Hart's way out. In: Coleman J (ed) Hart's postcript. Essays on the postscript to the concept of law. Oxford University Press, Oxford, pp 149–191
Shapiro SJ (2011) Legality. Harvard University Press, Cambridge
Tusset G (2007) The social reality of law. In: Comanducci P, Guastini R (eds) Analisi e diritto. Giappichelli, Torino, pp 179–198
Ullmann-Margalit E (1977) The emergence of norms. Clarendon Press, Oxford
Vilajosana JM (1997) El significado político del derecho. Fontamara, México
Vilajosana JM (2003) Hechos sociales y Derecho. In: Diciotti E, Velluzzi V (eds) Ordinamento giuridico, sovranità, diritti. Giappichelli, Torino, pp 41–63
Vilajosana JM (2006) El positivismo jurídico convencionalista. In: Ramos Pascua JA, Rodilla MA (eds) El positivismo jurídico a examen. Estudios en homenaje a José Delgado Pinto. Ediciones Universidad de Salamanca, Salamanca, pp 521–538
Vilajosana JM (2007) Identificación y justificación del derecho. Marcial Pons, Madrid
Vilajosana JM (2008) A las puertas del paraíso. Respuesta a Luís Prieto Sanchís. Anuario de Filosofía del derecho 25:507–536
Vilajosana JM (2010a) El derecho en acción. La dimensión social de las normas jurídicas. Marcial Pons, Madrid
Vilajosana JM (2010b) Eficacia normativa y existencia del derecho. Teoría & derecho. Revista de pensamiento jurídico 8:103–118

Cooperative Conventions, Rules of Recognition and Institutional Practices

Rodrigo E. Sánchez Brigido

Abstract According to Sánchez Brigido, after abandoning the idea that the rule of recognition is a coordinative convention in Lewis's sense, Postema offered a new, more sophisticated version of conventionalism. According to this new version, the rule of recognition should be understood, not as a coordinative convention, but as a cooperative convention. The paper examines Postema's cooperative convention account. It claims that it is unsuccessful for a crucial reason: certain features of officials' practice show that there might be a practice constitutive of a rule of recognition but there need not be any cooperative problem to be solved. Uncertainty, interdependence and mutually conditional preferences (the conditions that define a cooperative problem) need not be present. The paper also suggests that a proper account of rules of recognition should recognize that the practice constituted by such a rule should be understood, not as a cooperative convention, but as a special type of institutional practice.

1 Introduction

A central feature of law is that its existence depends on human actions and attitudes. It is a social phenomenon. But it is also a normative phenomenon, for law is associated with reasons for actions in several ways. One aspect of its normative character is that legal rules are invoked to justify interventions on individuals' basic goods. Rule-applying officials, in effect, invoke the very same practice they are involved in to provide reasons to apply such rules and therefore justify the interventions. To invoke a practice as a reason is problematic, however: it is not entirely clear how a social practice (in other words, a fact) can be invoked as a reason to act in a certain way, especially when said actions consist in applying rules that result in the intervention of citizens' basic goods. This is one of the problems related to the normativity of law, which I shall refer as *the normative problem*.[1]

[1] Another more important issue of the normative problem is whether there is an obligation to obey the law. This problem may be viewed as separate from the one I mention in this chapter, although

R. E. Sánchez Brigido (✉)
Universidad Nacional de Córdoba, Córdoba, Argentina
e-mail: rsanchezbrigido@csjn.gov.ar

L. Ramírez-Ludeña, J. M. Vilajosana (eds.), *Legal Conventionalism*, Law and Philosophy Library 126, https://doi.org/10.1007/978-3-030-03571-6_7

In a seminal work,[2] H.L.A. Hart claimed to give an account of the social character of law. He showed that when a legal system exists, a group of law-applying officials will follow what he called a "rule of recognition". Officials apply and implement certain rules identified as the law according to a set of common criteria, with general conformity in the population to such rules. His thesis was meant to explain how law is a social fact. But Hart's rule of recognition is also meant to explain the normative character of law. After all, the rule of recognition is a rule, and rules are seen as providing reasons for action.

Hart's answer to the normative problem was considered unsatisfactory by several critics. His account should have explained in more detail how a group of people (law-applying officials) using certain criteria could be seen as a reason to intervene in others' basic goods. After all, such practices are a fact. Thus, Hartian followers turned to an inquiry into the nature of the practice that is constitutive of a rule of recognition. Different theories emerged, all of them appealing to a common strategy: they tried to show that the practice constitutive of a rule of recognition belongs to a category of practices that are familiar to us, and the fact that those who are engaged in it invoke it as a reason for action is intelligible.

One such theory is legal conventionalism. Its central idea is that the practice constitutive of a rule of recognition is a convention, a type of practice in which participants, at least at first sight, can intelligibly invoke the practice itself (the convention) to justify their actions. In one of its versions,[3] legal conventionalism claims that the rule of recognition is a coordinative-convention in line with David Lewis.[4] Like the coordinative-convention of driving on the left, where every driver invokes the convention as a reason for him and others to drive on the left, legal officials invoke the practice of the rule of recognition (allegedly, a convention) as a reason for themselves and other officials to use the same criteria in order to identify the rules used to intervene in citizens' basic goods. Hart himself, in a postscript to his posthumously published book,[5] seems to have subscribed to the idea that the practice in question is indeed a coordinative-convention in this sense, with authors such as G. Postema and J. Coleman later developing the idea in more detail.[6]

Although the suggestion seemed attractive, this version of legal conventionalism was subject to various criticisms and eventually there was a general consensus to the

some authors (including the conventionalist authors I mention below) hold that they are related. See Postema (2011), p. 499.

[2] Hart (1994), pp. 114–117.

[3] Another version appealed to the idea of a constitutive convention and was elaborated by Marmor in several papers. *Social Conventions* (Marmor 2009) unifies his previous presentations. I am not able to consider this approach properly in this paper. However, the considerations I propose below suggest that Marmor's approach is mistaken. In a footnote below I say something more specific about it.

[4] Lewis (1969).

[5] Hart (1994), pp. 255–256.

[6] Postema (1982), pp. 165–203; Coleman (1982), pp. 139–641; Coleman (1998), pp. 381–425.

effect that these objections were conclusive. One of its proponents, Jules Coleman, even abandoned the approach.[7]

This consensus remained unchallenged for several years. In a recent work, however, Postema has reconsidered the issue and defended once more the idea of the rule of recognition as a convention. He readapts the idea of a coordinative-convention, appealing to the broader notion of a "cooperative-convention", and claims that this new, more sophisticated account can cope with the usual objections.

In the following sections, I shall examine this new defence of conventionalism, having criticized the previous version myself. Postema's work is a good opportunity to re-examine the scope of those objections.[8] I shall try to show that Postema's defence is unsuccessful, despite its new refinements. The crucial reason as to why the theory fails is that the constitutive practice of a rule of recognition belongs to a category of practices that one could call "institutional practices". A rule of recognition is the practice of an institution (the judiciary) to which certain actions are attributed. An institutional practice is neither a coordinative-convention, as legal conventionalists used to claim, nor a cooperative-convention, as Postema's more sophisticated version now claims. Institutional practice, in fact, has its own character.

First, I shall briefly characterize the notion of a coordinative-convention employed initially by legal conventionalists in Sect. 2 and Postema's more sophisticated version in Sect. 3. I will then consider how Postema readapted the idea of a convention to account for the nature of rules of recognition in Sect. 4 before examining if that idea can address the usual objections raised against this version of conventionalism in Sect. 5. In Sects. 6 and 7, I will argue that the theory fails, with the failure owed to the fact that the constitutive practice of a rule of recognition belongs to a different category of practices.

2 Coordinative-Conventions and the Initial Strategy of Legal Conventionalism

The notion of a coordinative-convention was originally developed by David Lewis. The basic idea is that there is a certain way to address "coordination problems", a type of complex social interaction situation that is solved through the emergence of specific patterns of conduct. A typical example of such a situation would be two people talking on the telephone when the connection is cut. Each person wishes to restore it, with neither caring who calls back and who answers. The only way to restore the connection is by one calling back and the other waiting for the call. They must decide whether to wait or call back without knowing how, and a coordination

[7] Coleman (2001), p. 98 ff.

[8] Sánchez Brigido (2010), pp. 40–43.

problem arises. A coordination problem is thus, roughly, a situation where there are two or more agents and two or more possible combinations of their actions such that each agent prefers that, if all but one person do their parts in that action-combination, the remaining person does likewise. Thus, if the telephone situation is solved the first time by the original caller calling back while the other waits to answer, this strategy may be followed the next time the problem occurs. If after several instances a pattern emerges, a social convention is then put in place.[9]

According to Lewis, a convention is a regularity (R) in the behaviour of the members of a group who are in specific situation S (a recurrent coordination problem) whereby (1) everyone conforms to R; (2) everyone expects everyone else to conform to R; and (3) everyone prefers to conform to R on condition that everyone does, since S is a coordination problem and uniform conformity to R is a combination of their actions such that no one would have been better off had any one agent alone acted otherwise.[10] Thus, in the telephone-call situation, everyone conforms to the regularity "original caller calls back, the other waits", expects everyone to conform, prefers everyone to conform if everyone does and, since agents are facing a coordination problem, everyone prefers that the other regularity be followed ("original caller waits, the other calls back") as long as everyone conforms to it. (It is possible that each agent cares about who calls. For instance, if the one who calls is to be charged, but still prefers above all to restore the connection.[11]

In its original version, legal conventionalism uses Lewis' notion of coordinative-convention in an attempt to account for the rule of recognition and the normative problem. The central idea can be put as follows: where there is law, a group of individuals must apply rules that satisfy certain criteria. Given that there will be a broad set of criteria from which to choose, the problem of which set to select can be seen as a recurrent coordination problem. It is also possible that each agent prefers, *ex ante*, a different set of criteria, but wants everyone else to choose the same set given that each agent choosing a different option would be tantamount to no legal system at all.[12] It is plausible to suppose that the problem would be solved by the emergence of a regularity of behaviour that fits the definition described above. Thus, the rule of recognition can be seen as a regularity and, consequently, a coordinative-convention. In fact, according to legal conventionalism, this would address the normative problem. Lewis-type coordinative-conventions are understood with the assumption that all participants are rational and wish to solve a coordination problem. Since regularities are the solution to such a problem, there are reasons for conforming to them.

Postema and Coleman were, as I said before, the main exponents of this approach. Despite its initial appeal, the approach was subject to numerous objections. To give an example, law-applying officials do not appear to face the stylized and restricted types of problems that participants in Lewis-like conventions do. In the latter case,

---

[9] See Lewis (1969), pp. 36–42.

[10] I am paraphrasing Lewis' first definition of conventions to show the core idea. See Lewis (1969), pp. 14, 42 and 78.

[11] Lewis' model is also designed to capture that situation. See Lewis (1969), p. 10.

[12] Coleman (1982), pp. 114–121. See also Postema (1982), p. 176 ff.

solutions are arbitrary in the sense that each participant prefers to act in accordance with a different regularity if others do. In that sense, the regularity that solves the problem in the telephone call situation (the original caller waits, the other calls back) is arbitrary since there is an alternative available (original caller calls, the other waits) that all participants would adhere to if others do the same. It is true, as conventional theorists remark, that arbitrariness in this sense does not mean indifference: participants can prefer one outcome to another if they prefer conformity over non-cooperation.[13] Nevertheless, there must be another pattern to which all would adhere. Claiming that the rule of recognition is a coordinative-convention implies, therefore, that each law-applying official prefers not only that everyone use a specific set of criteria, but also that another set of criteria be used if everyone were to be using it. This seems to be not conceptually necessary: one can easily think of cases in which law-applying officials did not think in such a way. In other words, it is perfectly possible that law-applying officials are unwilling to use a different set of criteria, even if others do.[14]

This objection, and others along similar lines, were considered decisive and interest in coordinative-conventions declined.

3 Postema's Sophisticated Version and Cooperative-Conventions

After many years, Postema has begun to defend this approach again, this time with a more sophisticated model. In his new version, Postema begins with a complex social interaction situation that he calls a "cooperation problem". In this sort of situation, he holds, rational strategic agents have certain preferences, but face a problem with three properties: (a) *rough coincidence of interest*, with each party more likely to benefit more by cooperation with others through a common scheme than by non-cooperation; (b) *mutually conditional preferences*, with certain actions or strategies being preferred to others that are available if, and only if, other parties also choose corresponding actions that are appropriate; and (c) *uncertainty*, a state of not knowing how other parties will act.[15]

A coordination problem such as the telephone call situation is a type of cooperation problem; the notion of a cooperation problem is much more comprehensive than the notion of a coordination problem. This notion gives Postema the possibility of characterizing the idea of convention in a new way. His characterization is different from Lewis', partially because, as I said before, it is based on the idea of a cooperation problem. According to Postema, conventions can be characterized in the following way:

---

[13] See Lewis (1969), pp. 76–80; Vilajosana (2010), p. 76; Marmor (2009), pp. 8–9.

[14] Marmor (2001), pp. 201–202; Shapiro (2002), pp. 392–393.

[15] Postema (2011), p. 489.

> A convention exists in a community when, with regard to a pattern or scheme of actions S, it is common knowledge among members of that community that (1) most members expect most of their fellow members to do their part in S, (2) most prefer (or have good reason) not to act unilaterally against this expectation, (3) most on the whole prefer general conformity to some such pattern or scheme to most members going their own ways, and (4) this common knowledge puts rational pressure on members of the community do their part in S. So understood, conventions are schemes of correlated actions that enable members of a community to solve the recurrent cooperation problems they face.[16]

This notion of convention, for Postema, gives an account of the idea of social facts with normative force. If the pattern of conduct is followed, the fact that others behave accordingly and are expected to do so creates rational pressure to behave in such a way when viewed in the light of familiar principles of practical reasoning. This rational pressure is internal to the framework of preferences and goals that can be achieved through out cooperation. This in no way implies, as Postema clarifies, that there are reasons to comply without considering the possibility of good reasons to seek cooperation. Yet it makes the practice intelligible.

Several features of this characterization are deserving of commentary.

First, this definition of a convention aims at improving Lewis'[17] and Postema's own characterization in an earlier work.[18] One aspect of this more sophisticated definition is that the cooperative-convention notion is much more comprehensive. It is important to remember that Lewis' conventions are solutions to coordination problems, while Postema's conventions may include coordination problems. Thus, Postema's characterization of a convention is not necessarily attached to the idea of arbitrariness. When a cooperation problem exists, solutions are not necessarily arbitrary in the way explained above. A cooperation problem could be a "stag hunt" or "security" game in which players are better off cooperating in the joint hunt of the "stag" (large prize) rather than hunting a hare (small prize) on their own, and no alternative regularity, and therefore no arbitrariness, exists. In this scenario, a cooperative convention could be required to hunt a stag, but not a hare.[19] This is a relevant point: Postema aims at giving an account of the rule of recognition in terms of a convention. One of the objections raised against that idea was that it implies that participants see the rule as arbitrary, something that does not seem applicable to the constitutive practice of the rule of recognition. The new idea of convention avoids that problem.

Second, even though the idea of a cooperation problem does not form part of conditions (1) to (4) of a convention (see above), Postema clearly thinks of it as a

[16] Postema (2011), p. 492.

[17] Postema understands that the notion of convention is useful to account for solutions to not only coordination problems but also cooperation problems. Furthermore, situations in which no solution could be achieved (e.g. prisoner dilemma situations) would be counterintuitively characterized by Lewis as solutions. Finally, for Postema, the idea of parties preferring any cooperative solution to no solution at all goes too far. In his understanding, it is not regularity that must be seen as a solution, but its outgoing character. See Postema (2011), pp. 489–491.

[18] Postema (2011), p. 492.

[19] Postema (2011), p. 522.

defining condition. Thus, he claims, as quoted above, that conventions are schemes of correlated actions that allow cooperation problems to be solved. If he did not think so, clause (4)—which, by definition, creates rational pressure to conform—would be completely dogmatic and capricious. The attempt to solve a cooperation problem allows the existence of this rational pressure to comply. What is more, as the notion of cooperation is implicitly included in the definition, there is common awareness among participants of a cooperation problem. The definition states, in reality, that not only are the circumstances described by clauses (1) to (4) common knowledge, but also the circumstances described by clause (5). In other words, it is common knowledge that a cooperation problem exists, and therefore community members are jointly aware of being in a situation where there are mutually conditional preferences, a rough coinciding of interests, and uncertainty: the three characteristics of a cooperation problem.

Third, an attempt to identify the methodological presuppositions of Postema's model may be worthwhile. For example, the feature I have just pointed out could raise questions about whether the theory is acceptable. If a convention requires common knowledge of all these facts, then the model is an over-rationalization of the beliefs and attitudes of those who are engaged in real conventional practices, and nothing would count as a convention. This kinds of question is, of course, part of a much more general methodological problem. Ultimately, the problem is how to establish a means to explain human activities.

The general problem cannot be considered properly in the present work. Nevertheless, I believe that certain claims by Postema give a relatively clear idea of his methodological assumptions. Postema states that the model works under the assumption that agents are rational, meaning they respect principles of instrumental and substantive rationality (they can recognize there may be substantive reasons, i.e. moral reasons, to solve the relevant cooperation problem). However, the model need not conclude that conventions are, in effect, reasons, because the agents could be mistaken about the substantive applicable reasons. This allows Postema to account for certain social phenomena without taking a stand on whether normative reasons really exist. In general, this is a kind of restriction that the positivist tradition is inclined to respect. Postema also explicitly states that the theory should be transparent, or in other words, that participants should recognize that they are dealing with a cooperation problem according to the features that characterize it.[20] This is consistent with the idea that the practice is, after all, constituted by human behaviour and human actions. However, the attribution of beliefs and attitudes has a limit, according to Postema:

> [I]t must be true that, when occasions arise in which acting to maintain group cooperation focused by the convention, or shifting to an alternative means of achieving the point of the practice when most others have done so, participants will behave in the cooperation-supporting way or come to see a significant discrepancy between their current understanding of their practice and their sense of what is required of them in the circumstances.[21]

---

[20] Postema (2011), p. 522.

[21] Postema (2011), p. 533.

Thus, the model does not require participants to actually have relevant beliefs, but rather something weaker: the attribution of attitudes that are counterfactual or dispositional. It is not necessary, for instance, for participants to actually believe that there is conditional interdependence because they may not even know of the concept of conditional interdependence. What must be true, if the preferences of the other participants were to change, is that they would react in a way that assumes that idea. Postema also appeals recurrently to the idea of explaining social practices in the sense of making them "intelligible", something that is not entirely clear (*"coordination is intelligible just when it can be seen in service of other intelligible ends, aims, values, or principles"*).[22]

Finally, I believe that Postema, who presents himself in the tradition of Hartian theory, would subscribe to the idea that the explanation is successful not only if it makes the practice intelligible but also if it does so by proposing a characterization of the necessary features of that practice and the features that make the practice what it is. To the extent that it proposes a characterization of conventions, it is a characterization that aims to account for the necessary features of conventions.[23]

These considerations are quite fragmentary, but I believe they could be brought together as part of a uniform methodological stance that would account for conventional practices and have two requirements. On one hand, the theory would need to show the features that necessarily characterize conventional practices. As human practices, these features should refer to a set of propositional attitudes (e.g. preferences or expectations). These beliefs and attitudes are attributed dispositionally or counterfactually. On the other hand, assuming that we are talking about imperfect rational agents, which normally recognize instrumental and substantial rationality principles, although they may make mistakes when identifying applicable reasons, and that they conceive of the practice in a certain way (i.e. providing reasons to act), the theory must make that self-conception intelligible. After all, the practices subject to philosophical explanation (conventions) are practices in which *we* participate. We recognize ourselves as imperfect agents and conceive the conventional practices we are involved in as providing us with reasons. To make, then, this self-conception intelligible implies the following: given the necessary conditions (according to the theory) for the existence of a convention to do p, doing p is the solution to a problem, and therefore there is a reason to do p under the assumption that participants believe that there are reasons for solving the problem.

This characterization of Postema's methodological presuppositions would account for the objection to over-rationalization, respect the positivist strictures that Postema subscribes to, and explain in what way the theory attempts to make a practice "intelligible".

Cooperative-conventions are therefore *normative facts*. When we consider the aim of solving a cooperation problem and assuming that participants respect certain instrumental and substantive rational principles, it is intelligible to say that certain

[22] Postema (2011), p. 531.

[23] This is the way Raz characterizes the aim of the analysis that, from my point of view, Postema is working on. See Raz (2013), p. 32 ff.

behavioural patterns (a set of counterfactual behaviours and attitudes that are necessarily constitutive of a cooperative-convention) are invoked as a reason for conforming to such patterns.

4 Cooperative-Conventions and the Rule of Recognition

The next step in Postema's strategy is to argue that the rule of recognition is a cooperative-convention and that therefore the normative problem can be solved. This strategy is guided by the same methodological presuppositions referred to above. The theory should account for the practice that is constitutive of the rule of recognition as a conventional practice, and therefore it should refer to a set of attitudes and beliefs that are dispositionally or counterfactually attributed to law-applying officials. This makes their self-conception intelligible, namely by the fact that the practice is invoked by them because it provides reasons for actions. The project appears promissory; after all, cooperative-conventions are normative facts in the aforementioned sense.

The argument that Postema provides is simple: the rule of recognition is the solution to a cooperation problem. Law-applying officials recognize the need to coordinate their law-applying decisions based on certain common criteria because no coherent, unified legal system would exist without doing so. Despite their disagreements (including disagreements on principles) on what the relevant criteria should be, they recognize the need to cooperate. If the practice of law-applying officials converges into regular patterns, and these patterns shape their mutual expectations, it would follow that rational pressure for every official to follow that pattern emerges in structured social interaction situations. Therefore, *"the "rule" instantiated in those regular patterns of behaviour and associated attitudes (i.e., reciprocal expectations) is a convention, whose normativity is explained by the fact that it solves the persisting cooperation problem faced by law-applying officials"*.[24]

Of course, Postema clarifies that this normative pressure does not mean that such reasons exist—reasons must be the right kind of reasons—nor does it mean that the rule generates moral reasons either. But it is possible that they do. According to Postema, for example, law-applying officials acquire a responsibility from the rules identified by the rule of recognition. Officials' preferences that structure their interaction with common citizens are not personal preferences, but are determined by their professional responsibility to maintain the integrity and unity of the law and also mediate between law and law-subjects. According to Postema, this professional responsibility could acquire a moral dimension for two reasons: when the need to coordinate efforts depends at least partially on moral considerations, and when considerations based on fairness are applicable, as would happen if officials generate legitimate expectations of conducting themselves in a certain way towards citizens

[24] Postema (2011), p. 494.

who are authorized to expect officials to seek coordination with them and therefore among the officials themselves.[25]

5 Objections and Replies

It is worth considering whether Postema's new version of conventionalism avoids the objections of the older version. One of these objections appeals to the idea that officials do not necessarily consider the relevant regularity to be arbitrary, and it seems that this objection can be avoided by applying the cooperative-convention model. The older model, nevertheless, faced other objections that must be considered.

5.1 The Idea of Obligation

Leslie Green objected to the conventional model based on the idea of coordinative-conventions (the objection applies to the cooperative-convention model as well) whereby said conventions are not necessarily seen to be generating obligations. This would be the case, on the one hand, when conventions are trivial. Patterns of behaviour related to fashion, for example, are a typical example of conventions that do not impose obligations. On the other hand, reasons generated by conventions (if any) may be based on personal preferences. In contrast, the rule of recognition is understood as generating reasons that do not depend on personal preferences.[26] Indeed, this reflects the idea of obligation: a reason that applies regardless of preferences or desires.

Postema is aware of this objection. He responds by holding that the details of the model must be filled in to account for specific conventions since a convention can acquire different shapes. He recognizes that some conventions can be trivial and others grounded on personal preferences. Nevertheless, some conventions can rest, he claims, on moral considerations. In fact, law-applying officials are bound to citizens by considerations of fairness, as the argument presented above would show.[27]

Postema's response is, to me, unclear on two crucial points.

First, he does not clarify whether the rule of recognition, in his view, should be regarded as the imposition of obligations or not. This is a very important point. If the rule is duty-imposing, the idea of obligation needs to be explained in accordance with the methodological assumptions described above. Thus, the model should attribute certain attitudes to law-applying officials (dispositionally or counterfactually). For instance, it should claim that certain normative considerations that

[25] Postema (2011), pp. 499–500.

[26] Green (1999), pp. 43–44.

[27] Postema (2011), pp. 501–502.

generate relevant duties are applicable, resulting in an obligation to follow the pattern. In other words, if the rule of recognition is seen to impose obligations, the theory should claim that such a rule is a cooperative-convention in which, in addition to the constitutive conditions of a cooperative-convention (clauses 1–5 mentioned above), clause (6), participants believe that a normative consideration that generates a duty, is applicable.

Second, it is not clear if Postema is actually claiming that the rule of recognition should be understood as a cooperative-convention in which, on top of the constitutive conditions of a cooperative-convention, participants believe that a specific moral consideration such as fairness is applicable.

In short, Postema's answer is not clear. If the rule of recognition is construed as duty-imposing, and if in the model he claims that its duty imposing character can be explained by virtue of the fact that participants believe in the promotion of a value such as fairness, the model should be modified. Postema has not yet made this modification, however, at least not explicitly.

5.2 *Unconditional Obligations*

Another objection raised against conceiving the rule of recognition as a coordinative-convention (an objection that also seems to apply to the idea of cooperative-convention) is that it cannot be seen as imposing the right kind of obligation: the obligation would be, at best, conditional on the remaining participants' preferences and conformity, whereas, in theory, legal authority binds in an unconditional way.[28]

Postema claims that the objection could be interpreted in three different ways, and he proposes three different responses accordingly. None of them, however, are satisfactory.

(i) Postema argues that if the objection rests on the idea that the obligation is unconditional by nature, the objection is then innocuous, since the reasons generated by cooperative-conventions are not necessarily based on personal preferences.[29]

It is important to note that this answer is unsatisfactory for the reason mentioned previously. Postema claims that there might be cooperative-conventions "not necessarily" based on personal preferences. If true, such duty-imposing conventions would be unconditional. However, as I said before, Postema needs to provide something more. If the rule of recognition is regarded as duty-imposing, and therefore its normative force is not based on personal preferences, the model must be attributed to participants' specific beliefs and attitudes; in other words, the model must be modified. And Postema has not proposed the relevant modifications.

---

[28] Green (1998), p. 121.

[29] Postema (2011), p. 502.

(ii) The second way to understand the objection that Postema addresses is that if the objection claims that obligations cannot be dependent on compliance by others, then the objection is not plausible: *"Although some obligations hold regardless of the behaviour of others, others, especially those which serve values or principles the realization of which requires collective effort, are reasonably regarded as compliance-dependent. There is no reason why we should not think them obligatory or binding even if conditioned on the general compliance of others".*[30]

The idea here is that there are principles or values, and the fulfilment of them demands cooperation and is therefore dependent on everyone's activity. The rule of recognition would be, then, the solution to such a cooperation problem. However, once again, it should be noted that Postema does not say in a conclusive way that the rule of recognition should be seen as binding, nor is he saying conclusively that such a feature can be explained in terms of participants seeing their practice as serving substantive values or principles. If he wishes to claim that the rule of recognition is necessarily a binding cooperative-convention, he nevertheless must attribute some normative beliefs to participants to be consistent with his methodological presuppositions. However, as I said before, Postema has not proposed the necessary modifications to the model.

(iii) The third way to understand the objection that Postema considers is that unconditional obligations are to be understood in a special way, i.e. as authoritative obligations in line with Raz. According to Raz, an obligation to do p is authoritative when it works as a particular type of reason: not only as a reason to do p, but also as a reason not to act on the balance of reasons in favour or against doing p.[31] If the duty-imposing nature of the rule of recognition according to the objection is to be explained by appealing to the idea that it promotes substantive values such as fairness, then it would not have an authoritative character.

Postema answers that if the rule of recognition is not regarded as duty-imposing but only as an identificatory rule, then the objection has no force. If, on the contrary, it is seen as a binding rule, it is reasonable to ask whether it has an authoritative character or if it merely provides significative, strong moral reasons for complying (supposing that the cooperation that promotes that value is achieved by the rule). Postema agrees that it is not clear how the debate between these two possibilities must evolve.[32]

Notably, Postema's answer is unclear once again. It seems to me that the problem is not about how to understand rules, whether under Raz' conception of rules or another's. Such a problem is related to the nature of rules and practical reasoning. The problem is that Postema does not have a clear stance on whether the rule of

---

[30] Postema (2011), p. 502.

[31] See Raz's postscript in Raz (1990).

[32] Postema (2011), p. 503.

recognition is necessarily duty-imposing or not. If it is, Postema seems inclined towards explaining its duty-imposing character by attributing to participants the belief that the rule promotes substantive values. Again, such an explanation would require modifying the model, which Postema has not yet proposed.

6 New Objections

Let us take stock. There are two points on which Postema's answer is not clear. On one hand, he must take a side on whether the rule of recognition is regarded as a duty-imposing rule or not. On the other hand, if it is duty-imposing, the model should explain why participants see it as such. Postema's only answer is that participants might believe that the rule is necessary for the promotion of a substantive value such as fairness. But then the model should be modified, and Postema has not explained how such a modification is to be done.

Both points are important. As I shall attempt to show, Postema must recognize that the rule of recognition is duty-imposing. Besides, even if his model is modified in the most plausible way to capture that feature, the rule of recognition cannot be seen as a cooperative-convention. In fact, the rule of recognition is not a cooperative-convention regardless of how the model is modified.

6.1 The Binding Character of the Rule of Recognition

Different reasons have been proposed to justify the idea that the rule of recognition must be regarded as duty-imposing and that is the standard way to understand the Hartian theory.[33] In my view, the rule should be seen as duty-imposing for a specific reason: law-applying officials are necessarily members of the judiciary and the judiciary is an institution, with the rule of recognition structuring that institution. Since the rules that structure any institution are duty-imposing, the rule of recognition acquires this characteristic.

Let us take any example of an institution (non-governmental organizations, financial entities, government departments, etc.) and we will see that there is a conceptual link. No institution exists unless the activity of its members is regulated by certain rules that are followed by all of them. In fact, the idea of an institution is necessarily linked to the idea of certain rules followed by the members of that institution. Furthermore, members in an institution believe that, *qua* members of the institution, they are bound to follow the relevant rule and therefore they necessarily view rules as generating obligations. No institution would survive if participants considered their activities (the activities regulated by the institutional rules) to be

[33] Raz (1990), p. 146; Raz (1980), pp. 198–199; Raz (1979), pp. 92–93; Hacker (1977), p. 23; MacCormick (1981), pp. 105 and 109.

merely optional. Thus, the rule of recognition, which regulates the activity of the members of the judiciary, must be duty-imposing. Without it, the judiciary would be unrecognizable.[34]

6.2 Modifying Postema's Model

Given that the rule of recognition is duty-imposing, Postema's methodological assumption requires attributing some belief (dispositional or counterfactual) to members of the judiciary to make intelligible the idea that they are bound by the rule. One way to do so, which Postema himself seems inclined towards, is to attribute to members of the judiciary the belief in the applicability of a moral consideration, such as fairness. It is important to note, however, that the model would then be easy to impugn. There is no reason to assume that participants should regard the rule of recognition as duty-imposing for the same reason, nor is there reason to think that the reason is fairness. Thus, it is possible, for instance, that members of the judiciary see themselves to be under the relevant duty because the rule promotes some substantive values. But it is also possible (and, I would say, true in most current legal systems) that they have different views on which value is being promoted (fairness, social justice, freedom, or a combination of those values, which sometimes are in conflict).

A simple way to overcome this inconvenience is to attribute to participants the belief that solving the cooperation problem will promote values, goods, or principles without specifying what the relevant values, goods, or principles are. The model could state something along the following lines: (1)–(5) conditions are met and (6) participants believe that solving the relevant cooperation problem (i.e. use unified criteria in order to identify the rules applicable to citizens) promotes a value, principle, or substantive good. This would make intelligible their belief to be under the duty of following the convention.

6.3 The Problem

According to the new model, then, with a rule of recognition a group of individuals can understand that certain common criteria for identifying legal norms is needed to promote certain values (e.g. fairness, social justice, or democratic government). This is the problem they must solve from their own point of view and it is the application of moral considerations that explains their belief in being duty-bound to use the convention. According to the new model, since the situation described above is a cooperation problem, the situation must be characterized using three features:

[34] For a more complete justification of why this is a necessary feature of the judiciary, together with other features I mention below, see Sánchez Brigido (2010), Chapter 1.

interdependence, mutually conditional preferences, and uncertainty. It is clear, however, that in this regard the new model is unsatisfactory.

Let us consider uncertainty. According to Postema, it is uncertain how others will act when faced with the cooperation problem. But it is clear that this condition might not be satisfied. For instance, in small and highly homogeneous groups, there are common and uniform beliefs about what things are important and about how those things should be promoted. Religious groups are an example of this, with fundamentalist legal systems based on religious dogmas. Religious dogmatism is dogmatic because no doubt exists. Therefore, there would be no uncertainty whatsoever as to the criteria of validity. In other words, it is perfectly possible to have complete consensus on the sources of law. Of course, this type of situation need not be due to dogmatism. In non-dogmatic groups, the situation may be similar. There may be no doubt that certain criteria will be applied while others will not. I do not want, of course, to exaggerate the point. The idea is not that the absence of doubt about the sources of law means that no debate will take place on which norms satisfy those criteria—it very well could take place. However, the debate is compatible with general agreement on the relevant criteria. Moreover, I do not wish to say that there would be complete certainty about how others will act. What I mean is that no radical uncertainty such as the one a cooperation problem requires need exist. It is not true, then, that in every instance of the constitutive practice of a rule of recognition, participants face a cooperation problem (nor is it true that participants should conceive the situation in that way). Hence, it is not true that a rule of recognition is necessarily a cooperative-convention.

Next, we can consider the condition of mutually conditional preferences. We must recall that the idea is that certain strategies or actions are preferable to other available ones if, and only if, others also choose correlated actions. According to the modified model I have proposed, however, it is not true that the relevant individuals will use the strategy (employ a certain set of validity criteria) *if* the others do so. The fact that others use or adopt certain criteria is not, according to the model I have suggested, enough to adopt the same criteria. Conformity by others is a way to achieve the promotion of the relevant value and, accordingly, such conformity is only a necessary condition. Thus, the defining clause of the model should be modified, and, at best, it should be understood as follows: certain strategies or actions are preferred to other available ones *only if* others also choose correlative actions. This is a much weaker clause.

The weaker clause is, nevertheless, still inadequate. The clause assumes that each participant has an available course of action only if others take a certain course of action. The result (the solution that is being sought) is that everyone carries out, individually, the relevant actions. But the solution is the mere sum of the relevant actions. Moreover, this implies that each of the relevant actions can be characterized separately from the actions of others as follows: despite the conditional quality of the actions, there is a plausible description of each action that is independent from the descriptions of the other actions; each action (as described) is carried out under the condition that the other participants perform other actions. The telephone-call situation (a coordinative practice and therefore a cooperative practice) illustrates this point. Each participant has a possible course of action (to call back or wait) and the solution is the addition of the individual actions (one calls back and the other waits). Actions are conditional, with each action able to be characterized independently from the others and carried out individually under that description, even if it may not be rational to do so.

Clearly, this cannot be a necessary feature of the constitutive practice of the rule of recognition. The judiciary is an institution. Another necessary pre-analytic feature of this institution is that a certain action or activity is attributed to the institution itself. The institution evaluates the behaviour of citizens applying norms that satisfy certain criteria. This is a common feature of many institutions: financial entities lend money, armed forces defend certain territories, charity organizations assist people in need, and so on. The activity belongs to the institution (none of the members can do it individually), and is not just the mere sum of individual actions. In addition, this implies that the actions of each individual cannot be characterized independently from the actions of others. In other words, individual actions can only be described adequately as contributions to the institutional activity and, accordingly, the description of each action is not independent from the descriptions of the actions of other participants. Thus, the condition of weak, mutually conditional preferences is not satisfied. This condition is not only necessary, but should be abandoned.

Let us look at the condition of interdependence. The model can no longer attribute participants personal preferences that are incompatible with the idea of duty. The basis of interdependent preferences is that it should be more likely that *each individual* benefits more from cooperation with others through a common scheme than through no cooperation. If personal preferences are no longer at stake, the condition must be changed. Let us assume that the condition is changed for the following clause: "it is more probable to benefit with cooperation than without it". The clause does not need to be satisfied either. So far, I have assumed that in all instances participants see what they do as promoting a value, a good, or a principle. But not even that is true. It is a normal for many institutions' members to be alienated. In other words, they may not share the values or principles that the institution promotes. Insofar as they act as members of the institution, they present themselves as respecting that value, but they do not have to believe in the real importance of that value. Thus, the condition of interdependence that the modified model retains is not satisfied either.

In fact, it is precisely because of the need to avoid the difficulties of alienation that many institutions incorporate members through contracts, promises, or oaths. These methods voluntarily create an obligation to perform a certain course of action when that course of action is not seen as particularly valuable. This is typical of more developed institutions as well as the judiciary. It is therefore possible that members consider themselves to be under a duty not because they believe that the practice they are contributing to promotes a substantive value, but because of normative considerations that are, to use a common label, content-independent.[35] Thus,

[35] Raz (1972), p. 95; Raz (1986), pp. 35–36.

it need not be true that members believe they are obligated because they are promoting a good or a substantive value.[36]

7 Conclusions

I have aimed to show that Postema's sophisticated version of the conventionalist model is unable to overcome the objections of the first version.[37] Postema's response to the objections appeals to the idea of conditional obligations based on the belief of participants that a certain moral value (fairness) may be promoted by a convention that solves the cooperation problem. A brief survey of certain necessary features of the judiciary, however, shows that its existence does not involve a cooperation problem: the condition of mutually conditional preferences is never satisfied because conformity by others is insufficient for compliance and, most importantly, because the action of each member cannot be described regardless of the actions of other members and the institution as a whole. The condition of uncertainty may not be satisfied either because there can be no doubt of how others may act. Likewise, the condition of interdependence may not be satisfied; the possibility of alienation or participants having assumed obligations regardless of the content makes this clear.

The main reason for why the model fails is because the constitutive practice of the rule of recognition is an institutional practice. In every instance of the constitutive

[36] According to Marmor, the rule of recognition must be understood as a type of constitutive convention, a sort of constitutive rule in Searle's sense. In Marmor's model, other conditions must exist, but this one is essential. If true, a rule of recognition can exist without a cooperation problem (Marmor 2006, pp. 357–359). Postema addresses this objection by claiming that this confuses the temporal pre-existence of a cooperation problem with its pre-existent logic (Postema 2011, p. 531). It is hard to understand what Postema is trying to say with this. He may be claiming that no cooperation problem is necessary *before* the rule emerges, and that it is sufficient that the rule *functions* to solve a cooperation problem. Whatever the force of this answer, however, the objection I propose in the text is immune to it. The objection is that none of the three defining conditions of a cooperation problem is necessary and in fact one of them (the mutually conditional preferences condition) is never satisfied, either *before* the rule emerges or *during* its existence. This does not mean Marmor's model is right. While I am unable to include a full explanation here, three points are worth mentioning. First, Marmor believes that the rule is constitutive since before the rule there can be no officials. I have tried to show how such a claim is mistaken in another work (Sánchez Brigido 2010, Chapter 9). Second, even though the idea of the constitutive rule is well oriented, the rest of Marmor's model is not. On one hand, Marmor does not attribute any belief to participants, even though he understands that a moral reason may exist to follow the rule. This does not make what participants do intelligible. Moreover, it implies abandoning the methodological stricture mentioned before; to determine the nature of institutional practices, the theory should ascertain that moral reasons exist and identify which moral reasons are applicable. On the other hand, Marmor believes that the rule regulates how to promote certain values that can be promoted in alternative ways. And I do not see why asserting that any value that a rule of recognition promotes (if the idea that *must* promote something is admitted) must be this kind of value.

[37] I have not addressed in the present chapter whether Postema's theory may be challenged by other reasons, such as the existence of disagreement. For Postema's answer, which I am unable to consider here, see Postema (2011), pp. 538–542.

practice of the rule of recognition, several individuals do something together using the same criteria of validity. "Doing something together" is the institutional activity, and the judiciary, like many other institutions, is constituted by a group of people whose actions are articulated by rules in which members believe they have a duty to follow *qua* members because they consider certain normative considerations to be applicable (whether content-dependent, content-independent, or both). Such are the necessary features of an institution and of the judiciary. These features are not explained by conventionalism in any of its forms. An alternative model is necessary. It is necessary to explain how features are interrelated, what it means to have a duty "*qua* member", and what "doing something together" consists of. Moreover, this account should be provided in a non-circular manner, without appealing to the same idea of a group or institutional practice, among other challenges.[38]

Acknowledgements I am grateful to Hernán Bouvier and Juan Iosa for their comments on an earlier version of this work.

References

Coleman J (1982) Negative and positive positivism. J Leg Stud 11:139–164
Coleman J (1998) Incorporation, conventionality and the practical difference theory. Leg Theory 4:381–425
Coleman J (2001) The practice of principle. Oxford University Press, Oxford
Green L (1998) The authority of the state. Clarendon Press, Oxford
Green L (1999) Positivism and conventionalism. Can J Law Jurisprud 12:35–52
Hacker P (1977) Hart's philosophy of law. In: Hacker P, Raz J (eds) Law, morality, and society: essays in honour of H.L.A. Hart. Oxford University Press, Oxford
Hart HLA (1994) The concept of law, 2nd edn. Clarendon Press, Oxford
Lewis D (1969) Convention: a philosophical study. Harvard University Press, Cambridge
MacCormick N (1981) H.L.A. Hart. Edward Arnold, London
Marmor A (2001) Legal conventionalism. In: Coleman J (ed) Hart's postscript: essays on the postscript to the concept of law. Oxford University Press, Oxford
Marmor A (2006) How law is like chess. Leg Theory 12:347–371
Marmor A (2009) Social conventions. Princeton University Press, Princeton
Postema G (1982) Coordination and convention at the foundations of law. J Leg Stud 11:165–203
Postema G (2011) A treatise of legal philosophy and general jurisprudence. Springer, Dordrecht
Raz J (1972) Voluntary obligations and normative powers. Proc Aristot Soc Suppl 46:95
Raz J (1979) The authority of law: essays on law and morality. Oxford University Press, Oxford
Raz J (1980) The concept of a legal system. Clarendon Press, Oxford
Raz J (1986) The morality of freedom. Clarendon Press, Oxford
Raz J (1990) Practical reason and norms. Oxford University Press, Oxford
Raz J (2013) Entre la autoridad y la interpretación. Marcial Pons, Madrid
Sánchez Brigido R (2010) Groups, rules and legal practice. Springer, Dordrecht
Shapiro S (2002) Law, plans, and practical reason. Leg Theory 8:387–441
Vilajosana JM (2010) El derecho en acción. Marcial Pons, Madrid

[38] I have tried to face those challenges in Sánchez Brigido (2010), chapters 6, 9, and 10.

On Identifying the Law and Its Supposed Conventional Foundations. A Set-Theory Approach

Giovanni Battista Ratti

Abstract The paper explores some possible applications of some elementary notions of set theory (such as "intersection", "union", and "difference") to two age-old and intertwined problems of legal philosophy: the identification of law and the rational reconstruction of an ultimate rule of recognition. The main results of the inquiry are the following. (1) Contrary to a widespread view, "law" does not denote a unitary set of rules, but rather a family of sets, the main relations among which are examined in the paper. (2) Contrary to what the strong version of legal conventionalism advocates, there is a conceptual space to regard the rule of recognition as the overlapping of several sets of criteria of identification that are used within a certain community. Amongst other things, this thesis renders the famous Dworkin's critique against conventionalism harmless.

1 Foreword

The identification of law (as a set of legal norms)[1] and the analysis of the conceptual reconstruction of the ultimate rule of recognition of a legal system are two crucial and intertwined problems in legal philosophy. In this paper, I will explore how some basic contributions from logic—in particular, some elementary notions of set theory, such as "intersection", "union", and "difference"—can help one approaching these two problems from a partially new analytical perspective.[2]

[1] Here I shall use "norm" and "rule" synonymously.

[2] Set theory is one of the fundamental parts of mathematical logic and is the product of some investigations seeking satisfactory definitions of "number" and "infinity". For my discussion of the basic elements of set theory, I am highly indebted to Berto (2007, pp. 145 ff.); Lemmon (1965, appendix B); Quine (1961, 1963), Quine (1974, pp. 235 ff.); Russell (1918); Suppes (1960).

G. B. Ratti (✉)
Department of Law, Tarello Institute for Legal Philosophy, University of Genoa, Genoa, Italy
e-mail: gbratti@unige.it

L. Ramírez-Ludeña, J. M. Vilajosana (eds.), *Legal Conventionalism*, Law and Philosophy Library 126, https://doi.org/10.1007/978-3-030-03571-6_8

Set theory has proved relevant not only in the context of the foundations of mathematics, but also in other fields of scientific enquiry. Yet, although many legal-theoretical issues could be clarified by taking advantage of the achievements of set theory, legal theory has seldom used these achievements; and only in relation to a very limited array of issues, most importantly the structure and the dynamics of legal systems.[3]

In this paper, I will try to demonstrate that a set-theory approach allows one to maintain the following propositions in relation to the two problems mentioned above. First, contrary to the received view, "law" does not denote a unitary set of rules, but rather a family of sets. Second, set theory can show that the rule of recognition, qua set of criteria of identification of the valid rules in a certain legal system, does not necessarily rest on a convention-based and convergent practice, but can be the product of several relations between different sets of criteria in use in a certain community. Such relations can be illuminated, I submit, by means of a set-theory analysis.

In Sect. 1, I provide an introductory explanation of some basic notions of set theory. In Sects. 2 and 3, I apply these notions to the mentioned issues of the identification of law and of the rational reconstruction of the ultimate RR.

2 Some Elementary Notions of Set Theory

For the sake of the analysis to be carried out in this paper, it will suffice to introduce the definitions of the basic set-theory concepts, to briefly touch upon the main logical operations which can be carried out on sets, and, as a preliminary step, to analyze the ways they can be identified.

2.1 The Concept of Set

In mathematics, "set" denotes a collection of objects of any kind, with regard to which it is possible to determine, by means of some definitional criteria, whether a certain object belong to this collection or not. The objects which belong to a set are called "elements". When a set has other sets as its elements, it is usually called a "set of sets" or, more often, a "family of sets".

It must be noted that the mathematical concept of a set is, in principle, recursive, since it is possible to determine, in a finite number of passages, the relations existing between a certain object and a certain set. However, recursivity can never be absolute, for at least two reasons. First, there are sets which do not allow for an autonomous determination in a recursive fashion: this is what happens with "correct"

[3]Alchourrón and Bulygin (1971, 1979); Rodríguez (2006), pp. 242–276; Ferrer Beltrán and Rodríguez (2011).

mathematical systems (i.e. those systems which demonstrate only truths), which are the object of the famous Gödel's incompleteness theorems. Second, it is possible that a set, abstractly well formed, is doubtfully applied to particular states of affairs, so that its determination *in concreto* cannot be wholly recursive.

2.2 *The Identification of Sets*

A set can be identified extensionally, by enumerating its elements one by one. It can also be identified intensionally, by establishing the criteria which the objects must match in order to belong to it. This second identifying strategy becomes necessary when one comes to deal with sets that, for empirical or conceptual reasons, are not susceptible to extensional identification.

The extensional determination of a certain set is usually represented by the enumeration of all the elements which compose it between braces (or curly brackets). For instance, if we want to identify the set α, comprised of the authors of the *Principia Mathematica*, we shall write {Alfred, Bertrand}.

By contrast, the so-called "principle of comprehension", which underlies the intensional identification, may be expressed by stating that any property F determines a set, and, more precisely, the set of the objects which are characterized by the possession of the property F. As a consequence, a certain object a may be regarded as a member of that set if, and only if, it possesses such a property.[4]

A second fundamental principle of set theory—the so called "principle of extensionality"—states that two sets may be considered identical if, and only if, they have the same elements.

The extensional identification of a certain set can always be traced back to its intensional identification, but not vice versa. Indeed, the extensional identification of a certain set is often impossible, whether for conceptual reasons, such as when the set to be identified is infinite (e.g. the set of natural numbers), or for empirical reasons, such as when the set to be identified, though finite, is not capable of being completely known, due to the limited epistemic faculties of human beings (e.g. the set of all living animals).

Hence, one can point to two relevant consequences.

First, it is surely possible to know a set which is not liable of being extensionally identified, but such knowledge can never be complete, that is, it will never bear upon all of the elements of the set. In such cases, we can only obtain knowledge deriving from the *intensional characterization* of the set at hand.

[4] This apparently intuitive and innocuous principle leads to the well-known Russell's paradox. Since in what follows I will not deal with questions which generate such a paradox, I will use this principle as a simple means of analysis. However, I am well aware that some more complex versions of this principle may avoid such paradoxical outcomes. For one of these versions, see Suppes (1960), p. 7. For discussion on Frege's reply to Russell's paradox, see Quine (1955), pp. 145–159.

Second, one must observe that, from an epistemic perspective, two different intensional presentations of co-extensional sets may be not equivalent. For instance, I may know the extension of the works written by Cicero without knowing that the set of his works may also be presented as "the works by Mark Tully".

As a matter of course, it is possible that two co-extensional sets may be different regarding the property, or collection of properties, which allows their identification: in this case, they are not co-intensional. Take for instance the set of musicians that, while playing in a band, had seventeen number 1 singles between 1963 and 1970 and the set composed of the members of *The Beatles*. Both sets have the same extension, although the properties which allow their identification are different.

In the legal domain—it can be noted—legal theorists are often interested in the intensional determination of the set of legal rules, whereas jurists, judges, and lawyers are instead interested in their extensional determination.[5]

2.3 Logical Operations on Sets

The main logical operations which can be carried out on sets are the following: (1) *union*, (2) *intersection*, (3) *difference*, and (4) *complementation*.

(1) Given two sets α and β, their *union* consists in determining the set of all the objects which are members of the set α *or* of the set β. The union of the sets, say, α = {1, 2} and β = {2, 3} is, very simply, {1, 2, 3}.
(2) Given two sets α and β, their *intersection* consists in determining the set of all the objects which are members of *both* α and β. The intersection of the above mentioned sets is {2}.
(3) Given two sets α and β, we call *difference* the set of all the objects which belong to a set, but not to the other set. Unlike union and intersection, difference is not commutative: the order of the sets changes the outcome. The difference between α and β is the set of elements which belong to α, but not to β—in our example: {1}. By contrast, the difference between β and α is the set of the objects belonging to β, but not to α—in our example: {3}.
(4) Given a certain set α, we can carry out its *complementation*, which consists in determining the complementary class of α, which is composed of all the objects which do not belong to α. This class is usually represented by the notation α'. Complementation presupposes the previous identification of the *universe of*

[5]An important concept of set theory, which will not be used in this essay, is that of "inclusion". Inclusion is the relation between two sets α and β, such that every element of α is also an element of β. One should distinguish *improper inclusion*, which admits the possible identity of both sets, from *proper inclusion*, which excludes it. In other words, a set α *improperly* includes another set β, when the latter is a subset of the former, i.e. all the elements of β belong to α, which may (but need not) contain other elements. By contrast, a set α *properly* includes another set β when the latter is a subset of the former, which, in turn, needs to contain other elements (since, as has been affirmed, both sets cannot be identical).

discourse within which it is carried out.[6] Without this previous operation, complementation would be indeterminate, since the complementary class of a certain class α would be made of all the infinite classes belonging to any universe of discourse.

Union, intersection, and complementation allow one to identify some logical relations among systems which are analogous to De Morgan's laws for propositional calculus[7]: the complementation of the intersection of sets α and β is equivalent to the union of the complements of α and β. Analogously, the complementation of the union of α and β is equivalent to the intersection of the complements of α and β.

3 The Identification of Law in the Light of Set Theory

Several interesting theoretical problems stem from the transposition of the issue of the extensional or intensional identification of sets into the legal domain.

A first step in analyzing the identification of legal systems consists in determining what are the objects of which such systems, qua sets, are made of.

(a) The first candidates, at least if we think of wholly codified legal orders,[8] are *rule-formulations* such as the provisions of written legal documents (a constitution, a legal code, a statute, a judicial sentence, etc.). In this case, legal orders are simply regarded as sets of written down sentences.
(b) A second option is to conceive of the members of legal orders as the *meanings attached* to such rule-formulations, that is rules. Accordingly, legal orders are regarded as sets of rules corresponding to certain rule-formulations.
(c) Another option consists of regarding legal orders as a set of rules *plus* their *logical consequences*, in accordance with certain standards of inference previously established. Consequently, such sets would be made of expressed norms (provided with an authoritative formulation) and implicit norms (i.e. logical consequences).

Each of these three options merits discussion.

[6]This operation brings about a partition in the universe of discourse. Suppes (1960), pp. 83 ff.

[7]As is known, for the laws of De Morgan, the negation of the conjunction of two propositions is equivalent to the disjunction with both original propositions denied, and the negation of the disjunction of two propositions is equivalent to the conjunction of both original propositions denied.

[8]By a "wholly codified legal order" I mean one in which the legal sources are all written down in legal documents. By "legal sources", I mean, following Ross (1958), p. 77: "the aggregate of factors which exercise influence on the judge's formulation of the rule on which he bases his decision".

3.1 Discussion of Case (a)

Regarding the first case—law as a set of texts—it seems easy to envisage an extensional identification of a legal set. One only needs to single out the rule-formulations, which have been enacted by a certain subject or organ, within a certain social community where, as it were, a minimal institutionalization of normative production exists.

As Bulygin (2015, p. 172) points out, "if a legal system is to be conceived as a set [...], then it must be a momentary system". By contrast, if one examines a certain legal system from a diachronic point of view, one should regard it as a sequence of different sets of rule-formulations. Such a sequence is diachronically developed by any change in the extension of the original set and of each single momentary subsequent set: what may be done by addition, subtraction, or substitution of rule-formulations. In jurists' jargon, the first two operations are called "enactment" and "repeal", whereas the third one is but the repeal of a rule-formulation which is accompanied, at the same time, by the enactment of a rule-formulation which did not belong to the set.

In addition to the simple extensional determination, one can ponder whether it is possible to identify the intensional properties which allow one to delimit a certain set of rule-formulations as legally relevant,[9] so that they can be distinguished from legally irrelevant rule-formulations.

A first criterion refers to so-called "formal existence", that is the simple utterance or emission by a subject or organ (not necessary competent from a legal point of view) of a certain sentence which has a prescriptive function. The provisions of the first constitution of a certain legal system may be regarded as having the properties of having been enacted by the subject or organ vested with de facto power within a certain society.

A second criterion refers to so-called "factual existence" or "effectiveness", i.e. the circumstance that some rule-formulations are, as a matter of fact, used by the members of that society, and in particular by legal appliers, to derive norms which are capable of justifying their decisions (cf. Ross 1958, p. 77).[10]

Although the intensional identification of a set of rule-formulations seems quite easy, Alchourrón and Bulygin (1979, p. 69) hold the view that the rule-formulations of the first constitution "are not defined by reference to a certain property or set of properties, but *by enumeration*" (i.e. they are only liable to being extensionally identified). It is not clear why Alchourrón and Bulygin maintain that no intensional determination is possible in regards to such rule-formulations. Probably, this thesis is based on the exigency of being able to clearly determine the set of the "first sources" of a certain legal systems: what may not be an easy task by means of an exclusively intensional identification of the legal sources in force.

---

[9] Bulygin (2015), pp. 243–246.

[10] Obviously, this list of criteria is far from being complete: many other criteria might be formulated.

However, it seems apparent that, regarding any extensionally determined set, one can find a collection of intensional properties which allows one to identify its elements. Moreover, we cannot even extensionally identify the set of rule-formulations in force within a certain community if we do not have a criterion at our disposal which allows us to delimit such formulations within the broader set of prescriptive sentences in use by such a community.

3.2 *Discussion of Case (b)*

A second option, as we have seen, consists in regarding legal systems as sets of expressed rules, i.e. meanings attributed to rule-formulations. More precisely, according to this case, law would be made of at least two connected sets of sentences: the set of rule-formulations and the set of rules (Guastini 2011a, p. 65).

The fact that a connection between rule-formulations and rules is required allows one to avoid some paradoxical consequences which stem from conceiving rules as merely abstract entities, similar to propositions or numbers (according to the so-called "hyletic conception of norms").[11]

Indeed, if rules are regarded as abstract entities, it is quite difficult to connect their existence with acts of enactment or repealing. Hence, it would be difficult (if not even impossible) to provide a genuinely extensional determination of a legal system, regarded as a set of eternal and a-temporal rules, unless one wishes to regard the set of so-conceived rules as the universal class of rules: what seems to be clearly unfruitful at the level of the analysis of *actual* legal systems.

From a theoretical point of view, it is preferable to connect the identification of a normative set to the act of ascribing a certain meaning-content to a given rule-formulation. On such a perspective, a legal system, regarded as a set of rules, may be extensionally identified insofar as interpreters ascribe an array of meanings to the set of legal sources. Of course, the ways in which these acts of attribution of meaning are conceived have evident repercussions on the identification of normative sets. Let me elaborate.

(i) If one postulates a one-to-one correspondence between rule-formulations and rules—as neo-formalistic doctrines of interpretation would have it[12]—then the act of attributing a meaning to a legal source would be, in the great majority of cases, a cognitive activity, a mere discovery, and interpretative sentences could be regarded as true or false.

By contrast, (ii) if one holds—as seems more plausible—that such one-to-one correspondence cannot be maintained, then the act of attributing a meaning to legal sources would be a genuine ascription, an act of volition (not of cognition), so that

[11] Cfr. Alchourrón and Bulygin (1979) and Bulygin (2015), ch. 9.

[12] For a paradigmatic example of a neo-formalistic theory of legal interpretation, see Marmor (2005).

interpretative sentences would lack truth-values. The genuine cognitive identification of all the meanings potentially ascribable to a certain rule-formulation would bring about a plurality (a "frame", according to the well-known Kelsenian metaphor)[13] of interpretative options.

For the first theory of interpretation, the extensional identification of a legal system, regarded as a set of expressed norms, is quite easy, insofar as it is possible to identify the set of the rule-formulations in force, and their corresponding meanings.

By contrast, according to the second doctrine, the extensional identification of a legal system is far more complex. Such identification consists in spotting the relations between rule-formulations and the different meanings which can be ascribed to each of them. Let $\{s_1, s_2, s_3 \ldots s_n\}$ be the set of legal sources, and $\{r_1^a, r_1^b \ldots r_1^n\}$, $\{r_2^a, r_2^b \ldots r_2^n\}$, etc., be the sets of meanings (i.e. of rules) which can be attributed to legal sources. From this perspective, the legal system is a sort of *union of sets* made of the sentences enacted by the lawgiver and the rules which are regarded as synonymous to them.[14] To these sets, one should also add the set of the interpretative sentences formulated by jurists and officials which relate legal sources to rules (which, in turn, are but sentences).

The identification of such a "macro-set", though abstractly possible, is empirically difficult and not very interesting for jurists. Normally, jurists want to reconstruct the interpretation "in force" of a certain set—usually, a very limited one—of rule-formulations. Such rules-formulations do not necessarily belong to the legal system where these jurists operate, but they are simply applicable, in that from them one derives norms which are regarded as acceptable foundations for the (judicial) solution of a certain legal issue.[15]

Consequently, "law", in its ordinary usage, denotes different sets of normative elements (and different relations among such sets).

(1) In a first sense, "law" denotes the set of rule-formulations, which have been enacted and have not yet been repealed by normative authorities at a certain moment.
(2) In a second sense, "law" denotes the set of rule-formulations "in force", i.e. used by the members of the community as the bases for the solution of certain legal questions.
(3) In a third sense, "law" denotes the union of the sets of rules which are derived, by means of interpretation, from formally valid rule-formulations.
(4) In a fourth sense, "law" denotes the macro-set, which is composed of the union of the micro-sets of rules which are derived from a certain set of rule-formulations in order to solve a determined legal question.[16]

---

[13] Kelsen (1992), p. 80.

[14] Guastini (2011b), pp. 227–230.

[15] Ferrer Beltrán and Rodríguez (2011), p. 80.

[16] It is worth observing that some, or even all, of the formulations used in deciding a legal issue may not belong to the legal system. The officials that should decide the issue may sometimes resort to

(5) In a fifth sense, "law" denotes, as it were, a "cluster of relations", which regard at least three sets: the set of legal sources, the set of the rules which can be derived from legal sources by means of interpretation, and the set of interpretative sentences which relate the elements of the first two sets.

3.3 Discussion of Case (c)

In classical logic, not only does a set contain expressed sentences (usually called "axioms"), but it also contains all their logical consequences (so-called "theorems"). If we apply this idea to the legal domain,[17] then legal systems should be regarded as made of both the set of expressed rules and the set of the rules which can be derived from them by means of some rules of inference.

In logic, it is a widespread thesis that the logical consequences of a certain set of sentences are infinite, so that the set of these consequences—that is, the "system" in a Tarskian sense[18]—is extensionally undetermined (though it can be intensionally determined).

The main attempt to use the Tarskian concept of system in the domain of legal philosophy is by Alchourrón and Bulygin (1971).[19] More than once, the two Argentine authors affirm that normative micro-systems built by jurists, through the combination of the relevant operative facts of rules, are made of *all the logical consequences* of the expressed rules.

However, it is quite clear that such normative systems are not composed of all the logical consequences, but only of all the *relevant* logical consequences. There are many rules which can be derived from the expressed ones, which are not among those which are brought about by the combination of relevant properties. Indeed, it suffices to add any irrelevant property whatsoever to the antecedent of an expressed rule to derive logical consequences which are not among those which may be derived by combining relevant properties.[20] It follows from that that, since marginal properties are *infinite*, the set of all the logical consequences of a certain set of expressed rules cannot be extensionally identified.

This result can be generalized, by affirming that no set of rules, developed as a Tarskian system, is liable to being wholly identified in an extensional mode, unless

normative systems which are not even legal (e.g. moral systems). In such cases, the analysis based on set theory allows one to show that, in the ordinary jargon, some elements which are dubbed as "legal" belong, actually, to its complement, that is the non-legal.

[17] For discussion cf. Raz (1994), ch. 10.

[18] Tarski (1983), pp. 346–350.

[19] On rules logical consequences (or, as he dubs them, "juridical consequences") see also MacCormick (1983), pp. 249–254.

[20] For instance, the statute that provides that one is entitled to inherit if declared an heir by a valid will, entails the norm, derived by adding an irrelevant property, that if one has been declared an heir by a valid will and is blue-eyed (*irrelevant property*), then that person is entitled to inherit. I draw the example from Dworkin (1986), p. 351.

one has a criterion of relevance at one's disposal which allows relevant consequences to be distinguished from irrelevant ones.

The "defeasibilist turn" in legal theory has made the problem under examination even more pressing.[21] Since defeasibilism holds that the relevant properties of rules are not determined once for all,[22] it follows from this that the whole extensional identification of legal systems is impossible.[23] Moreover, the issue of the defeasibility of rules can be regarded as relevant regarding different normative levels, up to the ultimate criteria of identification of a legal system. Affirming that the RR of a certain legal system are defeasible is tantamount to affirming that law cannot be identified at the extensional level *and* that its intensional identification is dubious, since the properties presumptively apt to identify it are only contributory (and not sufficient) conditions for the legality of rules.[24]

Another fundamental question regarding the identification of legal systems which contain derived rules concerns the very criteria of derivation (i.e. the rules of inference). Guastini has repeatedly maintained,[25] in arguing against the defenders of the Tarskian conception of normative systems, that, *as a matter of fact*, the great majority of the unexpressed norms within the legal domain are not the outcome of logically stringent reasoning, but of logically invalid inferences. Normally, many such logically invalid inferences (which bring about new legal rules) are expressly authorized (if not imposed) by the legal sources or by the constructive practice of the legal community. More often than not, such productive inferences generate different and incompatible outcomes. In this case, law can be reconstructed, from the perspective of the analysis of derived norms, not as a unitary system, but as a family of alternative sets, composed of a common normative basis and by wholly or partially different derived rules.[26]

---

[21] On the defeasibilist turn, see generally Ferrer Beltrán and Ratti (2012a, pp. 11–38); Ferrer Beltrán and Ratti (2012b).

[22] This entails the rejection of the rule of inference usually called "enrichment" or "strengthening of the antecedent". Enrichment is the rule of inference according to which, given a certain conditional "$p \rightarrow q$", one can derive an entailed conditional in which the original antecedent is enriched by adding whatever sentence "$p \& r \rightarrow q$". An example can clarify it. If we have the conditional "If I dive into the pool, then I get wet", then we can derive the conditional "If I dive into the pool and it's Friday, then I get wet".

[23] Caracciolo (2012), pp. 218 ff. As Jorge Rodríguez has pointed out to me, here two conceptually different problems are intertwined: (1) if one accepts enrichment, from a certain normative basis one could derive many irrelevant consequences, not extensionally identifiable. (2) If one assumes that relevant properties are indeterminate, then enrichment is rejected, and no consequence can be univocally derived from the verification of certain facts. In both cases, the set of consequences is not extensionally determinable, but for different reasons.

[24] Cf. Ferrer Beltrán and Ratti (2010); Ferrer Beltrán and Ratti (2012a, pp. 11–38); Ferrer Beltrán and Ratti (2012b).

[25] See Guastini (2011a, b).

[26] A set-theory notion which perhaps is useful to capture the idea of different normative systems derived from the same normative basis is that of "symmetrical difference", which consists of the operation that allows one to identify the elements that belong, alternatively, to one or the other of two sets.

4 The Rule of Recognition in the Light of Set Theory

The issue of the identification of law can be also approached by resorting to Hart's famous concept of an ultimate rule of recognition, which is also liable to be fruitfully analyzed in terms of set theory. According to Hart, the rule of recognition (henceforth: RR) is the secondary rule which allows one to identify the norms that belong to a certain legal system.

In Hart's work, the RR is characterized by two main aspects.

First, it is a positive and customary rule that prescribes a certain behavior to judges, one which consists in identifying certain sentences by means of some criteria that it furnishes (Hart 1994, pp. 101, 109–110).[27]

Second, its prescriptive character depends on a complex and convergent practice of identification of law that works as "a public, common standard of correct judicial decision" (Hart 1994, p. 116).[28]

Besides this, it is not very much clear what the *logical status* of RR is.[29]

Without claiming to be exhaustive, we can observe the following.

(a) Common-law legal theory has shown itself inclined to conceive of the RR as a genuine duty-imposing rule.[30] In particular, it was generally argued that, despite the hesitations and the tensions which are present in the work of Hart,[31] the fact that the RR supervenes on a customary practice (i.e. that it is a "social rule") necessarily renders it a duty-imposing rule. In particular, such a rule imposes the duty of recognizing and applying all and only such provisions that satisfy the criteria of validity set on the in the very RR.[32]

By contrast, (b) Civil-Law legal theory has repeatedly characterized the RR as a conceptual rule. Indeed, the RR has been generally considered—especially after the

---

[27] See Green (1996), p. 1697.

[28] Coleman (2001a), p. 118.

[29] See Jori (2010), p. 55.

[30] Marmor (2001), p. 193.

[31] It is worth recalling at least four shortcomings affecting the RR that can be found in Hart's work. First, there is the famous paradox that consists in determining who are the officials whose practice produces or constitutes the RR, for the concept of "official" is parasitic to that of RR (for an attempt to solve the paradox, see Coleman (2001a), p. 121). Secondly, Hart introduces the concept of RR to distinguish between primitive and advanced legal systems: however, as Bobbio (2012), p. 160 has shown, all normative systems (the most primitive included) need a RR. Moreover, if the RR, qua social rule, is a duty-imposing rule, then the very distinction between primary and secondary rules collapses, for at least a secondary rule—the RR, in fact—has the same characteristics as the primary rules. Finally, as Bobbio (1994), pp. 241–242 has also shown, the RR, in so far as it allows one to identity the rules of change (which are secondary rules regarding the primary rules of conduct), is a third-order norm, which is at a higher level than secondary rules in general.

[32] A paradigmatic formulation of this stance is found in Lamond (2013), p. 115: "the rule of recognition is a duty-imposing rule: it not only provides the criteria for the identification of the rules of the system but imposes a duty on officials to use those criteria in identifying the laws of the system". See also Raz (1979), p. 93. Partially contrariwise, see Coleman (2001b), pp. 74 ff.

pioneering work made by Bulygin in the mid-seventies[33]—a recursive definition of "valid law", which allows one, in a finite number of passages, to identify the norms which compose a certain legal system.

Both reconstructions are affected by some theoretical difficulties, on which some comments are in order here.

The Common-Law discussion—inaugurated and, in a certain sense, mislead by Hart himself—systematically conflates the issue of the normativity (viz. the binding force) of the use of the criteria of identification of a legal system with another issue concerning the content of such criteria.

Put it briefly, the RR can be given, from this perspective, the following logical form (That reads: "It is obligatory to apply a criterion according to which a norm *a* belong to the class of the norms *x*, characterized by the property *F*, if and only if *a* is characterized by *F*".):

$$\mathrm{OA}\left(a \in \{\mathrm{x} \mid F\mathrm{x}\} \leftrightarrow Fa\right), \tag{1}$$

where "O" represents the normative character "obligatory", "A" denotes the action of applying a certain standard, and the complex formula "$(a \in \{\mathrm{x}|F\mathrm{x}\} \leftrightarrow Fa)$" represents the so-called principle of intensionality, according to which a certain object *a* belong to the set of objects *x*, characterized by the property *F*, if and only if *a* is characterized by *F*.

As it is easy to see, the criteria of identification constitute, in such a logical reconstruction, a part of the reference of the norm. They are, as it were, the object of the action consisting in applying a standard. In detail, they are a propositional content, since such criteria are not arbitrary (as the criteria framed in a genuine stipulation might be), but are actually practiced by the members of a certain society. It follows that such a propositional content describes the criteria in use within a certain community.

Consequently, the RR imposes on its addressees the duty of applying the criteria in use within the community to which they belong. As Bobbio (2012, p. 73) observes, the attempt—which is present in Hart and the subsequent literature—of founding all the rules on an ultimate RR fails in the very moment in which it derives the obligation of applying the criteria contained in it from the fact that such criteria are used in the corresponding political community. There is a naturalistic fallacy here, which affects the entire passage from the effectiveness of the criteria to their purported normativity.[34]

One can also notice that, given that (1) is a deontic sentence, it can also be interpreted descriptively. So interpreted, (1) affirms that there exists, in a certain com-

[33] Now collected in Bulygin (2015), pp. 117–123.

[34] Coleman (2001a, b), pp. 119–121 tries to reply to the argument at hand with one that reaches the conclusion that the RR is "a reason for officials because an aspect of it—the internal point of view—is a cause for them" (p. 120). This argument—if correct—avoids the fallacy, but needs to explain how norms can be actually generated by "a system of stable reciprocal expectations" (p. 119).

munity, a rule which imposes the duty of applying the criteria in use in that community. However, since for logical reasons such a rule cannot be a part of the system that it allows recognizing by means of the criteria of identification it contains, then it cannot but be an extralegal rule. From this, one can derive the somewhat paradoxical result that (1), descriptively understood, describes the membership in a certain extralegal normative system of the rule that provides the duty of applying certain criteria of identification of another normative system. In order to elude such paradoxical results,[35] the Common-law positivistic theory has maintained the view that law is based on a sort of convention or agreement among judges, on which the RR supervenes.[36] In other words, the validity of the rules of a certain legal system lies on a rule whose existence originates (not from another extralegal norm, but) from the fact of being actually practiced by judges, i.e. of being effective.

As is widely known, this view has been repeatedly attacked. In particular, Dworkin "second" challenge to legal conventionalism consists in maintaining that, since there are disagreements on the ultimate foundations of legal systems, the notion of a RR proposed by Hart and legal conventionalism at large is an unsatisfactory explanation of what happens in our legal systems.[37]

In particular, since there are abundant disagreements between judges over basic legal issues, the tenet that, at the basis of the legal systems, there is a generally practiced RR, is quite implausible. This, according to Dworkin, implies a remarkable consequence: since the system cannot receive a conventional foundation, it can only have a *moral* foundation.

Civil-law legal theory seems, on the one hand, able to prevent the paradoxical results reached by Common-law legal philosophy, and on the other, to be invulnerable to the Dworkinian attack. Indeed, many legal theorists in the Civil-law tradition hold neither that the RR is a duty-imposing rule nor that it is the product of a social practice grounding such an obligation. Instead, most of these theorists regard the RR as a recursive definition of "valid law".[38]

For instance, in the *locus classicus* of such a reconstruction, one can read the following characterization: "The rule of recognition, being a definition, lacks truth-value. Although one definition may for several reasons prove more convenient than another, it is clear that, in principle, anyone is free to adopt whatever definition he prefers. Among the many possible definitions of 'valid law', however, there is one that deserves special attention: the one effectively used 'either by courts or other officials or private persons or their advisers'" (Bulygin 2015, p. 120).[39] Shortly

[35] See Marmor (2001), pp. 215–216.

[36] Coleman (2001b), pp. 78–81.

[37] See Dworkin (1986), pp. 34–35.

[38] But see Pino (2012), pp. 265–299 who conceives it as a tool to determine the "applicable law".

[39] Here Bulygin quotes Hart (1994), p. 101. In Bulygin's formulation, the definition shared by the members of the community seems to be the content of a lexical definition (not of a stipulation). However, Bulygin probably intends to state that members of that society adhere to a stipulation, from the internal point of view, and in so doing they use the definition to guide their "identification practice" and criticize those who do not adhere to it.

after, one can read: "Moreover, we speak of *one* legal system only when the *same* rule of recognition is generally used by a given social group. [...] The statement that a given criterion or set of criteria us effectively used by the community and by courts is an empirical statement, a statement of fact" (*ibidem*).

From these statements, one can derive what follows: (1) there are numerous recursive definitions of "valid law"; (2) where a unique legal order exists, there is a definition (called "definition in use"), among the possible ones, which is generally used and can be described by means of a factual proposition.

From propositions (1) and (2), it is possible to derive another consequence. The sentence that contains the criteria of identification of the norms that belong to a certain legal order is ambiguous, for it is liable to express either a stipulation (and, as such, is arbitrary) or a proposition bearing on the use of such a stipulation (and, as such, is objective in that it is empirically verifiable). That the definition of "valid law" may not be arbitrary depend on the fact that such a definition is actually in force in a certain social group.

On these bases, Ricardo Caracciolo (1994, pp. 73–74) maintains that the RR is best understood as a "descriptive sentence which just identifies [...] the criteria used by officials and, consequently, can be true or false". This occurs for its content depends "ultimately on the actual use by the officials of the criteria it mentions. Such a use consists in the application of the norms that satisfy such criteria. Since officials will always use some criteria, whatever they might be, to apply a norm, it follows that any norm they apply more or less regularly is, with more reason, a norm of the system".

From this twofold reading of the RR, some relevant theoretical consequences follow.

The first view (i.e. the RR is a definition) implies that, when there are several definitions in use in a certain social group, there is not only one legal order in that group, but several normative systems (possibly legal systems), since, among the members of that society, different definitions of "valid law" are in use. However, it is not impossible that such definitions partially overlap, and so allow one to identify a kernel of norms that is common to the different normative systems that stem from such definitions. Whenever this occurs, the RR is the product of the overlapping of the several definitions in use.

On the second view (according to which the RR is a descriptive sentence), it is plausible to maintain that when lawyers disagree about the criteria of identification, the RR receives a complex formulation, aiming at describing the different practices of identification in force among the different members of that group. In this sense, it is the (correct) descriptive formulation of the RR that allows one to determine the possible relations (intersection, union, difference, etc.) of the several definitions of "valid law" which are used in a certain society.

It is possible to analyze the possible effects on these views of the Dworkinian attack predicated on the idea that disagreements are an element which directly undermines the notion of a RR.

The first reconstruction, which regards the RR as a definition, can reply as follows. For a RR to exist, it is sufficient that, when in a certain society there are several definitions of "valid law", they overlap in a relevant way, so that a great part of the legal sentences which are supposedly identified by means of the different rules of recognition are actually the same. There is no need of agreement or convergent practice regarding the criteria of identification of a legal order for it to exist. There is only the need that there is a common criterion or a common set of criteria (even if it is simply the product of the overlapping of different criteria or sets of criteria) that is used by the members (and especially the officials) of a certain community. We are thus in the following situation: several definitions of law exist and they intersect regarding the recognition of certain rules.[40]

Better put, the RR in force is constituted by the area of overlapping of the different definitions in force. In formal terms, we can imagine a situation in which the following sentences (2) and (3) are (the rational reconstructions of) the definitions which are used in a certain society, and (4) is the definition (viz. the "real" RR) one can derive from the intersection of the sets identified by means of (2) and (3) (The symbol "∩" represents the intersection.):

$$\left(a \in \{\mathrm{x} \mid F\mathrm{x}\} \leftrightarrow Fa\right) \tag{2}$$

$$\left(a \in \{\mathrm{x} \mid G\mathrm{x}\} \leftrightarrow Ga\right) \tag{3}$$

$$\left(a \in \{\mathrm{x} \mid F\mathrm{x} \cap G\mathrm{x}\} \leftrightarrow (F \,\&\, G)a\right) \tag{4}$$

This succinct logical analysis suggests that there is no (conceptual) need of any agreement or convention regarding the criteria of identification of a legal order. For it to exist one only needs that there is actually a common criterion or set of criteria (even if it is the product of the overlapping of several criteria or sets of criteria) which is used by the members (and mostly by the officials) of a certain community.

This explains why, though the Dworkinian critique can have a certain strength against legal conventionalism regarded as an explanation of the origins of legal systems, it has none against the deflationary thesis that regards the RR as a simple conceptual rule, not necessarily found on agreement or convention.

Concerning the second view, which regards the RR as a descriptive sentence, the Dworkinian attack is ever more irrelevant. This is so, for it is always possible to determine a posteriori what the (supposed) criteria of identification of a certain set of norms are, although one denies—as Dworkin does, through the argument from disagreement—that the RR supervenes on a convergent social practice. Dworkin's critique, at best, might weaken the conception of a RR as a social rule (resulting in the deflationary view we have just outlined), but it cannot subvert at all the reconstruction of the RR as the description of the criteria actually in use in a certain

[40] This view is developed in Dolcetti and Ratti (2013), pp. 313–314.

society (whatever such criteria might be). It is interesting to notice that, from this descriptive stance, the set of criteria of identification that are widespread in a certain society may be the result of *any* operation on sets: union, intersection, difference, or complementation. Consequently, the resulting RR is liable to be analyzed as followed.

In the first case, the union of all the sets of criteria used in a certain society form the RR: so, all the criteria, which are used by some more or less relevant sector of the officials or the people at large, are to be regarded as criteria of legal validity. Of course, problems arise at the operative level when such criteria prove incompatible.

In the second case, the intersection of the sets of criteria used in a certain society form the RR: this means—as we have previously seen—that the RR contains only the common elements of all the sets of criteria.

In the third case, the RR contains the difference between a certain set of criteria and other sets of criteria. For instance, if we regard law as a special case of social practices, we need to determine what the law is (or contains) by working out the difference between the sets of the criteria that determine social practices at large and the set of the criteria that identify social, but not legal, practices.[41]

Finally, the fourth case is characterized by a negative criterion: what is law in a certain society is the product of the complementation of all the criteria that, for some reasons, are excluded from legal relevant ones. This is a seldom-used tool, for obvious reasons: it has the tendency to include into the legal domain whatever cannot be qualified by means of the criteria of identification of other normative sets.

5 Concluding Remarks

In this paper, I have tried to show, at a preliminary stage, that a set-theory approach can prove fruitful for jurisprudence.[42] In particular, I have done so by demonstrating the following propositions. First, the idea of law as a unitary legal system is illusory, as soon as one realizes that law is composed of many sets, whose mutual relations are in need for a careful explanation (part of which has been put forward here). Second, by breaking down the concept of a RR in a series of more nuanced notions, which can be analyzed by means of set theory, one is in a far better position in order to assess the idea that law, through the notion of a RR, has convention-based origins and to examine the critiques that have been framed against this idea.

[41] See Marmor (2001, p. 216).

[42] Other legal theoretical insights provided by a set-theory approach can be found in Ratti (2012, ch. 1), Ratti (2018).

References

Alchourrón CE (1987) On the philosophical adequacy of set theories. Theoría – Segunda época 5–6:567–574
Alchourrón CE, Bulygin E (1971) Normative systems. Springer, Wien
Alchourrón CE, Bulygin E (1979) Sobre la existencia de las normas jurídicas. Oficina latinoamericana de investigaciones jurídicas y sociales, Valencia (Venezuela)
Berto F (2007) Logica da zero a Gödel. Laterza, Bari
Bobbio N (1994) Contributi ad un dizionario giuridico. Giappichelli, Torino
Bobbio N (2012) Studi per una teoria generale del diritto (1970). Giappichelli, Torino
Bulygin E (2015) Essays in legal philosophy. Oxford University Press, Oxford
Caracciolo R (1994) La noción de sistema en la teoría del Derecho. Fontamara, México
Caracciolo R (2012) Acts, normative formulations, and defeasible norms. In: Ferrer Beltrán J, Ratti GB (eds) The logic of legal requirements. Essays on defeasibility. Oxford University Press, Oxford, pp 209–222
Coleman J (2001a) Incorporationism, conventionality, and the practical difference thesis. In: Coleman J (ed) Hart's postscript. Essays on the postscript to the concept of law. Oxford University Press, Oxford, pp 99–147
Coleman J (2001b) The practice of principle: in defence of a pragmatist approach to legal theory. Oxford University Press, Oxford
Dolcetti A, Ratti GB (2013) Legal disagreements and the dual nature of law. In: Waluchow W, Sciaraffa S (eds) The philosophical foundations of the nature of law. Oxford University Press, Oxford, pp 301–321
Dworkin R (1986) Law's empire. Fontana, London
Ferrer Beltrán J, Ratti GB (2010) Validity and defeasibility in the legal domain. Law Philos 29:601–626
Ferrer Beltrán J, Ratti GB (2012a) Defeasibility and legality: a survey. In: Ferrer Beltrán J, Ratti GB (eds) The logic of legal requirements. Essays on defeasibility. University Press Oxford, Oxford, pp 11–38
Ferrer Beltrán J, Ratti GB (eds) (2012b) The logic of legal requirements. Essays on defeasibility. Oxford University Press, Oxford
Ferrer Beltrán J, Rodríguez JL (2011) Jerarquías normativas y dinámica de los sistemas jurídicos. Marcial Pons, Madrid
Green L (1996) The concept of law revisited. Mich Law Rev 94:1687–1717
Guastini R (2011a) Interpretare e argomentare. Giuffrè, Milano
Guastini R (2011b) La sintassi del diritto. Giappichelli, Torino
Hart HLA (1994) The concept of law, 2nd edn. Oxford University Press, Oxford
Jori M (2010) Del diritto inesistente. ETS, Pisa
Kelsen H (1992) Introduction to the problems of legal theory (1934). Clarendon Press, Oxford
Lamond G (2013) The rule of recognition and the foundations of a legal system. In: Duarte D'Almeida L, Edwards J, Dolcetti A (eds) Reading HLA Hart's the concept of law. Hart, Oxford, pp 97–122
Lemmon EJ (1965) Beginning logic. Nelson & Sons, London
MacCormick DN (1983) On legal decisions and their consequences: from Dewey to Dworkin. N Y Univ Law Rev 58:239–258
Marmor A (2001) Legal conventionalism. In: Coleman J (ed) Hart's postscript. Essays on the postscript to the concept of law. Oxford University Press, Oxford, pp 193–217
Marmor A (2005) Interpretation and legal theory, 2nd edn. Hart, Oxford
Pino G (2012) Farewell to the rule of recognition?. Problema. Anuario de Filosofía y Teoría del Derecho 5:265–299
Quine WVO (1955) On Frege's way out. Mind 64:145–159
Quine WVO (1961) Mathematical logic, Rev edn. Harvard University Press, Cambridge
Quine WVO (1963) Set theory and its logic. Harvard University Press, Cambridge

Quine WVO (1974) Methods of logic, 3rd edn. Routledge & Kegan Paul, London
Quine WVO (1980) From a logical point of view. Nine logico-philosophical essays, Rev edn. Harvard University Press, Cambridge
Ratti GB (2012) Diritto, indeterminatezza, indecidibilità. Marcial Pons, Madrid
Ratti GB (2018) Cornici e insiemi. In: Chiassoni P, Comanducci P, Ratti GB (eds) L'arte della distinzione, vol II. Marcial Pons, Madrid
Raz J (1979) The authority of law. Essays on law and morality. Clarendon Press, Oxford
Raz J (1994) Ethics in the public domain. Clarendon Press, Oxford
Rodríguez JL (2006) La tensión entre dos concepciones del sistema jurídico. Análisis filosófico 26:242–276
Ross A (1958) On law and justice. Stevens & Sons, London
Russell B (1918) Introduction to mathematical logic. Allen & Unwind, London
Suppes P (1960) Axiomatic set theory. Van Nostrand, Princeton
Tarski A (1983) Logic, semantics, metamathematics, 2nd edn. Hackett, Indianapolis

Part III
Conventions and Legal Interpretation

Conventionalism Unchained and Sceptical. A Defence of a Quasi-Realist Account of Legal Statements Against Dworkin's Criticisms

Federico José Arena

Abstract Dworkin famously argued that Hart's practice theory is not able to give an account of legal duties and therefore that it is a bad theory of law. Conventions were then proposed as a substitute for the practice theory capable of showing the existence of legal duties. In this text Arena examines two different conventionalist strategies that have been proposed as answers to Dworkin's criticisms—Marmor's constitutive conventionalism and Postema's constructive conventionalism. Arena claims that both proposals remain captive of Dworkin's premises and that this has led them to overstate the cooperative dimension of legal practice. Dworkin's argument is based on the premise that without explaining the existence of legal duties a theory would be unable to explain some essential features of law: judges' statements of duty and disagreements. Arena argues against this premise by claiming, first, that judges' statements of duty are just a projection of their attitudes both on the action considered mandatory or forbidden and on the conventional interpretative method they use to ground that statement. Second, that this projectivist perspective may account for judges' talk in terms of truth value and for their disagreements. On the one hand, by following a quasi-realist schema, Arena claims that judges must earn their right to talk about truth and, on the other hand, he claims that judges' disagreements are genuine disagreements in attitudes.

1 Premise

After Ronald Dworkin's attack against Hartian positivism different authors, including Herbert Hart himself, sought in conventions a way out to his objections. According to Dworkin, legal duties are an essential trait of law, without them there are many features of law that would remain unexplained. He famously argued that Hart's practice theory is not able to give an account of that trait and therefore that it is a bad theory of law.[1] Conventions were then proposed as a substitute for the

[1] The first one that labelled Hart's proposal in *The Concept of Law* (Hart 1994) as "the practice theory of norms" was, to my knowledge, Joseph Raz in Raz (1990), p. 51.

F. J. Arena (✉)
Conicet (U.N.C.) – Universidad Blas Pascal, Córdoba, Argentina
e-mail: fjarena@conicet.gov.ar

L. Ramírez-Ludeña, J. M. Vilajosana (eds.), *Legal Conventionalism*, Law and Philosophy Library 126, https://doi.org/10.1007/978-3-030-03571-6_9

practice theory capable of giving support to the existence of legal duties. According to conventionalism's main thesis legal duties are conventional.[2] However, Dworkin remained unconvinced and rearranged his arguments claiming that conventions would not do the trick.

It seems to me that conventionalists have so far remained captive of Dworkin's own premises and that this has led them to defeat. In order to succeed, conventionalism should set itself free from those premises. I do not think so just because of a libertarian feeling regarding conventionalism, but because I think those premises are erroneous.

Dworkin's argument is based on the premise that a good theory of law should explain the existence of legal duties. Dworkin has persuaded conventionalists that without explaining the existence of legal duties a theory would be unable to explain two essential features of law: (1) the fact that judges claim/assume/presuppose that there are legal duties and (2) the fact that judges disagree about the content of those duties. The thesis according to which explaining those two traits requires showing the existence of legal duties is the premise that strikes me as ill-founded and that conventionalism should to get rid of. This would require cutting different chains that keep conventionalism captive. I should warn that as in every liberating process, conventionalism will not be the same at the end of it.

I argue against Dworkin's premise by claiming, first, that judges' statements of duty are just a projection of their attitudes and that judges project their attitudes both on the action they consider mandatory or forbidden and on the conventional interpretative method they use to ground the statement. Second, that judges' discourse and disagreements may be accounted for under this projectivist perspective plus a quasi-realist schema. On the one hand, projectivism makes room for judges' talk in terms of truth value via the quasi-realist thesis according to which people using language to express their attitudes, may earn their right to talk in terms of truth by producing an improved set of attitudes. On the other hand, judges' disagreements about the ground of their statements of duties are just disagreements of attitudes regarding the interpretation of the normative provision, i.e., regarding which is the best interpretative method.

I will proceed as follows. First, I will introduce Dworkin's criticism and the premises on which it is based. Second, I will examine the answers that conventionalism has proposed to those criticisms and show why they are not able to escape from Dworkin's premises. Third, I will show why Dworkin's premises are ill-founded and how this opens an alternative for conventionalism. This alternative involves endorsing some legal realist thesis and that is why I will call it "sceptical conventionalism".

---

[2] Following some common usage between legal philosophers, I will use "conventional" as conveying the meaning "determined by (or based on) a convention". Besides, as I will only refer here to conventionalism in the legal domain I will use "conventionalism" for short, avoiding the longer "legal conventionalism".

2 Caging Conventionalism. Dworkin's Argument

According to Dworkin the law does not simply advise citizens and judges about what they may or may not do; "it provides what they have a duty to do or no right to do".[3] He claims that legal theory has had a hard time trying to explain such duties.[4] Conventionalism is an attempt to explain how legal duties arises. According to conventionalism's core thesis, that I will call "conventionality thesis",[5] legal duties are conventional.[6]

From Dworkin's perspective, the conventionality thesis has two possible forms. It can be either a thesis about how conventions *constitute* legal duties or a thesis about how conventions *justify* legal duties. Under the first form it amounts to the claim that the convention determines the existence and the content of the duty. Under the second form it amounts to the claim that the convention gives support to the existence of the duty and partially determines its content.[7]

Dworkin accepts that conventionalism may have some allure given that almost everyone agrees that certain human arrangements, such as legislature and precedent, make the law that counts in their lives.[8] However, Dworkin claims that both forms of conventionalism are deemed to fail as theories of legal duties. The arguments designed to show that the constitutive form fails are set up mainly in *Taking Rights*

---

[3] Dworkin (1978), p. 48.

[4] Dworkin (1978), p. 49. He also says that "[e]very legal philosopher, with the exception of the most extreme of the American legal realists, has supposed that in at least some cases the judge has a duty to decide in a particular way, for the express reason that the law requires that decision" (Dworkin 1978, p. 49). Some pages earlier, Dworkin has derided legal realists by accusing them of witch hunting. See Dworkin (1978), pp. 15–16. As I argue below, legal realist's main thesis may be recovered without implying, using Dworkin caricature, the charge of sorcery.

[5] Several authors have used the label "the conventionality thesis" to name the core claim of conventionalism (even if they disagree about its content). See Coleman (2001a), p. 357, Postema (2011), p. 483 and Bayón Mohino (2002a).

[6] There is not much that can be said in advance about the specific sense in which a legal duty is supposed to exist, because the discussion is, precisely, about the conditions for the existence of a legal duty.

[7] "The fact that a practice [...] exists *justifies* asserting a normative rule to that effect—not because the practice *constitutes* a rule which the normative judgment describes and endorses, but because the practice creates ways of giving offense and gives rise to expectations of the sort that are good grounds for asserting a duty [...] or for asserting a normative rule [...]." (Dworkin 1978, p. 57). The italics are mine.

[8] Also, if conventionalism were right, the existence of the duty would be just a matter of mere social facts, i.e., the existence of the uniform social practice. Plainly, the fact that this would render the conventionality thesis compatible with legal positivism has been one of the reasons why many philosophers—that take themselves to be positivists—have placed their trust in conventionalism. The compatibility with positivism has been one of the chains Dworkin has used against conventionalism. I will not indulge here in the analysis of the relationship between conventionalism and positivism.

Seriously and restated in *Law's Empire.*[9] The arguments designed to show that the justifying form is misled are set up mainly in *Law's Empire*.

The constitutive form of conventionalism would be the one defended by Hart in his book *The Concept of Law*. According to Hart's theory, as presented by Dworkin, legal duties are *constituted* by a uniform social practice of recognizing these rights and duties.[10] Dworkin's attack is deployed in several steps. His strategy is to cage conventionalism in a philosophical corner and then to draw a door through which conventionalism could escape. Sadly, the offered exit is just the entrance to another, smaller cage.

The first cage is built around the vegetarian example. Conventionalism cannot account for duties as the one defended by a vegetarian in a non-vegetarian society. For in this scenario conventionalism can only see the vegetarian as wishing that there were a duty. But that is not what the vegetarian wants to say, because he is claiming that a duty already exists even though society has not yet recognized it. In this case we cannot explain the assertion of the existence of the duty on the basis of the speaker's acceptance of a convention because such a social practice does not exist. In order to get out of this cage conventionalism should avoid claiming that all duties are constituted by a uniform social practice; it should limit the scope of the theory to already existent practices.[11]

Unfortunately, this would lock conventionalism up into another cage, because it still fails to notice the distinction between *concurrent* morality and *conventional* morality. Although in both cases there is a uniform social practice, in the case of conventional morality the members of the community "count the fact of that agreement as an essential part of their grounds for asserting that rule",[12] whereas in the case of concurrent morality they do not. In this last case they believe that the duty would still exist even if the practice were to fade away.[13] So, the theory is now cornered in conventional morality.[14]

But again, the exit is just an illusion. The theory is not even an adequate account of conventional morality "because it cannot explain the fact that even when people count a social practice as a necessary part of the grounds for asserting some duty, they may still disagree about the scope of that duty".[15] Indeed, judges very often disagree about the existence and content of legal duties, mostly because "[t]hey have different theories about how statutes and past decisions should be read".[16]

---

[9] This is a bit stretchered. From a chronological point of view, in *Taking Rights Seriously* Dworkin attacks positivism and only in *Law's Empire* conventionalism explicitly becomes his target.

[10] Dworkin (1978), pp. 49–50.

[11] Dworkin (1978), pp. 52–53.

[12] Dworkin (1978), p. 53.

[13] Dworkin (1978), pp. 53–54.

[14] Hart seems to have accepted this narrower scope for his theory in his manuscript notes posthumously published as "Postscript". See Hart (1994), pp. 255–256.

[15] Dworkin (1978), p. 54.

[16] Dworkin (1986), p. 122.

Dworkin introduces some examples to show that this is the case, I will focus here on two of them: Riggs v. Palmer[17] and TVA v. Hill.[18] In both cases there is a disagreement about the existence and content of a duty. In Riggs the majority considers that there is a legal duty to deny Elmer the inheritance of his grandfather, whereas the minority considers that there is a duty to award him the inheritance. In TVA the existence of a duty to enjoin the completion of Tellico dam is affirmed by the majority and denied by the minority. Apparently, these are disagreements. Dworkin claims that they are not empirical disagreement, because there is no discussion about the facts of the case, nor about the facts regarding the meaning of the text.[19] According to Dworkin they are disagreements about the grounds of law, i.e. about what determines the existence and content of the duty.[20]

In these cases there is neither convergence nor conforming behaviour. The conventionalist cannot say that in those cases the duty is uncertain, because that would amount to abandon the thesis that duties are constituted by convention. For even though all facts about social behaviour are known the content of the duty is not.[21] When disagreement of this kind arises, Dworkin claims, conventionalism is constraint to say that there exists no duty.[22]

So, the theory must be weakened even more and "it must be held to apply only in cases, like some games, when it is accepted by the participants that if a duty is controversial it is no duty at all. It would not then apply to judicial duties".[23] This is the tiny philosophical corner that Dworkin reserves for conventionalism. Conventionalism seems only capable of explaining duties that arise within games, where a duty is not a duty if there is no agreement about it.[24]

---

[17] This case was already introduced in Dworkin (1978) and rebaptised as "Elmer's case" in Dworkin (1986), pp. 15–20.

[18] Rebaptised as "The Snail Darter Case" in Dworkin (1986), pp. 20–23.

[19] Actually, there are several empirical disagreements between the majority and the minority that makes Dworkin reconstruction somehow tricky. For instance, regarding the impact the fact that Congress authorized and appropriated new funds for the construction of the dam after the snail darter was declared an endangered species may have on the counterfactual intentions of the Congress.

[20] I will avoid here the label "theoretical" that Dworkin uses in *Law's Empire* for disagreements about grounds, because I think that the label carries some ambiguity. Below, after discussing conventionalism, I will introduce further precisions regarding the characterization of disagreements.

[21] Dworkin (1978), p. 55.

[22] Dworkin argues that the only way to understand the disagreement (and the fact that judges issue that kind of statements) is to opt for his interpretive theory, according to which the existence of a duty depends on the best moral/institutional argument on its behalf. That is, the duty exists when it can be defended on the basis of the best moral/institutional argument. See Dworkin (1986), pp. 238–258 for an outline of how this would work in actual legal practice.

[23] Dworkin (1978), p. 55.

[24] If the advocate of conventionalism wanted to argue that the cases of disagreement can be understood as cases were people having stated the existence of the duty for some cases urges to extend its application to the new cases, then it would be subject to the vegetarian objection. See Dworkin (1978), p. 55.

Dworkin draws a little exit door but like Alice falling down the Rabbit-Hole conventionalism is too small to reach the key that opens it. In order to reach the key conventionalism has to be strengthened, it should turn into a justifying—and not a constitutive—theory of duties. However, once it is strengthened conventionalism would not be able to pass through the door. In *Law's Empire* Dworkin claims that even if conventionalism were to turn into a justificatory theory, it would fail as a justification of legal duties.

As a justificatory theory conventionalism would claim that legal duties arise because conventions about which institutions should have power to make law and how instantiate the ideal of protected expectations. This is so because conventions "give fair warning by making the occasions of coercion depend on plain facts available to all rather than on fresh judgments of political morality which different judges might make differently".[25]

Dworkin raises two objections against the claim that the ideal of protected expectations is instantiated by legal conventions. On the one hand, conventionalism cannot show how being tied to the content of conventions may realize the ideal in cases where conventions run out. On the other hand, surprise (i.e., the frustration of expectations) is not always wrong.

Under the first objection, strengthened conventionalism would not be able to overcome the objection from disagreement. Conventionalism must accept that convention cannot offer any useful advice to judges in those cases "in which the explicit extension of the various legal conventions contains nothing decisive either way, and the judge therefore must exercise his discretion by employing extra-legal standards".[26] But if conventionalism concedes that its proposal does not apply to the major part of the cases that arrive to courts, then the defence of protected expectation is weakened.

This gives room to the second objection. The frustration of expectations is wrong only when the one who frustrates them has intentionally encouraged the expectation. If conventionalism were practiced and announced by public institutions, then it would be unfair for those institutions to abandon it. "But this is not true of us, as the argument up to now has established".[27] That is, given the existence of disagreements authorities cannot be charged with encouraging the expectation that they would abide by a convention.

To resume, Dworkin's attack to conventionalism has as departing point the fact that judges claim that there are legal duties. According to Dworkin explaining these claims requires showing that there are legal duties. The proposal advanced by conventionalism is that legal duties are conventional duties and that a convention exists when there is convergence. Dworkin's criticism points to the further fact that judges sometimes disagree about the content of those duties and that even in those cases judges claim that there are legal duties. In cases of disagreement there is no convergence and, therefore, there is no convention. This fact shows that the convergence is

[25] Dworkin (1986), p. 117.

[26] Dworkin (1986), pp. 128–129.

[27] Dworkin (1986), p. 141.

not conventional and, hence, that conventionalism, in either form, is not even a good explanation of convergence cases. That is to say, conventionalism cannot show how legal duties arise.

The first evading strategy that conventionalism might attempt is to hold that judges are wrong in claiming that there are legal duties in cases of disagreement. The mistake would result from the fact that in cases of disagreement there is no convergence and therefore there is no convention. By giving this answer, conventionalism would be explaining judges' claims about the existence of legal duties, but at the price of espousing a local variant of an error theory. Judges' claims that there are duties imposed by conventions are correct in cases of convergence. Error theory conventionalism only adds that those statements are irremediably false in cases of disagreement.[28]

However, espousing a local error theory of this kind has some undesirable consequences. For instance, an error theory explains judges' claims only if they are unaware of the error. That is to say, once judges have been alerted of their error, they should, *ceteris paribus*, change their behaviour. In other words, once judges are aware of the fact that there are no duties in cases of disagreement, it would be suspicious if they were to keep using the same language instead of modifying or replacing it to avoid the error.[29]

As a rejoinder, the supporter of the error theory could try to show that there are some considerations, external to the way in which judges conceive of the practice, such as social utility, legal enforcement, effort saving, etc., that would justify the continued use of that language even if judges were to discover (or were actually conscious of) the error.[30]

Nevertheless, it seems to me that this position would be uncomfortable for conventionalism. By espousing a local error theory conventionalism would suffer from a kind of schizophrenia in as much as it gives judges statements two different statuses in defining the existence of legal duties. In other words, conventionalism

[28]The error theory is local because its scope is limited to statements issued in cases of disagreement. A global error theory would be a theory that claims error regarding (almost) all statements of duty (see Mackie 1977, pp. 15–49). There is another difference between this local error theory that I have sketched and John Mackie's well-known Error Theory in the moral sphere. The difference is that the falsity of statements of duty is contingent in the first case (disagreements are a contingent feature of legal practice) and necessary in the second case (Mackie claims that the moral world is necessarily non-existent because of the properties that moral facts are deemed to have).

[29]As Simon Blackburn claims: a language that contains an error would be affected "in something like the way in which phlogiston theory or witchcraft explanations are so tainted. If we come to believe in this error, one response is to abandon the whole thing: [...], just as we have grown out of phlogiston and witchcraft theories" (Blackburn 2005, pp. 326–327).

[30]Conventionalism may try out here what Scott Shapiro has named "the repair argument": "In systems of separated powers, where legislatures alone are authorized to make law and judges are required to apply it, it is dangerous for judges to admit that they are exercising discretion and attempting to repair the law. Courts preserve their legitimacy when they act as though there really is law 'out there' to discover rather than admitting that the law is sometimes indeterminate and that they are filling in the gaps" (Shapiro 2007, p. 39).

would be claiming that the behaviour of a group of people (including their statements) constitutes in some cases the content of duties and in other cases are plainly wrong. This is not to say that conventionalism cannot claim that judges can be mistaken in some cases. The problem is that the basis of the mistake cannot be that bees do not know what honey is.

This might explain why no conventionalist has indeed taken the option of a local error theory. Indeed, conventionalists have tried to leak out by exploring other alternatives.

3 Captivity. Kinds of Conventionalism

Even if the advocates of conventionalism have taken different routes; it strikes me that so far all forms of conventionalism have remained captive of Dworkin's premises. They all accept the Dworkinian thesis according to which the explanation of (1) the fact that judges claim/assume/presuppose that there are legal duties and (2) the fact that judges disagree about the content of those duties requires showing that there are legal duties. Thus, all of them have sought to explain, first, how conventions give rise to duties in cases of convergence and, second, how that explanation can be extended to, or accommodated in, cases of disagreement. They diverge regarding the specification of the conventionality thesis and the explanation they give to cases of disagreement. First, some philosophers have purported to defend conventionalism staying within the field of a constitutive relationship between convention and duty. As mentioned above, this seems to have been Hart's attempt in *The Concept of Law*, so I will call this position Hartian conventionalism.[31] This kind of conventionalism had historically two versions. On the one hand, a version based on coordination conventions advanced, but then abandoned, by Jules Coleman.[32] On

[31] In fact, in his manuscript notes posthumously published as "Postscript", Hart, on the one hand, seems to explicitly recognize that his original theory embraced conventionalism (see for instance: "Certainly the rule of recognition is treated in my book as resting on a conventional form of judicial consensus" (Hart 1994, pp. 266–267). On the other hand, Hart points that it is a mistake to restate his theory as an "interpretative" or justifying theory. First, because an "interpretative" theory of positivism is not a "plain-facts theory" of positivism. Second, because "[w]hereas Dworkin interpretive theory in all its forms rests on the presupposition that the point or purpose of law and legal practice is to justify coercion, it certainty is not and never has been my view that law has this as its point or purpose. Like other forms of positivism my theory makes no claim to identify the point or purpose of law and legal practices as such" (Hart 1994, p. 248). Still, there is no complete agreement between Hart's readers regarding his endorsement of conventionalism. For instance, Leslie Green and Julie Dickson claim that Hart's theory in *The Concept of Law* was not conventionalist and that the *conventionalist turn* took place later on with the posthumous publication as "Postscript" of his manuscript notes. See Green (1999), pp. 37–41 and Dickson (2007), pp. 382–386. Dickson even doubts that the *conventionalist turn* actually took place, see Dickson (2007), p. 385 fn. 43.

[32] To my knowledge, the first time in which Coleman endorses this thesis is in Coleman (2001b), p. 117 ("I explicitly characterize the rule of recognition as a coordination convention"). In previous articles he mentions the possibility but does not explicitly embrace it; see Coleman (1982). However, he abandons this idea in Coleman (2001a), p. 374 and fn. 30.

the other hand, a version based on constitutive conventions that has been advanced by Andrei Marmor.[33]

Second, some philosophers have purported to defend a strengthen version of conventionalism. For example, Gerald Postema has defended what he calls Constructive conventionalism. According to Postema legal duties stem from the "general political-moral concerns" that legal conventions are there to satisfy.[34]

All these alternatives may be also classified in internalist and externalist versions of conventionalism. According to internalism, legal duties exist in virtue of some elements of conventions themselves. An internalist version is held by those philosophers that consider the practical capacity of conventions as stemming autonomously from their constitutive elements. Marmor seems to privilege an internalist version.[35] According to externalism, legal duties arise only if conventions relate in the right way to non-conventional norms. Postema, for instance, seems to privilege an externalist version of the practical capacity of conventions.

There are further differences between these two strategies. Constructive conventionalism is, I would say, a local theory, whereas Hartian conventionalism is global. Local theories purport to show how duties stem from *legal* conventions. On the contrary, global theories seek to explain legal duties by explaining the normativity of conventions in general.

3.1 Hartian Conventionalism

Hartian conventionalism accepts the thesis according to which there are legal duties, but adds that in order to explain how conventions can give rise to duties it would be necessary to specify what a convention is. Two different sets of conditions have been proposed for the existence of a convention, those that define a coordination convention and those that define a constitutive convention. The different versions of conventionalism diverge on which one of these conventions gives rise to legal

[33] Marmor (2009).

[34] Postema (1982), pp. 165–203 and with substantial adjustments Postema (2011), pp. 483–545. Other versions of this kind of conventionalism have been advanced, with different nuances by Dimitrios Kyritsis (2008) and Govert den Hartogh (2002). However, Kyritsis' and den Hartogh's versions are somehow different from Postema's position in as much as they defend the thesis according to which conventions have the capacity to justify by themselves the existence of duties in general. Postema purports only to show how legal conventions, given certain conditions, may generate duties. See Postema (2011), p. 497 for an assessment of the difference.

[35] Even if he is in an unstable middle way. On the one hand, he claims that a condition for the existence of a convention is that there are normative reasons to follow the regularity of behaviour and that "reasons for action are closely tied with the idea of value" (Marmor 2009, p. 5). This seems to imply that the existence of a convention necessarily implies that there are normative reasons to follow it. On the other hand, he claims that constitutive conventional duties are conditional. Indeed Marmor says that "conventional practices create reasons for action only if the relevant agent has a reason to participate in the practice to begin with. [...] The obligation to play by the rules [...] must come from moral and political considerations" (Marmor 2009, p. 168). More on this below.

duties. To my knowledge, after Coleman retreat, coordination conventions are no longer proposed as a constitutive version of Hartian conventionalism, so I will not deal with them in this section. Yet, I will have more to say on coordination conventions in the next section, regarding Postema's proposal. Here I will discuss the version based on constitutive conventions.

According to Marmor, constitutive conventions are a system of rules that have basically the following functions: (i) they define the practice, (ii) they regulate conduct within it, and (iii) they define some of the values that are inherent to the practice and the kind of evaluative discourse that applies to it.[36] In other words, they define the practice and how to be part of it. Clearly enough, this characterization relies on John Searle's distinction between regulative rules and constitutive rules.[37] Regulative rules are rules that regulate forms of behaviour that exist prior to, and independently of, the creation of the rule (e.g., "it is mandatory to use a tie in the exams"). Constitutive rules are rules that create and define new forms of behaviour. Searle claim that the distinction can be framed mainly on the basis of the following two criteria: (i) In the case of regulative rules, as long as the description does not make reference to the rule, the action could have been described in that way even if the rule did not exist. For example, it is possible to describe certain actions as "to smoke in closed places" before the existence of the rule "It is forbidden to smoke in closed places". On the contrary, in the case of constitutive rules, the behaviour in conformity to the rule can be now described in terms that could not have been used if the rule had not existed. Even if it is possible to describe an action as "to make the ball trespass the white line under the crossbar and between the posts" before the existence of the rules of soccer, it is not possible to describe an action as "to score a goal" before those same rules exist. (ii) Regulative rules have the form: "Do X" or "If you do X then Y", whereas constitutive rules have the form "X counts as Y in context C".[38]

Marmor proposes to conceive of constitutive rules, not as rules that constitute particular actions or "new forms of behaviour" but as rules that constitute a social practice, that is to say, as rules that constitute activities.[39]

Our author claims that constitutive conventions, as a kind of social rules, may give rise to duties: "Social rules can determine their ought, as it were, by being followed (viz., regarded as binding) by a certain community, just as the rules of chess determine their 'ought' within the game that is actually followed by the relevant community".[40] Once we are engaged in a chess game, rules of chess determine our duties within the game. In the same way, if judges were to identify certain norms as

[36] Marmor (2009), pp. 36–37.

[37] See Searle (1969). Even if he was not the first to frame the distinction, it appears in the work of John Rawls (1955) and Alf Ross (1968).

[38] See Searle (1969), pp. 33–36.

[39] "It is only when we have a whole structure of rule-governed activity, with some complexity and interconnections between the rules, that we can say that we have a social practice constituted by rules" (Marmor 2009, pp. 34–35).

[40] Marmor (2009), p. 161.

law by following criteria determined by a systematic set of rules, they would be engaged in a practice that defines and constitutes their duties.[41]

Now, is there a set of constitutive rules that defines the practice for the identification of law and determines how to be part in it? It seems to me that constitutive conventions, useful as an account of game-like activities, cannot be extended further to cover the activity of judges because of the differences between this two kind of social practice. In fact, the identification of law takes place in a context of interaction with an open structure. The open structure of the interaction implies that there is neither a sharp demarcation between participants and nonparticipants nor, obviously, a sharp detachment from real-life concerns. So, there is no sufficient basis to claim, as in games, that there are rules that define how to be part of it and how to behave within it.

Therefore, if constitutive conventions are regularities of behaviour that take place under game-like structures of interaction, given that judges activity regarding the identification of legal duties does not take place in a structure of that kind, it is not possible to claim that legal duties arise from a constitutive convention.

Maybe, to face this challenge Marmor could say two things: first, that rules constituting legal practice (at least the one telling how to identify the law) have been codified and that this is a sufficient basis for the existence of a constitutive convention. Second, that in particular cases there is a clear demarcation of participants, e.g., the parties of a contract, the wedding partners, judges themselves, and so on.

However, I think that there are two further circumstances that preclude the possibility of claiming that judges' activity regarding the identification of legal duties is regulated by a constitutive convention.[42] These circumstances have to do with the assumption, behind Marmor's theory, that legal practice is a cooperative activity.

---

[41] As I have said at the beginning of this section, Marmor is in an unstable position. This instability may be a consequence of the following dilemma: either Marmor explains conventional duties by arguing that conventions are tied to values via reasons for action, but then he cannot account for silly or bad constitutive conventions; or he claims that the rules of the practice just prescribe mere modes of conduct within it and that the duty, if there is one, must come from moral considerations, but then he must isolate conventions from reasons and values. In a later work, Marmor tries to answer this objection and seems to opt for the second horn of the dilemma. Indeed, he claims that: "reasons for having a convention might be defeated, sometimes immediately and unquestionably so, by reasons not to have it. Unfortunately, the counter-reasons in play are not always recognized by those who convention it is. That is why bad conventions often exist and sometimes persist for a long time" (Marmor 2011, p. 497). But this answer falls short of the target: the fact that a reason for following a practice may be defeated by another does not prove that the practice is morally isolated, because moral reasons may be defeated.

[42] Vilajosana has defended a thesis according to which at the foundation of law there are conventions with a constitutive dimension (see Vilajosana Rubio 2010, pp. 471–501). Even if his proposal is close to Marmor's, Vilajosana claims that coordination and constitutivity do not exclude each other. Therefore, according to Vilajosana there is no categorical dichotomy between coordination and constitutive conventions; it is just a distinction between several dimensions of conventionality (see Vilajosana Rubio 2010, p. 487 fn. 49). To my mind, since the positive conditions for a convention to have a constitutivity dimension are the same as the positive conditions for a convention to be constitutive, the objections apply also to Vilajosana's proposal.

Marmor accepts that his account is compatible with the perspective that a certain cooperative aim or intention is a condition for the existence of some social practices. However, Marmor claims that this compatibility does not implies that cooperation is a condition for every social practice. So, according to Marmor, cooperation is not a necessary feature of his account.[43] He also claims that his theory is not "meant to say anything about the metaphysics of social reality" and so that it has no bearing on Searle's thesis regarding the role of collective intentionality in explicating social reality.[44]

Yet, if we give a second look to his theory, it will become evident that cooperation between the individuals involved is a necessary condition for the existence of a constitutive convention as conceived by Marmor. And this is so because this is the only way in which behaviour may give place to constitutive rules. To see why, I will recall Searle's ideas about constitutive rules and institutional facts. These ideas are applicable to Marmor's theory about constitutive rules and constitutive conventions without carrying the metaphysical load. Marmor defines conventions (be it of coordination or constitutive) by saying that "there is a group of people, a population, P, that normally follow R in circumstances C", where R is a rule. So, if the convention is of coordination the rule is regulative, and if the rule is constitutive, the convention is constitutive. But he assumes by fiat that the same kind of behaviour is sufficient for considering that a group of people follows a regulative or a constitutive rule. Given that Marmor does not offer a story about how the behaviour of people may give rise to a constitutive rule, let us turn back to Searle's argument.

Searle's idea is very simple, constitutive rules allow people to assign functions to objects that cannot be performed by the object's physical properties. It is well known the example of the primitive tribe that builds a wall around its village and assigns to it the function of limiting its territory even if the wall gradually decays and no longer can repel foreigners.[45] Searle claims that the assignment of function can be attained only if the people involved share certain states of mind, what he calls collective intentionality: "the crucial element in collective intentionality is a sense of doing (wanting, believing, etc.) something together, and the individual intentionality that each person has is derived from the collective intentionality that they share".[46] In Searle's words: "the collective imposition of functions on objects where the function assigned to the object cannot be performed solely in virtue of the object's intrinsic physical features [...is..] a matter of human cooperation. [...T]he collective imposition of function, where the function can be performed only in

[43] It seems to me that Marmor is nudged to this conclusion because he bases his defense of constitutive conventions on the idea that even if some conventions are there to solve coordination problems, not all of them are. See Marmor (2014), pp. 84–85 where he concedes that even if constitutive conventions may solve social problems, these are not coordination problem in Lewis strict sense.

[44] Marmor (2009), pp. 53–54.

[45] Searle (1995), pp. 39–40.

[46] Searle (1995), pp. 24–25.

virtue of collective agreement or acceptance, is a crucial element in the creation of institutional facts".[47]

This explanation as to how human behaviour may give rise to constitutive rules shows why constitutive conventions are rooted in cooperation, without necessarily carrying the metaphysical load that Marmor disowns. Without cooperation, i.e., without people assigning to certain behaviour the same meaning (or function), there are not rules constituting a practice. For an activity to be defined and constituted by a regularity of behaviour, that behaviour must comprehend people cooperation regarding the conditions for being part of the activity and regarding how to behave within it. Therefore, cooperation is necessary for the existence of a conventional constitutive rule, that is, for constitutive rules that are not institutionally enacted.[48]

Given that cooperation is also a key feature of Postema's theory, let us explore the claims of strengthen conventionalism before discussing how this kept conventionalism captive of Dworkin's premises. As we may see at the end of next section, the failures of both kind of conventionalism stem from the same fact.

3.2 *Constructive Conventionalism*

This kind of conventionalism accepts the Dworkinian thesis according to which there are legal duties and the thesis that conventionalism should explain how conventions may justify that duty. So, it tries to reach the key in order to pass through the last tiny door drawn by Dworkin. Constructive conventionalism trusts to have found the growth cake in the value of cooperation.

According to Postema it is possible to show that judges identify and apply the law on the basis of conventions and that those conventions impose duties. The argument is that once the convention is stabilized it will generate the expectation that judges will continue complying with it. Under certain conditions the fact that these expectations are created gives raise to the duty of following the convention. In his earlier works Postema thought of these conventions as coordination conventions[49] (or "Lewisian conventions"), in his more recent works he advances a broader concept of convention that he calls "Humean conventions" linked with cooperation and not just coordination.[50] However, even with these changes, the function of conventions within Postema's theory remains mostly the same. So, I will start by introducing Lewisian coordination conventions and Postema's argument regarding how they

[47] Searle (1995), p. 39. And also: "Because physical features specified by the X term are insufficient by themselves to guarantee the fulfillment of the assigned function specified by the Y term, the new status and its attendant function have to be the sort of things that can be constituted by collective agreement or acceptance" (Searle 1995, p. 44).

[48] Marmor explicitly characterizes his theory as a theory of conventional (non-institutionally enacted) constitutive rules. See Marmor (2009), pp. 35–36.

[49] Postema (1982).

[50] Postema (2011), pp. 486–492.

explain legal duties. Then I will introduce some of the objections and Postema's answer based on Humean cooperation conventions. Finally, I will argue that notwithstanding Postema's efforts, these changes keep conventionalism captive of Dworkin's premises.

A coordination convention is a regularity of behaviour that solves a recurrent coordination problem. This is the idea of convention introduced by David Lewis in his book *Convention.*[51] According to Lewis, a convention exists, even without an agreement, in certain situations of social interaction that have specific properties. These are situations in which two or more individuals, with similar interests, face two or more possible courses of action. Each option satisfies their interests in a similar way provided that both of them take the same course of action. For instance, we can imagine two friends facing a situation of this kind when they have decided to meet without specifying the place and without being able to communicate before the meeting. In their situation, many solutions are available (several places for their meeting) and to each friend it is not too important which particular solution is chosen, each of them only cares for the place to be the same as the one chosen by the other. The situation becomes problematic because even if everyone's interests are the same, there are many options (at least more than one) that satisfy them. Lewis called "a coordination problem" the kind of situation that I have described.

When a situation of this kind is recurrent, i.e., it verifies with certain regularity, the solution attained once can generate, between the agents, mutual expectations about the behaviour of others that can drive them to converge in that same solution the next time. Once the group of friends has met in one bar they would tend to go back to that place. The relevant thing about this regularity is not so much the way in which it emerged, but the fact that it started to be repeated. In that case a coordination convention will be born.[52]

According to conventionalism, judges face a coordination problem. Judges purport to guide the behaviour of citizens and to accomplish this end they need to give citizens the chance to identify law. This would be impossible if judges were to decide cases in disparate ways. For that problem to be solved, and for judges to effectively comply with their professional task, they must converge in the identification of law. In particular, judges should maintain the unity and integrity of their

[51] Lewis (1969). The label "coordination convention" is not Lewis'. Actually, Lewis attempted to answer Willard Quine's objection against the possibility of a conventional foundation for logic and language. Lewis was interested in showing that one of the premises of Quine's argument, i.e., that the existence of a convention depends on an agreement, is false. In fact, Lewis purported to provide an explanation of the general concept of convention, hoping to capture "our common, established concept of convention" (Lewis 1969, p. 3). After some criticism (see Jamieson 1975), pp. 73–81, Lewis only conceded that there may be derivative usages of "convention" that do not meet "the defining conditions" of his "central concept" (Lewis 1976, pp. 113–114).

[52] When an alternative emerges as a solution it is said to be *salient*. An alternative can be made *salient* in different ways, e.g., by being chosen by an authority, by an agreement, or just spontaneously or by chance. However, once the same solution starts to be followed, its salience comes from this fact, i.e., being a precedent, and not so much from how it originated. All that counts for its subsistence is its recurrent capacity to capture the attention of all the people involved in the coordination problem. See Lewis (1969), p. 38.

activity.[53] If the convergence on identification stabilizes, a coordination convention will be born. The existence of that convention will create in the citizens the expectation that judges will keep identifying law in such and such way.

Still, not all expectations, even if reasonable, impose to an agent the duty to meet them.[54] According to Postema, the obligation emerges only "when the context in which expectations arise and are sustained is closely analogous to a cooperative enterprise for mutual benefit in which considerations of fair play require conformity".[55] The conformity is required when the frustration of the expectation would be unfair. The frustration of an expectation is unfair when those who encouraged it frustrate the expectation.

These considerations, the argument continues, make it mandatory for judges to comply with the conventions on which basis they identify the law. Indeed, the relationship between judges and citizens, while interdependent, is asymmetrical. Judges conceive of, and they demand others to conceive of, their activity as authoritative, and this is clearly a way to induce expectations. This type of activity requires, according to the doctrine of political responsibility, that judges act on the basis of a "general public theory" and therefore each judge should (i) secure consistency regarding the activity of other judges and (ii) respect the legitimate and reasonable expectations of citizens regarding his activity.[56]

In this way, given that induced expectations should be respected, and given that citizens are entitled to expect that judges will conform to the convention, judges have a duty to respect the coordination conventions on which basis they identify the law.[57]

The problem with conventionalism in this coordination vest is that, contrary to what Postema claims, judges do not seem to face a coordination problem when they are in the business of identifying the law. That is to say, the conditions that define a coordination problem as a particular kind of strategic interaction are not present in the activity of judges.[58] A coordination problem is a situation in which participants have ex-ante preferences that are structured in a certain way, i.e. their interests are similar. But in the legal domain, where charges and benefits must be distributed,

---

[53] "Citizens react to, and attempt to anticipate or predict, the law-applying activities of the judiciary as a hole. Thus, if the activity of law applying is to achieve the ends of the law in a reasonably efficient manner, it must be possible to view the activity of law applying as governed by some reasonably coherent pattern. This requires that judges seek to coordinate *their* law-applying activities in order to achieve something tolerably close to a norm of what I have called 'institutional coherence'" (Postema 1982, p. 193).

[54] As, in the example mentioned by Postema, the fact that during his diary promenades Kant would pass at an exact hour every day at a lady's window and the fact that on that basis the lady would form the expectation that he would pass every day at that hour, do not impose to Kant the duty to satisfy that expectation. See Postema (1982), p. 180.

[55] Postema (1982), p. 180.

[56] Postema (1982), p. 197.

[57] Postema (1982), pp. 196–197 and Postema (2011), pp. 498–500.

[58] Coleman himself raised this kind of objection in Coleman (2001a), p. 374. It is advanced also in Celano (2010b), p. 328.

interaction problems are of several different kinds and complexities. To conceive the activity of judges as solving a coordination problem would be to distort the kind of situation in which they act. Using the same game-theory terminology, the situation seems better described as a case of prisoner's dilemma or as a fair play problem, where there is a radical conflict of interests.[59] Coordination conventions are not solutions to this kind of problem. It is true, coordination problems may have different degrees. In pure cases there is a perfect coincidence of interests and in less pure cases agents have contrasting personal preferences regarding the different alternatives. However, a situation in which there is a radical contrast between preferences is not a coordination problem, because the fact that others behave in certain way is not necessary a reason to behave in that same way.

In short, if coordination conventions are regularities of behaviour that solve recurrent coordination problems, then, given that judges do not face a coordination problem, it is not possible to claim that legal duties arise from a coordination convention.

Even if not explicitly, Postema offered an answer to this objection in his recent works. I think we may consider as such his arguments in favour of a broader concept of convention as solution, not just to coordination problems, but to cooperation problems in general, which include forms of interaction where conflicts of interest prevail.[60] Postema claims that this can be done by adjusting Lewis' account in two ways. First, by weakening the requirement for a strategy to be a solution. All we need for having a solution to the cooperation problem is that "at least one set of coordinated strategies available to the parties is preferred by all to any set that is the result of parties going their own way (even though that one set may not be optimal from the point of view of each party or even of the group as a whole)".[61] Second, by enhancing the kind of facts that determine the content of the conventions. "What is essential to the capacity of conventions to solve cooperation problems [...] is not the regularity of behavior, but rather the salience of the pattern or scheme of action which the regularity's publicity creates.".[62] Thus, under this new version, conventions between judges regarding the identification of law "are schemes of correlated actions that enable members of a community to solve the recurrent cooperation problems they face"[63] by "anchoring" everyone's expectations to a single solution.[64]

---

[59] While a situation of the kind of the prisoner's dilemma involves only two people, a problem of fair play involves a group of people. See Celano (2010a), p. 312.

[60] "[..F]ollowing Hume, we can identify coordination elements in other kinds of games in which conflict is more pronounced, not only so-called Battle of the Sexes games, but also iterated prisoner's dilemma and hawk/dove games with uncertain termination points. We can refer to these as 'cooperation problems,'" (Postema 2011, p. 489). Eerik Lagerspetz proposed a very similar strategy in Lagerspetz (1995).

[61] Postema (2011), p. 491.

[62] Postema (2011), p. 491.

[63] Postema (2011), p. 492.

[64] This broader conception of conventions has also an impact on Postema's answer to Dworkin's objection from disagreement. In his earlier work Postema argued that disagreements are just new

It seems to me that by broadening it, the concept of convention loses explicative power. Coordination conventions *à la* Lewis have explanatory power thanks to their limited scope. However, I will not dwell here with Postema's proposal regarding the concept of convention. Instead, what I will try to argue is that the assumption, common to Postema's and Marmor's theories, about the cooperative nature of legal practice as a whole—including the activity of judges aimed at determining the existence and the content of legal duties—is unwarranted. Postema explicitly expresses this claim and, as I have tried to show, Marmor is committed to it once we dig into the Searlian foundations of constitutive conventions.

As I have said at the end of the discussion of Hartian conventionalism, there are two circumstances that preclude the possibility of claiming that judges' activity is cooperative, at least regarding the determination of the existence and content of legal duties. Therefore, it also precludes the possibility of conceiving of their activity either as a constitutive convention or as a cooperation convention.

An essential feature of social actions is that the outcomes people want to produce or prevent are determined by the actions of other agents. That is, the agent finds himself in a situation in which the attainment of a result requires not only an action of him, but the contribution of other agents as well. The social outcome would not occur if all the parties did not do their part. So, for there to be cooperation, each agent must be able to assume that other members of the collective enterprise will also do their parts. Therefore, cooperation requires the existence of an epistemological basis for the formation of an expectation about other agents' cooperative attitude. That is why one of the major difficulties that the explanation of social actions must face is the problem of the knowledge of other participants' attitudes. The question is crucial because without some reliable information about other participants' contribution, individuals will not have sufficient reasons to engage in the activity. It is in virtue of this fact that a theory of a cooperative enterprise must offer a story about how that information is to be gathered.

The theories of constitutive and cooperation conventions that I have just introduced offer an explanation of how the structure of the situation may give a good epistemic basis for the formation of the expectation about other participants' cooperative attitude. First, regarding paradigmatic cases of constitutive conventions, i.e. game-like activities, due to the close structure of the interaction, it does not appear

coordination problems "within a (partially solved) coordination problem. [...] This can be solved in essentially the same way as any other coordination problem is solved, namely, by exploiting the mutual expectations that already obtain in the situation" (Postema 1982, p. 178). However, this answer was insufficient because if disagreements are coordination problems, it must be accepted that prior to the decision there is no solution, so there is no previous convention. Instead, based on the idea of convention as "schemes of correlated actions", Postema's more recent answer is that "[c]onventions, on this view, are not static, fixed points, determined strictly by descriptions of the convergent behavior from which they emerge, but rather relatively stable nodes in a dynamic matrix, the full significance of which cannot be appreciated if removed from this matrix. It is that matrix, available to all and to which all contribute, that gives practical force to particular conventional arrangements and provides resources to enable participants to solve novel situations that arise in the course of the practice" (Postema 2011, p. 495). Where "novel situations" includes disagreements.

to be problematic for an agent with a cooperative attitude to form the relevant expectation regarding the fact that other agents share that attitude. That is, the clear identification of participants, the detachment from other real life concerns and the stability of the interaction give a good epistemological basis for the agent to hold the expectation that others will do their part in the cooperative enterprise.[65] Second, as we have seen, a common way to solve coordination problems is by taking advantage of some salient event. An alternative of action is salient when it "stands out from the rest by its uniqueness in some conspicuous respect".[66] Once salience has been noted by several agents and the problem has been solved one or more times, coordination can be achieved by precedent. So, when salience occurs there is a sufficient basis, according to the story, for each agent to form the expectation about other agents' cooperative attitude.

However, it seems to me that the solution given for game-like activities and coordination problems cannot be extended further to cover legal practice, and hence, that there is no sufficient epistemological basis for each agent to form the necessary expectation about other agents' cooperative attitude. The first, less important, problem is that each agent cannot rely on the belief that she shares with others the same belief about which is the function of each legal institution. As it has been pointed out, many legal institutions do not have a clearly shared function. "For example, what is the purpose of our marriage, divorce, property and inheritance laws? Anything that can be said about it is banal or obviously concocted – for example, that the purpose of the rules of divorce is to enable people to have reasonable access to divorce".[67]

The second, more important, problem is the way in which judges and lawyers discuss the identification of the law. As Dworkin showed, from a historical perspective legal practice often changed in response to arguments made in the context of adjudication, lawyers "often call for changing even settled practice in midgame".[68] For instance, as pointed by Dworkin, relevant changes in the theory of legislation[69] and in the doctrine of precedent were made inside the context of legal adjudication. These changes were changes within judicial practice; they were neither the result of special agreements about having a new set of rules, as would be the case in game-like activities,[70] nor the result of the salience of a new fact, as it would be in the case of coordination conventions. Conventions can also change, but once people are engaged in the practice, a sharp distinction is made between arguments about and arguments within the convention. This distinction is not made by judges and lawyers

[65] Searle (2010), pp. 54–55.

[66] Lewis (1969), p. 35.

[67] Ross (1958), p. 147.

[68] Dworkin (1986), p. 138.

[69] Theories about "how far and in what way legislative intention is relevant in reading statutes" (Dworkin 1986, p. 137).

[70] To conceive of this activity as a game-like enterprise would be like conceiving of a game in which certain moves within it count in favour or against opposite ways of keeping score.

in many cases, so the formation of an expectation about other participants' cooperative attitude would be unwarranted.

The third, equally important, problem is that the existence of duties is questioned not only in the middle of the game, but it is also the case that the content of legal provisions suffers from a high degree of indeterminacy. As a matter of fact, given the availability of several methods of interpretation, every normative provision can be interpreted as expressing different norms. The main sources of indeterminacy are, as Guastini remarks: "(i) the plurality of interpretive methods; (ii) juristic theories (so-called 'legal dogmatics' in continental jurisprudential language), and (iii) the sense of justice of interpreters, i.e., their ethical and political preferences (be they expressly declared by means of value judgments or not)".[71] Within legal practice there is a large set of accepted interpretive methods that is sufficient to produce a great deal of incompatible and/or competing results. "Take, for example, an Italian constitutional provision referring to 'statutes'. Arguing *a contrariis*, one can conclude that such a provision applies to any kind of statute and only to statutes. Arguing by analogy, one can conclude that the provision at stake applies to statutes as well as to executive regulations (since both are 'sources of law'). Arguing by the distinguishing technique, one can conclude that, since the class of 'statutes' includes different subclasses (constitutional and ordinary, on the one hand; state and regional, on the other), the provision—in the light of its *ratio*—only applies to one of such subclasses".[72] Given this level of indeterminacy, the expectation about other agents' cooperative attitude would be unwarranted, because each agent may interpret the provision according to his interests.

Thus, my point is that for there to be cooperative behaviour each agent must have a cooperative attitude, that is, a disposition to do her part in the collective enterprise. It also requires for each agent to form an expectation regarding the fact that others have that same attitude. This last requirement is satisfied only if agents have a sufficient epistemological basis to form the expectation that other agents have the cooperative attitude. A theory that purports to explain that social fact must offer an account of how the epistemological basis for holding the expectation is formed. It seems to me that even if paradigmatic cases of constitutive conventions and coordination conventions may satisfy this requirement, we cannot extend the solution to legal practice. In this last case it is dubious that such a basis exists. The fact that legal norms are discussed in midgame and the fact that the result of legal interpretation is highly indeterminate preclude the possibility of saying rightly that in the legal context there is a sufficient epistemological basis for the formation of an expectation that other agents have a cooperative attitude, and hence, it also precludes the possibility of saying rightly that the identification of law is defined and regulated by a cooperative enterprise.

To sum up, the two versions of conventionalism discussed so far (Hartian/constitutive and Constructive/justificatory) purported to answer Dworkin's objection by

---

[71] Guastini (2011), p. 148.

[72] Guastini (2011), pp. 148–149. Bruno Celano has defended a non-cooperative view of legal interpretation too in Celano (2005), pp. 99–114 and in Celano (2017).

fine-tuning the concept of convention. I have argued that both versions fail in their endeavour because the conditions for the existence of the particular kind of convention each of them advances are not present in legal practice. I think that the reason for this failure is that conventionalist have remained captive of Dworkin's premises and that this has led them to overstate the cooperative nature of legal practice. The argument so far is that cooperation does not occur within judges' activity of the identification of law. Contrary to what both versions seem to presuppose, there are portions of legal practice that have an agonistic character, such as the activity of judges aimed at the identification of the content of legal duties. If this is so, and given that cooperation is a necessary condition of both Marmor's constitutive conventions and Postema's cooperation ones, we must conclude that, at least regarding the identification of legal duties, there is not a convention of either of this two kinds. Therefore, neither Hartian conventionalism nor Constructive conventionalism can explain the existence of conventional duties and they cannot even start to elaborate a way out of the objection from disagreement.[73]

So, the lesson that, it seems to me, we can gather from this failure is that even if legal practice has elements of cooperation, those elements do not extend to the point of determining the existence and content of legal duties. To say it another way, the existence and the content of legal duties are not determined by cooperation, even if participants in legal practice cooperate in other ways. As I will claim below, legal participants cooperate, for instance, regarding the identification of legal provisions and regarding the set of available methods to interpret those provisions. In legal practice there may be conventions regarding how to identify legal provisions and conventions regarding the different ways in which they can be interpreted. However, cooperation does not extend to the fixation of one particular meaning, that is to say, there are no conventions determining the meaning of one particular normative provision and hence, there are no conventions determining the existence and the content of legal duties. Before fleshing out these bold statements I will, in the next section, offer a way of breaking Dworkin's chain by challenging his premises.

[73] I have mentioned Postema's answer to the objection above. Just for completion, Marmor's answer to the objection from disagreement is a *reductio ad absurdum*: "we can only make sense of such disagreements on the basis of the assumption that there are rules of recognition that constitutes, *inter alia*, the court system and the legal authority of judges" (Marmor 2009, p. 163). In other words, according to Marmor, the existence of disagreements between judges presupposes the existence of judges and the existence of judges presupposes the existence of constitutive conventions. Even if we concede this point to Marmor, it seems to me that it does not solve the problem. To answer Dworkin's objection, we need to show that, notwithstanding the disagreement, there are constitutive conventions determining the content of the duty, not just who should identify it.

4 Breaking the Chain

The difficulty that have brought us here is that judges talk as if there were legal duties and as if those duties could be the object of propositions, that is, as if they could be described, even in cases of disagreement. The discussion so far has taken us to the point where no version of conventionalism is able to show that those statements refer to conventions. Dworkin has claimed that even if conventionalism seems capable of showing how judges statements of duty can be true in cases of convergence, it is impossible for them to show how they can be true in cases of disagreements and this renders the apparent explanation in cases of convergence deceptive. I have added, following some sceptical arguments, that conventionalism is not even a seemingly good explanation of convergence cases, because conventionalism presupposes cooperation whereas legal practice is characterized by conflict and indeterminacy.

I have argued that conventionalism has arrived at this critical point because it has remained captive of Dworkin's premises, i.e., that the only way to explain judges' claims and disagreement is to show how legal duties exist, and those premises has impelled conventionalists to exaggerate the cooperative nature of legal practice.

In order to set itself free conventionalism must break that chain and that is what sceptical conventionalism does.

4.1 Sceptical Conventionalism

Sceptical conventionalism is not blind to the fact that judges claim that there are legal duties, even in cases of disagreements, and concedes that a theory of law cannot just get rid of this trait of legal practice. However, it breaks the Dworkinian chain according to which judges' claims about the existence of legal duties can only be explained by showing how those duties exist. Indeed, contrary to the previous versions of conventionalism (that from now on I will call "cognitive conventionalism"), sceptical conventionalism rejects the thesis according to which there are legal duties.

Now, in order to succeed sceptical conventionalism has to show that even if they do not make reference to anything in the world (because there are no legal duties), judges—seemingly denotative or representative—statements, can be explained without falling into an error theory.[74] This is the alternative I would like to explore here.[75]

Thus, it would be necessary to show that for judges to claim, without falling into error, that there are legal duties it is not necessary that the entity to which they seem

---

[74] In this case, given the claim that there are no legal duties, it would be a global error theory.

[75] I have tried to show how projectivism plus quasi-realism can solve some other problems regarding legal statements in Arena (2012), pp. 185–201 and Arena (2013), pp. 417–438.

to refer exists. This may be done by sharpening the comprehension of those statements:

(i) They are propositional reflections of judges' evaluative attitudes (projectivist thesis).[76]
(ii) To assert that a legal duty exists is nothing other than express one's attitude towards the accomplishment of the action.[77]

According to the projectivist thesis then, judges' attitudes are the answer to some properties of the world around them. Thus, what they consider a perception of duties (or a sensibility towards duties) is just a function of stimuli/beliefs to responses/attitudes. For example, if Morena sees Luca using drugs and says "That is plainly wrong!" projectivism claims that given a set of facts, i.e., Luca performing some actions, Morena perceiving those actions and Morena's beliefs (about what Luca is doing, his intentions, and the effects of his actions), an emotion of disapproval raises in Morena. Morena projects her emotion into the world and then she exclaims "That is plainly wrong!". This is why Morena "judges the world to contain a certain quality, and her doing so is not the product of her tracking a real feature of the world, but is, rather, prompted by an emotional experience".[78] When judges engage in a discourse about duties they actually use language to project attitudes.

The second trait implies that, when a judge utters a statement of duty she is expressing an attitude ("*voicing certain attitude*").[79] What she does when she says that something is due, or correct or compulsory is to express ("*avow*") her practical point of view.[80] To say that there is a duty to ϕ is to express a certain attitude regarding the state of affairs in which ϕ is the case and to be motivated to act in consequence.

However, when uttering statements of duties judges not only avow an attitude regarding the action at stake. They are also claiming that there is an interpretative method supporting the association of that duty to the normative provision. In this sense, when a judge defends the existence of a duty, she also expresses an attitude towards the method used to associate that meaning to the normative provision. Thus, the statement consists in the affirmation, by the judge, that the meaning that she associates with the text is the best choice given the interpretative methods that are in

[76] Blackburn (1998), p. 77. "We project an attitude or habit or other commitment which is not descriptive onto the world, when we speak and think as though there were a property of things which our sayings describe which we can reason about, know about, be wrong about, and so on" (Blackburn 1984, pp. 170–171).

[77] Blackburn (1998), pp. 77–83.

[78] Joyce (2007). See Blackburn (1998), pp. 4–8.

[79] However, "[t]o hold a value, then, is typically to have a relative stable disposition to conduct practical life and practical discussion in a particular way: it is to be disposed or *set* in that way, and notably to be set against change in this respect. This way of being set is such as to align values and motivations" (Blackburn 1998, p. 67).

[80] "'Avowal' here means that we express this state, make it public, or communicate it" (Blackburn 1998, p. 68).

place. To give a full account of judges' statements of duty more has to be said about interpretative methods.

4.2 *The Route to Freedom*

Legal interpretation is the activity of associating a meaning (a norm) to a normative provision. From this point of view an interpretative statement has the following form: "T means N", where T stands for the legal text (or normative provision) and N for its meaning (the norm).[81] There is a clear sense in which conventions have a place in legal interpretation.[82] Terms and expressions do not have a natural or intrinsic meaning; on the contrary, the users of language give terms and expressions their meaning. However, this simple claim does not offer an account of the complexity of legal interpretation. For instance, it is blind to the fact that the alleged determinacy of meaning in ordinary discourse does not necessarily translate to the legal domain.[83] It would also be reductionist, because it would neglect other kinds of interpretative codes or methods besides ordinary meaning.

Indeed, there are several interpretative methods allowing to establish, in different ways, the meaning of normative provisions. Each interpretative method determines the specific processes through which judges may associate a meaning to a normative provision. In other words, within legal interpretation, ordinary meaning does not exhaust the set of interpretative methods.[84] Within a legal community, each interpretative method contains a set of rules or directives regarding the interpretation of legal provisions. These rules or directives may be of three different kinds: (1) primary directives, (2) secondary directives; (3) axiological directives.[85] For instance, the interpretative method of the legislator's intention contains, in most legal cultures, the primary directive according to which the meaning should match with the "intended meaning" or the "purpose" of the legislator; the secondary directive specifying that the method should be applied only when literal meaning is not clear; the axiological directive specifying that the method should be used in cases where the authority of the legislator is in need of reinforcement. Clearly enough, it is a contingent matter which directives are contained in each interpretative method and which particular interpretative method should be used in a case.

---

[81] Guastini (2011), pp. 138–161.

[82] As from now on I will refer only to interpretation in the legal context, I will use just 'interpretation' for short.

[83] For an argument in this sense see Chiassoni (2000), p. 94.

[84] "The simple rule of literal meaning is just one of several possibilities in which [interpretative] conventions could be framed; and, specially, the claim that within legal practice this simple rule is the only interpretative convention is clamorously denied by the facts" (Bayón Mohino 2002b, pp. 63–64). The translation is mine.

[85] Chiassoni (2004), p. 63 and Chiassoni (2007), pp. 79–80.

These directives constitute a basis for the (relative) evaluation of the result of an interpretation, allowing us to evaluate, at least relatively to the directives, the correctness of interpretative statements.[86] Moreover, participants do not see themselves as breaking the law or as having an apparent disagreement when they use another method of interpretation besides the literal or semantic simple one. Likewise, it is not the case that judges decide to interpret a certain text in an isolated way or on the basis of an interpretative method used only by her. On the contrary, they engage in an interpretative practice where the fact that other judges use a certain interpretative method is part of the reason for the use of that same method. So, interpretative methods are conventions regarding how to associate a meaning to a normative provision.[87]

A statement of duty like "There is a duty to deny Elmer the inheritance of his grandfather given that this matches with legislator counterfactual intentions" or "There is a duty to enjoin the completion of Tellico Dam given that this matches with the plain meaning of the normative provision" can be interpreted like the expression of two attitudes:

(i) An attitude of approval regarding the action due.
(ii) An attitude of approval regarding the method of interpretation.

In the usual expressivist reconstruction:

(i) Denying Elmer the inheritance of his grandfather—hooray!
(ii) Interpreting the provision according to legislative counterfactual intentions—hooray!

Or

(i) Enjoining the completion of Tellico Dam—hooray!
(ii) Interpreting the provision according to the plain meaning of the normative provision—hooray![88]

In what sense may the judge say that a duty exists if her statements express an attitude? Well, the truth of her statement would be a product of her own intellectual work and sensibility. According to Blackburn, to claim that there is a duty implies to claim that the attitude reflected belongs to the set of attitudes that have overcome every improvement test, or at least that are considered no susceptible of revision. In Blackburn's words: "the simple suggestion is that we define a 'best possible set of attitudes', thought of as the limiting set which would result from taking all possible opportunities for improvement of attitude. Saying that an evaluative remark is true would be saying that it is a member of such a set, or is implied by such a set. Call

[86] Chiassoni (2004), p. 103.

[87] This make interpretative methods closer to Marmor's constitutive conventions. However, I do not need to argue for or against that here. Marmor himself has some doubts about that. See Marmor (2011), pp. 498–499.

[88] Of course, this is still a rough picture of interpretative statements.

the set M*. Then if *m* is a particular commitment, expressing an attitude *m*: *m* is true = *m* is a member of M*".[89]

Paraphrasing Balckburn, a judge *has to earn* her right to talk of legal truth. Given that truth has subjective sources, such as attitudes, needs and desires, her right depends on her capacity to form an improved set of attitudes, where coherence and consistency are respected.[90]

So, the theory may accommodate the propositional grammar of judges' statements even if there are no legal duties. A judge may claim that there is a duty to deny Elmer the inheritance of his grandfather or that there is a duty to enjoin the completion of Tellico dam, without the duty coming from the existence of some fact. By uttering that statement, the judge is expressing her attitude, her point of view, or maybe her desire regarding the state of affairs in which the duty is accomplished. This expression allows us to identify how the world should change in order to adjust itself to the attitude of the judge and which should be the behaviour of the rest of the officials if they were to respect judge's statement.[91]

Having said that, we can turn to the last link in Dworkin's chain: the objection from disagreement.

4.3 Dworkin's Last Link: Disagreements

Dworkin's argument from disagreement against Hart's positivism has produced a considerable amount of literature. A full assessment of that debate is not only beyond my competence, but it seems to me that it would take me beyond the

---

[89] Blackburn (1984), p. 198. Oddly enough for my project, Blackburn seems explicitly to endorse something like cognitive conventionalism. He claims that the truth value of a legal statements is grounded in facts about human arrangements, actions, and decisions. So that a judge's statement of duty is true if those groundings support the judgment that it is (Blackburn 1984, pp. 205–210). However, of my arguments against cognitive conventionalism are good, then they would apply to Blackburn's reconstruction of legal truth.

[90] Blackburn (1984), pp. 197–202.

[91] Certainly I am not the first to defend a view of legal statements in an expressivits vein. Scandinavian Legal realist have long ago advanced this claim. I will end this text in debt with them and the reader because a precise assessment of the relationship between the proposal made here and Scandinavian legal realism remains a job for a further occasion. More recently, Kevin Toh has also defended an expressivist account of "committed legal statements". At the beginning, Toh has defended it as an interpretation of Hart's theory in *The Concept of Law* (Toh 2005), pp. 75–123; later, with additions and improvements, he has defended it as what he thinks is the correct view of legal statements (Toh 2011), pp. 107–137. Even if I have profited reading his work, there are differences between his view and mine. On the one hand, Toh does not introduce Blackburn's quasi-realism and prefers Gibbards account (Gibbard 2003). On the other hand, Toh purports to combine expressivism with Hart's idea of the rule of recognition, which I do not. This Hartian leg of Toh's proposal has attracted criticism not only as an erroneous reading of Hart (see Swaminathan 2014), pp. 87–117 but also in virtue of its difficulties to cope with conventionalism' problems: among others, disagreements and overestimation of cooperation. My view is closer, I think, to the proposal hinted by Shivprasad Swaminathan in Swaminathan (2016), pp. 231–266.

structure of this work. So, in this last section I will just outline the way in which sceptical conventionalism may accommodate disagreements, whereas a more detailed and extended treatment of the argument remains a task for a different occasion. In any case, it is important to be clear about the point at stake, at least what I take it to be, so let me introduce some further precisions about the objection. Sometimes Dworkin claims that legal theory should account for genuine disagreements,[92] and other times he claims that legal theory should account for theoretical disagreements.[93] Dworkin does not say that only theoretical disagreements are genuine, but it is hard to discern what exactly he means by these two terms. So, just to avoid a mere terminological issue, we may, following Dworkin himself, distinguish between four kinds of genuine disagreements: empirical, borderline cases, structural and grounding. All these kinds of disagreements are genuine because people involved discuss on a shared basis, and I take the basis to include two elements: meaning (or concept) and object (or state of affairs). From this point of view, a disagreement is genuine if people involved associate the same meaning (or concept) to the terms they use and if they refer to the same object (or state of affairs).

So, genuine empirical disagreement arises when people assign different truth value to empirical statements because they have different believes regarding whether a state of affairs is the case. So, people may disagree about the truth value of the statement "Duchamp's urinary is art", because even if they agree on the meaning (or conception) of art (e.g., "original work that represents nature") and even if they refer to the same object, they disagree whether the state of affairs "Duchamp's urinary is an original work that represents nature" is the case. One of them believes that the urinary is just an industrial object, whereas the other, concede me the example, believes that the urinary has been handmade by Duchamp and that it is a representation of a Roman fountain.

Border-line cases disagreements arise when people sharing a common basis, disagree whether a particular object is within the scope of the meaning (or concept). For instance, if two people use the term "book" with the same meaning, they may disagree whether the object that is on the shelf and has a thin set of pages is or is not a book. Two people may have this kind of disagreement regarding the statement "Duchamp's urinary is art" because they may have different opinions regarding how many properties the urinary shares with what it represents and so they disagree whether it is in fact a representation, and hence they disagree whether it is art.

Structural disagreements arise between scientists when they discuss about the structure of natural kinds. I will not indulge in the analysis of this kind of

---

[92] "If this simple picture of when genuine disagreement is possible exhausts all possibilities, it must apply to legal concepts, including the concept of law" (Dworkin 1986, p. 45). And more explicitly in Dworkin (2017), p. 2110: "But making sense of our intellectual life requires that we have at least some way of distinguishing genuine from illusory disagreement".

[93] "Unfortunately for these theories, this picture of what makes disagreement possible fits badly with the kind of disagreements lawyers actually have. [..M]uch disagreement in law is theoretical rather than empirical" (Dworkin 1986, p. 46).

disagreements because it is not relevant for the present discussion (i.e. conventionalists and Dworkin agree that legal disagreements are not of this kind).

Finally, grounding disagreements arise when people discuss about what makes a statement true, that is, about which are its truth conditions. Again, people disagreeing about the truth value of the statement "Duchamp's urinary is art" have this kind of disagreement if one of them claims that the statement is false because **art** is just an original work that represents nature, and the other claims that it is true because **art** is what an artist points as art.

With this categories in mind, let us turn back to Dworkin's objection. The problem with cognitive conventionalism is that grounding disagreements are not possible regarding conventional concepts because conventional concepts have their content determined by users' shared criteria of use. Given that for there to be a conventional concept users must share a set of criteria, there cannot be a conventional concept when there is a disagreement about the criteria. Therefore, an apparent grounding disagreement about conventional concepts is either an empirical disagreement about which are indeed the shared criteria or a deceptive disagreement, i.e. people are just talking pass each other.

For instance, if **art** is a conventional concept, then a disagreement about the truth conditions of the statement like "Duchamp's urinary is art", is either an empirical disagreement about which are the conventional criteria for something to be art or a deceptive disagreement because one of them uses the word "art" as "original work that represents nature" and the other uses it as, let us say, "pointed as art by an artist". Regarding conventional concepts there cannot be genuine disagreement about criteria of use. The only kinds of disagreement available are either empirical disagreements about the actual criteria or about the state of affairs referred to by the concept or borderline-cases disagreements.

Dworkin claims that genuine grounding disagreements are possible only regarding what he calls interpretative concepts, that is, concepts which content is determined by the theory that presents under its best light the practice in which the concept is used.[94] **Art**, according to Dworkin, is an example of an interpretative concept. So, under his view, people discussing about Duchamp's urinary are neither having an empirical disagreement nor a deceptive one, but a genuine grounding disagreement about which is the best theory of the practice where **art** is used. The disagreement is genuine because they are talking about the same paradigmatic cases of what they consider to be art.

However, if the objection against cognitive conventionalism were just that it must say that disagreement between Earl and Gray in Riggs v. Palmer or between Powell and the majority in TVA v. Hill were either an empirical disagreement or a deceptive disagreement, it would not be such a strong objection because even if they are not grounding disagreements, empirical disagreements are certainly genuine. So, if this had been the objection, cognitive conventionalism could answer that it

[94] Dworkin has a proposal as to how this metaphor should be understood. See Dworkin (1986) and, with more details, Dworkin (2011). But I do not need to enter in its details for the argument I am presenting here.

can make room for genuine disagreements regarding the grounds of statements of duty. To claim that cognitive conventionalism does not make room for genuine disagreements because they cannot account for grounding disagreements would beg the question. Unfortunately, I think that the problem for cognitive conventionalism is deeper. An empirical disagreement is genuine if people are referring to the same state of affairs (e.g. the book on the shelf, Duchamp's urinary, shared criteria, etc.); the problem is that according to cognitive conventionalism the existence of that state of affairs (i.e., criteria of use), within legal practice, depends on judges' agreement, hence, given that judges actually disagree, there is no state of affair to which their apparent empirical disagreement may refer, hence, they do not share a common ground. This implies that cognitive conventionalism is constraint to say that judges are having a deceptive disagreement either because they are talking about inexistent criteria of use or because they are talking pass each other. In other words, assuming cognitive conventionalism it is impossible for judges to have a genuine disagreement when they disagree about the grounds of statements of duty.[95]

It is worthy to point out that to answer Dworkin's objection from disagreement it is enough to show how judges statements of duties can be true in cases of disagreements, it is not necessary to show that they are indeed true. It seems to me that this is also what Dworkin theory allows us to say, i.e., that for judges' statements to be true they must result from the best political/moral argument that put legal practice under its best light, but from this it does not follow that all statements of duty are true, just that it is possible for them to be.

I think that Sceptical conventionalism has the resources to reach the same result without assuming that there are legal duties and without overestimating the cooperative nature of legal practice. As I have said in the previous section, typically, when a judge defends the existence of a duty she does it on the basis of an interpretative argument. So, she projects her attitudes both towards the action and towards the method she considers gives the best interpretation of the normative provision. That is why disagreements about grounds are typically associated with disagreements about interpretation, i.e., about the best interpretative method for the identification of the meaning of the provision. Indeed, if we take a closer look to the cases Dworkin uses in support of his objection, we will see that judges disagreeing about grounds where arguing about the best method for the interpretation of a normative provision.[96] In Riggs v. Palmer, Earl (writing for the majority) and Gray (in his dissenting opinion) discussed about the interpretation of statutory provisions that regulated testament. Whereas Gray argued in favour of a literal interpretation, Earl claimed that the interpretation must be based mainly on a counterfactual argument about legislative intent.[97] The same happened in TVA v. Hill, the majority considered

[95] So, as I have argued above, under the schema of cognitive conventionalism, judges claiming to disagree about the grounds of their statements of duty are either mistaken ("local Error theory") or disingenuous ("the Repair argument").

[96] See Ratti (2008), pp. 301–331 for a clear analysis of both decisions in this sense.

[97] See Canale y Tuzet (2014), pp. 196–197 for a reconstruction of the different interpretative arguments used by the majority in Riggs vs. Palmer. Actually, Canale and Tuzet show that the argument from principle plays just a subsidiary role in Earl's argument.

that the plain meaning of the Sect. 7 of the Endangered Species Act was clear enough and that it matched with the legislative intent as it could be gathered from legislative proceedings. On the contrary, Judge Powell in his dissenting opinion demanded to interpret the normative provision according to what he considered to be Congress' counterfactual intention.

In both cases, the majority and the minority agreed that the object of interpretation is a text issued by the legislative, they also agreed on the issue regarding the conditions for the existence of the duty: the result of the interpretation of the provision determines whether there is a duty or not and its content. But they had different attitudes regarding both the action at issue, i.e. "to award Elmer the inheritance of his grandfather" and "to enjoin the completion of the Tellico dam" and, most importantly for the present point, regarding the interpretation of the provision. Their talk in terms of truth and falsity was a consequence of the fact that they projected their attitudes onto the legal practice. They had a disagreement in attitudes and by projecting their preferences into the legal practice, they talked as if the property of being a duty and being the best method were part of that practice.[98]

On this basis, judges' discourse in cases of disagreement (in fact, in all cases) may be explained without restoring to an error theory. The theory can accommodate the existence of genuine grounding disagreements. Grounding disagreements are just disagreements in attitudes regarding methods of interpretation. And they are genuine disagreements because judges share a common ground: the object of interpretation, i.e., normative provision.

And again, also in cases of disagreements, judges must earn their right to talk of legal truth and this depends on their capacity to form an improved set of attitudes, where coherence and consistency are respected. Note that sceptical conventionalism does not claim that all statement of duty issued by judges in cases of disagreement have truth value, however, opposite to cognitive conventionalism and analogously to Dworkin's interpretative theory, it makes room for the possibility that they do.

5 Conclusion

Dworkin's objections to Hart are challenging. In this text I have claimed that philosophers who sought in conventions a way out to those objections have remained captive of Dworkin's premises. Cognitive conventionalists have so far shared with Dworkin the claim that to explain some essential features of law it is mandatory to show how legal duties exist. This is the chain that keeps them locked into a tiny philosophical corner. The illusion of freedom has impelled conventionalists to take charge of showing the existence of a convention that explains the existence of legal duties, leading them to overstate the cooperative nature of legal practice.

---

[98] Disagreements in attitudes as genuine disagreements is a thesis of Charles Stevenson, which *locus classicus* is Stevenson (1945), pp. 1–19.

In order to free conventionalism I have claimed that the explanation of judges' claims regarding the existence of legal duties and their disagreements does not require showing that those duties exist. In this sense, I have argued that when a judge claims that there is a duty she is voicing her attitude in favour of a state of affairs in which the due action is accomplished. Besides, judges do not utter those statements freely, they ground them in conventional interpretative methods. If our judge favours textualism she would be expressing a positive attitude towards deciding a case in that particular way on the ground that the best interpretation of the provision is the one that assigns to it its literal meaning. Thus, judges' statements of duty are just a projection of their attitudes regarding both the action at stake and the interpretation of the normative provision. From this perspective, disagreements about the grounds of statements of duty are just disagreements in attitudes, and these are genuine disagreements. Moreover, judges' talk about the truth or falsity of those statements can be retained under a quasi-realist schema. That is to say, the truth value of the statement depends on the fact of there being a set of improved attitudes from where the statement can be derived. If these arguments work, then it is possible to escape from Dworkin's premises, because now explaining legal language does not require showing the existence of legal duties.

Acknowledgments I would like to thank Pierluigi Chiassoni and Dimitrios Kyritsis for their insights and comments on previous drafts of this paper.

References

Arena FJ (2012) Antirrealismo moral vs. positivismo jurídico. Revista de Filosofía del derecho - Infojus 1(2):185–201

Arena FJ (2013) Una alternativa para el escepticismo interpretativo: convenciones y cuasirrealismo en la interpretación jurídica. Doxa 36:417–438

Bayón Mohino JC (2002a) El contenido mínimo del positivismo jurídico. In: Zapatero Gómez V (ed) Horizontes de la filosofía del derecho: homenaje a Luis García San Miguel, vol 2. Universidad de Alcalá de Henares, Alcalá de Henares, pp 33–54

Bayón Mohino JC (2002b) Derecho, convencionalismo y controversia. In: Navarro PE, Redondo MC (eds) La relevancia del derecho. Gedisa, Barcelona, pp 57–92

Blackburn S (1984) Spreading the word: groundings in the philosophy of language. Clarendon Press, Oxford

Blackburn S (1998) Ruling passions. Clarendon Press, Oxford

Blackburn S (2005) Quasi-realism no fictionalism. In: Kalderon ME (ed) Fictionalism in metaphysics. Clarendon Press, Oxford, pp 322–338

Canale D, Tuzet G (2014) Intenzioni del legislatore e ragionamento controfattuale. Analisi e diritto, 195–209.

Celano B (2005) Legal reasoning: three key issues, and what philosophy can(not) do about them. Analisi e diritto, 99–114

Celano B (2010a) [1997] Interazione strategica e convenzione. In: Celano B Fatti istituzionali, consuetudini, convenzioni. Aracne, Roma, pp 281–322

Celano B (2010b) [2003] La regola di riconoscimento è una convenzione?. In: Celano B Fatti istituzionali, consuetudini, convenzioni. Aracne, Roma, pp 323–341

Celano B (2017) Due problemi aperti della Teoria dell'interpretazione giuridica. Mucchi editore, Modena
Chiassoni P (2000) Interpretative games: statutory construction through Gricean eyes. Analisi e diritto 1999:79–99
Chiassoni P (2004) Codici interpretativi: Progetto di voce per un *Vademecum* giuridico. Analisi e diritto 2002–2003:55–124
Chiassoni P (2007) Tecnica dell'interpretazione giuridica. Il Mulino, Bologna
Coleman JL (1982) Negative and positive positivism. J Legal Stud 11(1):139–164
Coleman JL (2001a) The conventionality thesis. Philos Issues 11(1):354–387
Coleman JL (2001b) [1998] Incorporationism, conventionality and the practical difference thesis. In: Coleman JL (ed) Hart's postscript. Essays on the postscript to "the concept of law". Oxford University Press, Oxford, pp 99–148
den Hartogh G (2002) Mutual expectations. A conventionalist theory of law. Kluwer, La Haya
Dickson J (2007) Is the rule of recognition really a conventional rule? Oxf J Legal Stud 27(3):373–402
Dworkin R (1978) Taking rights seriously. Harvard University Press, Cambridge
Dworkin R (1986) Law's empire. Belknap Press of Harvard University Press, Cambridge
Dworkin R (2011) Justice for hedgehogs. Belknap Press of Harvard University Press, Cambridge
Dworkin R (2017) [1994] Hart's posthumous reply. Harv Law Rev 130(8):2096–2130
Gibbard A (2003) Thinking how to live. Harvard University Press, Cambridge
Green L (1999) Positivism and conventionalism. Can J Law Jurisprud 12(1):35–52
Guastini R (2011) Rule scepticism restated. In: Green L, Leiter B (eds) Oxford studies in philosophy of law, vol 1. Oxford University Press, Oxford, pp 138–161
Hart HLA (1994) [1961] The concept of law. In: Bulloch PA, Raz J (eds) 2nd edn. Clarendon Press, Oxford
Jamieson D (1975) David Lewis on convention. Can J Philos 5:73–81
Joyce R (2007) Moral Anti-realism. Stanford Encyclopedia of Philosophy. <URL: http://plato.stanford.edu/entries/moral-anti-realism/>, Accessed 26 Aug 2015
Kyritsis D (2008) What is good about legal conventionalism? Legal Theory 14(2):135–166
Lagerspetz E (1995) The opposite mirrors. An essay on the conventionalist theory of institutions. Kluwer, Dordrecht
Lewis D (1969) Convention. A philosophical study. Basil Blackwell, Oxford
Lewis D (1976) Convention: reply to Jamieson. Can J Philos 6(1):113–120
Mackie JL (1977) Ethics. Inventing right and wrong. Penguin, London
Marmor A (2009) Social conventions. From language to law. Princeton University Press, Princeton
Marmor A (2011) Conventions revisited: a reply to critics. Jurisprudence 2(2):493–506
Marmor A (2014) Convenciones, razones y derecho. In: Ramírez Ludeña L, Vilajosana Rubio JM (eds) Convencionalismo y derecho. Marcial Pons, Madrid, pp 67–88
Postema G (1982) Coordination and convention at the foundation of law. J Legal Stud 11(1):165–203
Postema G (2011) In: A treatise of legal philosophy and general jurisprudence, vol 11: Legal philosophy in the twentieth century: the common law world. Springer, Dordrecht
Ratti GB (2008) Los desacuerdos jurídicos en la jurisprudence anglosajona. Analisi e diritto, 301–331
Rawls J (1955) Two concepts of rules. Philos Rev 64(1):3–32
Raz J (1990) [1975] Practical reason and norms. Oxford University Press, Oxford
Ross A (1958) On law and justice. Stevens and Sons, London
Ross A (1968) Directives and norms. Routledge and Keagan Paul, London. Cited by the Italian Translation by M Jori. Direttive e norme. Giuffrè, Milán, 1978
Searle JR (1969) Speech acts. An essay in the philosophy of language. Cambridge University Press, London
Searle JR (1995) The construction of social reality. Free Press, New York
Searle JR (2010) Making the social world. The structure of human civilization. Oxford University Press, Oxford

Shapiro S (2007) The 'Hart-Dworkin' debate: a short guide for the perplexed. In: Ripstein A (ed) Ronald Dworkin. Cambridge University Press, Cambridge
Stevenson CL (1945) Ethics and language. Yale University Press, New Haven
Swaminathan S (2014) Toh's Hartian project: expressivist turn, relativist returns. Aust J Legal Philos 39:87–117
Swaminathan S (2016) Projectivism and the metaethical foundation of the normativity of law. Jurisprudence 7(2):231–266
Toh K (2005) Hart's expressivism and his benthamite project. Legal Theory 11:75–123
Toh K (2011) Legal judgments as plural acceptance of norms. In: Green L, Leiter B (eds) Oxford studies in philosophy of law. Oxford University Press, Oxford, pp 107–137
Vilajosana Rubio JM (2010) Una defensa del convencionalismo jurídico. Doxa 33:471–501

Conventionalism and the Causal Theory of Reference

Lorena Ramírez-Ludeña

Abstract An intuitive view of language is frequently assumed: words are related by competent speakers to descriptions that determine reference. Such a view is generally understood as convention-based in the sense that it emphasises the existence of conventions that determine what descriptions are relevant. However, this descriptivist approach has been shown to be problematic in reconstructing our linguistic practices. In contrast, the Causal Theory of Reference (CTR) provides a plausible account of our use of words. CTR has been understood to be a theory that provides a non-conventionalist approach to language and one that is committed to an implausible version of essentialism. In this chapter, Ramírez-Ludeña presents a version of CTR that addresses the criticisms it has normally received. She also shows the advantages of this version of CTR when compared to the traditional descriptivist model. In the legal field, CTR has been associated with non-positivistic conceptions about law. However, since CTR is not committed to essentialism but rather takes account of the way in which the community uses words, Ramírez-Ludeña also shows how the proposed model is compatible with conceptions in legal philosophy such as that of Hart, which emphasises the conventional character of law.

1 The Causal Theory of Reference and Semantic Conventionalism

An intuitive conception of language is frequently assumed: we associate words with descriptions, and then these words refer to the objects that have the properties contained in our descriptions. Words refer to objects with the properties we consider relevant, and speakers are competent inasmuch as they know the descriptions that constitute the meaning of those words.[1] Since it emphasises the existence of

[1] In philosophy of language, Frege (1998a), pp. 58–77, Frege (1998b), pp. 25–50, Russell (1905), pp. 479–493 and Russell (1910–1911), pp. 108–128 are considered the two most representative

L. Ramírez-Ludeña (✉)
Law Department, Pompeu Fabra University, Barcelona, Spain
e-mail: lorena.ramirez@upf.edu

L. Ramírez-Ludeña, J. M. Vilajosana (eds.), *Legal Conventionalism*, Law and Philosophy Library 126, https://doi.org/10.1007/978-3-030-03571-6_10

conventions in the community that determine what descriptions are relevant, this view is generally understood to be conventionalist.

This conception of language is intuitive because it provides a clear explanation of the relation of reference: the objects we refer to have certain properties that we consider relevant. And it easily explains the way we learn and show how words are used, i.e. by the use of descriptions. This conception is assumed, with varying degrees of sophistication and awareness, by many individuals. Moreover, it has had a strong impact on philosophers of language,[2] legal philosophers,[3] and legal scholars in general. For example, in criminal law, references to literal meaning are frequent, and the relevance of ordinary language—and the descriptions we normally associate with words—has been defended.[4] It is not surprising that descriptivism is assumed in the legal field: we decide what situations we want to regulate in a particular way, and this would imply that we decide which properties are relevant for the law to be applied.

This descriptivist approach has been shown to be problematic, however, in reconstructing our linguistic practices, as shown by supporters of CTR. Although they emphasise different aspects, it can be argued that they all share a negative thesis: speakers *do not* need to associate words with a set of descriptions in order to refer to objects.[5] Individuals, but also a community as a whole, often have poor and/or mistaken knowledge of those descriptions and yet are able to refer to objects. This is not too controversial if we think about proper names, such as "Olympia". "Olympia" is my daughter's name. We can refer to her without needing a description that selects her, and the descriptions we associate with her name may be wrong or suited to a different individual. In this sense, although it is difficult to deny that we associate certain descriptions, positive and negative connotations, and other elements with the words we use, these elements do not explain what we refer to or how.

How is that we are able to refer to objects that are often distant in time and space without descriptions? According to those in favour of CTR, reference is normally established by an act of ostension. A name is bestowed by a declaration such as "let us call this individual 'Olympia'". Subsequently, users of "Olympia" refer to the bearer of the name because they are part of a network, a chain of communication in which each link has received "Olympia" from a previous link and uses it with the intention of referring to the bearer at its origin of the chain. Therefore, according to

---

authors of this conception, which we could call "traditional". This is debatable, however, if one considers their writings. In any case, I am not interested in describing here the position of particular authors, but rather reconstructing what may be considered the traditional conception, which is intuitive and generally accepted, in order to understand the point of departure for those who defend CTR.

[2] Searle (1958), pp. 166–173.

[3] Some legal theorists have understood Hart (1994) in this way.

[4] That is to say, literal and ordinary meaning are frequently regarded as interchangeable. See Montiel and Ramírez-Ludeña (2010).

[5] In order to reconstruct the basic tenets of CTR, I have mainly taken into account Donnellan (1970), pp. 335–358, Putnam (1975), and Kripke (1980). Donnellan and Kripke basically focused on proper names, while Putnam explored natural kind terms.

CTR, subjects refer to an object based on their objective position in the chain of communication, without the need for descriptions to refer to the object.[6]

How can this model be extended to general terms? Following Putnam (1975), let us imagine that the term "water" was introduced by indicating a certain sample of the substance in a lake. This initial sample represents a paradigmatic instance and thereafter other samples are classified by their similarity to the paradigmatic case. According to supporters of CTR, what makes a particular sample *water*, and what determines the correct application of the term "water", may not be accessible to the speakers. The molecular structure H_2O is what determines what water is, and it determines therefore the domain of application of the term. But the scientific nature of water was discovered long after the term was introduced. Individuals lacking that scientific information were nonetheless able to refer to water and were considered competent.

It is frequently assumed that CTR is incompatible with conventionalism. This is because it is understood as being committed *at all times* to essentialism, and *in an implausible way*. Advocators of CTR are understood to be postulating the existence of shared underlying natures that are not immediately visible or observable and can only be discovered through scientific research and theoretical reflection. From this perspective, CTR provides a plausible explanation insofar as hidden natures are relevant. And they are relevant regardless of our linguistic practices. However, in the version I defend, commitment to essentialism is not inherent. Some samples are treated as paradigms, and others are classified as members of the same class because of their similarity to the paradigms. But this similarity may be superficial or focus on the function. The model, therefore, *does not require* that the relevant criterion is related to hidden natures. The criterion that is ultimately relevant depends on complex factors that are not semantic, but *deeply related to our interests and concerns*. The novelty of the version of CTR that I present here is that it leaves the door open to the idea that the criterion is related to elements that subjects do not know, transcending the entire community.[7]

It is important to note that since the question of which features are relevant is not answered in advance, it makes sense to reflect on the essential properties of objects and kinds. This then explains the reopening of the debate on essentialism, avoiding the prejudice arising from the assumption of the traditional model. However, the semantic conception of the supporters of CTR by itself cannot substantiate a metaphysical question such as whether there are essences or not.

The version of CTR that I am presenting here is compatible with the fact that different chains of communication may arise in connection with the same word, and that through the use speakers make of the words, a chain of communication that was anchored in certain objects undergoes changes, thus changing the reference as well. This view is also compatible with the idea that there are certain periods in which

[6] Regarding the notion of chains of communication, see Almog (1984), pp. 479–489.

[7] For emphasis on this point, see Martí and Ramírez-Ludeña (2016).

reference is indeterminate. These facts do not go against the characterization offered here, but rather show that it is plausible.[8]

To show this, let us examine different groups of cases, all with a legal impact. For the term "death", speakers generally understand that there is an underlying nature that has been gradually discovered by experts.[9] Although a loose use of the term is occasionally made, when relevant things are at stake such uses are understood by the speakers themselves as wrong. It is assumed that the term refers to a precise phenomenon that goes beyond the descriptions associated with it, with scientific discovery providing a better understanding of death. Thus, regarding a single chain of communication, the nature of the phenomenon, largely opaque to speakers, is relevant.

In contrast to the previous example, there are cases in which two chains of communication are consolidated. In Spanish, for example, the word "vacío" is used to refer to spaces that are empty and also with the same technical meaning as "vacuum". Thus, regarding the word "vacío" there are two uses, and two consolidated chains. Neither is seen as wrong and, depending on contextual elements and various non-semantic considerations, one or the other is relevant. In cases such as *vacío,* it is difficult, if not impossible, to allow indeterminacy to arise in the particular uses of the word and raise doubt about which chain of communication should come into play. For example, it would be absurd to invoke the expert's use of the word if it is made explicit in a contract that an apartment must be left *vacío.*[10]

Something similar happens in the case of the term "tomato". There is a botanical use, relating tomatoes to fruit, but also a culinary use, which includes them among vegetables. Unlike *vacío*, however, in certain cases doubts may arise as to which chain of communication is relevant. Such was the case with *Nix v. Hedden* (149 US.304, 1893), involving a disagreement about whether tomatoes were subject to taxation as vegetables. In that case, traders in tomatoes (Nix and others) claimed that Hedden (the tax collector) had to return the taxes already paid, arguing that tomatoes were not vegetables subject to the tax, but rather fruit, which was exempt. The court decided in favour of Hedden, not because it decided to ignore the *true nature* of tomatoes, but based on the relevant use of the term for the purposes of the regulation.[11]

A different problem is posed by "Madagascar". Originally, "Madagascar" was used to name part of the African continent but finally, through a widespread misconception, the term was anchored in an island as we know it today.[12] This involved a

[8] Martí and Ramírez-Ludeña (2016).

[9] For an analysis of this example and its legal consequences, see Moore (1985), pp. 277–398.

[10] The existence of two different words in English precisely shows how it is plausible to say that, regarding *vacío,* two different uses (ordinary and expert) must be differentiated. In English, a vacuum is a space from which most or all of the matter has been removed, or where there is little or no matter; in contrast, "empty" is used in a looser sense to mean, for example, to not contain any objects or people.

[11] Regarding this example, see Moreso (2010), pp. 15–47.

[12] For more on the case of Madagascar and the problems it could pose for CTR, see Evans (1973), pp. 187–208.

time period in which reference was not clearly determined. This example shows how it may be very difficult to determine when a new chain of communication takes place, and when one that was previously consolidated disappears.

The example of Madagascar helps us to understand the role of intentions and practices in the version of CTR that I present here. Typically, the speaker intends to use the word with the same semantic function as that of the people she acquired it from. But the intention of the speaker does not determine reference: at most, it may contribute to her joining a practice of usage in which the referent has already been determined.[13] What is required is that a practice be established. Proper names such as "Madagascar" are part of a language, and they must be embedded in a pattern of systematic use. This implies that grey areas may arise, that is, there may be uses of "Madagascar" for which it makes no sense to insist on determining whether one refers to the island or the mainland, since there was a period of time in which there was no consolidated practice.[14] In any case, the existence of grey areas does not mean that we can deny that "Madagascar" refers to the island today.

With respect to indeterminacy, similar difficulties to the Madagascar example are present in a case decided by the German courts, the question being whether certain types of fungi were included in hallucinogenic plants referred to in the legislation. In that case, it was not clear whether the best characterization of the situation was that the inclusion of fungi as a plant constituted a different use of the word "plant" or a deviant one.[15] In other words, the controversy lays in whether legal language made reference to expert use or if a new chain of communication had been generated by the legislator.

In conclusion, none of these cases undermine CTR. On the contrary, the notion of chains of communication allows us to offer a plausible characterization of what happens in each situation. Contrary to what might be assumed, in none of the cases may we conclude that the way we use the terms is irrelevant, something that would make these conceptions largely implausible. Our uses, complex and changeable as they are, are decisive. Thus, even in cases in which the relevant similarity is related to the nature of objects, and therefore opaque to users, it is this similarity that matters (and not, for example, external features) because we use the words in a particular way. It may be said, then, that our conventions regarding the relevant similarity

[13] Here I follow Martí (2015). In this regard, she claims that "[w]hen a speaker intends to follow a practice, to abide by the rule, it is the rule, and not his intention, that does the semantic work. The referential intentions of a speaker do not determine the reference of particular uses of expressions, and so they fall outside of the realm of semantics" (Martí 2015, p. 82, fn. 11).

[14] Establishing this practice requires success in making people use a name to refer to a thing, which in the case of Madagascar depended upon a combination of errors and power (Martí 2015, p. 86). In addition, Martí (2015, p. 87) argues that "we should not think that bestowing a name is an act; it is a process. It requires success in launching a practice, and launching practices is not something that occurs instantly".

[15] This case was discussed by German doctrine and jurisprudence and concluded with a decision by the *Bundesgerichtshof* (25.10.2006), which established that fungi were included in a regulation that refers to plants. For an analysis of this case, see Montiel and Ramírez-Ludeña (2010).

play a fundamental role, and therefore this version of CTR is not at odds with conventionalism.

CTR, as reconstructed here, has obvious advantages over the traditional model. As I have shown, they do not present a simplified image of the language of the law since they do not assume that we need to know identifying descriptions in order to refer to something. The recognition of different uses, some of them eminently legal, allows us to offer a more complete image of interpretative changes, indeterminacies, and disagreements.

We have already seen, according to CTR, that it is important to distinguish between existing and accepted uses that give rise to different chains of communication and uses that are seen as deviant but are allowed in certain contexts. Thus, the difficulties we face in accommodating the complexity of ordinary language may be recognised in the framework of CTR. Also recognised is how, when important issues are at stake, the taxonomies of experts may be considered determinant, though we might in general have a poor or defective knowledge of them.

As we have seen, the notion of chains of communication does not require the rejection of descriptions, which may allow us to provide a clear characterization of what happens in certain cases, nor does it force us to assume that hidden natures are always relevant, but only admit that the notion of chains of communication is compatible with them.

It may be said that, in the version I am presenting here, CTR does not appear to be significantly different from the traditional conception, or that both conceptions seem to be compatible. However, my claim is not that some terms work as descriptivists say they do, while others function according to CTR. In the version I am presenting here, almost all terms are used according to CTR, and only a few do so according to descriptivism from the very beginning, with words being associated with descriptions that play a mediating role in reference (i.e. technical words such as "triangle"). Usually, we make reference to things without mediating descriptions being necessary, with the relation of similarity to exemplars playing a fundamental role. External features that can be part of a description may then become relevant, as may hidden natures. Therefore, my version of CTR is in opposition to the descriptivist argument that descriptions always play a mediating role, because it denies that very thesis. My account may, however, accommodate cases in which descriptions become relevant, as I have shown.

It is important to note that in the version presented here, the notion of chains of communication is useful in understanding how language works with respect to conventional meaning. But, as the examples above show, doubts and disagreements may arise regarding the generation or extinction of a chain, and over which chain is relevant in a particular context. Such issues do not belong to semantics, however, in the sense that they cannot be decided by semantic considerations. Moreover, the fact that hidden essences are sometimes relevant does not mean that we must assume that there is just one correct way of naming things, or that we have to be committed to the immutability of the world. In fact, things could have been otherwise in many different senses.

First, we could have been different. We could have different abilities from the ones we now have and be able, for example, to see things we cannot see now. Consequently, we could have decided to group things in a different way than we do now. Nothing in the framework provided by CTR precludes that possibility. The main tenet of CTR is that given the history of the use of the word, our interests understood in a broad sense, and our discoveries, according to our practise the correct use of "water" depends on the nature of the substance, which we have established is H_2O.

Second, we could have chosen different words to name things in our language. I may have called my daughter "Sabina" instead of "Olympia". It is important to note, however, that when we describe other possible situations in which we use words in a different way, we use our language with our current meanings and references. Thus, we can acknowledge that Olympia could have not been called "Olympia" without posing any problem for CTR.

Third, as has been shown with the examples, CTR is not incompatible with changes in usage. In these cases, we would use the same word to refer to other things. This could be deliberate or not (e.g. Madagascar).

As happened with jade, the world could be different in the sense that we could have discovered that samples once grouped together did not share a common essence. This means that we could have discovered that what we called "water" was both H_2O and XYZ. And if we had discovered microscopic or other relevant differences, we probably would have concluded that those samples did not constitute a single class. Our reactions to those situations depend on multiple factors, such as for example whether we have other words to name similar things. However, given the history of the use of "water", our interests, and our discoveries, "water" depends on the nature of the substance, which we have established is H_2O.

In connection with the previous argument, it may be said that, since we can imagine a situation in which a substance looks like water and is found in the very places where we in fact find H_2O, but we discover it is XYZ, then the correct application of "water" does not depend on the substance being H_2O. However, as Kripke points out, we would only have the illusion that the connection between "water" and H_2O is contingent. Again, given the history of the use of "water", our interests, and our discoveries, "water" depends on the nature of the substance, which we have established is H_2O.[16]

Fifth, we often discover that the world is different from what we thought. Discoveries may lead us to exclude things from a classification we currently use. Since essences may be unknown to us, it is obvious that defenders of CTR are able to accommodate such situations.

Moreover, change is not problematic for CTR: relevant properties could change, or different objects even disappear. If all samples of H_2O changed to XYZ, would we say that water ceases to exist, or that "water" now refers to XYZ? Defenders of CTR may leave this question open: given the history of the use of the word and the

[16] See Kripke (1980), p. 102 ff.

nature of the world, "water" refers to H_2O. In other circumstances, the answer would depend on multiple complex elements.

The different situations illustrated above show how our linguistic conventions are relevant to the account provided by CTR. In the next section, this element will be of crucial importance to showing the compatibility between CTR and legal conventionalism.

2 The Causal Theory of Reference and Legal Conventionalism

CTR is generally understood to be committed to an essentialist view of meaning and to an anti-positivist conception of the nature of law.[17] In contrast, in this paper I have tried to show why CTR is not committed to hidden essences. Using several examples, I have argued that CTR is able to accommodate cases in which the relevant similarity is not a hidden essence as well as cases in which different uses and chains of communication coexist. As I have explained, the conception of semantics held by defenders of CTR cannot substantiate a metaphysical question such as whether essences exist. According to the version of CTR I am presenting here, we use terms by making some assumptions that may be essentialist, but this claim is *merely* semantic. Whether hidden natures do in fact exist is a different issue.

In the version of CTR defended here, our uses, complex and changeable as they are, are decisive. As we have seen, even in cases in which relevant similarity is related to the hidden nature of objects, and thus opaque to users, it is that similarity (and not a different one) that matters because we use the words in a particular way. That is to say, CTR requires us to take into account the conduct and attitudes of speakers in the use of words, providing a plausible account of ordinary language and its complexities while not being at odds with the conventional character of our language.

According to Hart, law tries to guide our conduct and it is to a large extent expressed in ordinary language. If ordinary language—and our linguistic practices in a broader sense—are better reconstructed in the way CTR claims, it seems reasonable to believe that the language of the law may be reconstructed in the same way. But it is also possible to understand, in a way that is compatible with this framework, how a new use or chain of communication that is characteristic of the legal field may arise. Moreover, as I have previously explained, and as Hart acknowledges, doubts and disagreements may emerge, and the notion of chains of communication is useful to reconstruct the situation. Therefore, it is not only that CTR does not seem to be at odds with Hart, but that Hart provides a powerful argument to

[17] See for instance Bix (1993), p. 162 ff., Marmor (2005), p. 65 ff., and Dworkin (2006), p. 19 ff. In fact, CTR has been defended by authors in the legal field who are not positivists, including Moore (1985), pp. 277–398 and Stavropoulos (1996).

consider it in the legal field: CTR reconstructs our linguistic practices, and our linguistic practices are relevant in the legal field.

It might be argued that even if CTR emphasizes the relevance of our usage and is not committed to essentialism, it is not compatible with Hart's conception, which emphasises the conventional nature of law.[18] But I believe that this is a mistake. The conventionality of law need not imply a descriptivist conception of our linguistic practices that requires the existence of shared and transparent descriptions constituting the meaning of words. It is important to note that I am not claiming that law as such is natural or functional[19] or that the word "law" is better reconstructed according to CTR.[20] I simply wish to emphasise that legal interpretation is sometimes better reconstructed by taking CTR into account, depending on how our contingent interpretative practices evolve. The relevant practice of identification (the criteria set out by the rule of recognition) determines which norms belong to the legal system. And CTR will provide a plausible reconstruction of the meaning of some words, depending on our interpretative practices, and on the behaviour and attitudes of the participants of the legal practice. Ordinary language is generally relevant, but nothing precludes the emergence of new usage.

In this model, certain conventional facts ultimately determine the requirements of the legal system without assuming a necessary connection between law and morality. In the version I am presenting, furthermore, it is not possible to establish in advance which terms operate in the way CTR claims and which terms do not. This all depends on our contingent interpretative practices: terms that work under certain assumptions outside the legal field may work in a different way within the legal context since it is accepted that new uses may arise.

Some may insist on the incompatibility between CTR and Hartian positivism by emphasizing that CTR leads us to accept that there may be no convergence on the particular requirements of certain legal systems when hidden natures are relevant—a view that would be rejected by positivists. However, this is not so problematic if we take into account the debate between inclusive and exclusive positivism.[21] Inclusive positivists argue that there may be a contingent connection between law and morality that is compatible with the main positivist tenets; the incorporation of morality ultimately depends on social facts. Therefore, the particular requirements of specific legal systems may not be transparent to participants in a way that is compatible with positivism. CTR would lead us to understand the interpretation of some

---

[18] Regarding the conventionality of law, see Marmor (2009) and Vilajosana (2010).

[19] Such is the case, for example, with Moore (1994), pp. 188–242.

[20] Coleman and Simchen (2003), pp. 1–41 argue this.

[21] Regarding inclusive legal positivism, see Waluchow (1994), Coleman (2001), and Moreso (2001), pp. 37–63. For a defence of exclusive legal positivism, see Raz (1979, 1994), Shapiro (1998a), pp. 469–508, Shapiro (1998b), pp. 33–64 and Shapiro (2011). It is important to note that Hart has normally been understood as an inclusive legal positivist. See the *postscriptum* in Hart (1994).

legal terms in the same way: meaning is not transparent but since this meaning ultimately depends on social facts, CTR need not be at odds with positivism.[22]

According to the version of CTR I have presented here, different doubts and disagreements, all of them compatible with the conventional nature of law, may arise. On the one hand, such doubts and disagreements may be in regard to hidden essences. But, as explained in the previous paragraph, in those cases the particular requirements of specific legal systems may not be transparent to participants in a way that is compatible with the conventional nature of law. On the other hand, doubts and disagreements may arise with respect to the generation or extinction of a chain, or the correct identification of the relevant chain in a particular context. However, as I argued in the previous section, such issues do not belong to semantics in the sense that they cannot be decided by semantic considerations. In the legal field, such doubts and disagreements are related to debates on legal interpretation and the general conception of law understood to be most plausible. According to Hart, some clear-cut cases exist, but there are also hard cases with no single correct answer. Although interpretative instruments play a role, in this context there are sometimes consolidated interpretations that do not raise questions. There are also cases where different instruments lead to the same solution. But in other cases, doubts may arise and the judge is said to have discretion.[23]

The abovementioned position depends on Hart's conception of law. According to the Hartian model, law is dependent upon a convergence in certain individuals' conduct and attitudes. In particular, officials use shared criteria to identify the law of their legal system and remain committed to them. Hart's emphasis on convergence seems to involve the position on interpretation that I have previously pointed out: when disagreement takes place, there is no legal solution to appeal to, and the judge has discretion to decide. In such cases, judges normally invoke socially accepted interpretative canons, such as the purpose of the rule or the intentions of the legislator, but Hart acknowledges that they are in fact creating new law.

The previous considerations lead us to reflect on an important methodological issue that has implications for jurisprudence. Conventional meaning plays a very reduced role and when doubts and disagreements arise non-semantic considerations become relevant. In the legal field, this means taking into account methods and other instruments of interpretation that are normally invoked by legal interpreters. But then, both the existence of a right answer and what kind of considerations are relevant when making a decision depend on the theory of law that is assumed or adopted. This implies that conceptions such as Hart's are not problematic because they assume an implausible conception about meaning. The relevant debate is not

---

[22] In fact, Hart explicitly acknowledges that there may be uncertainty in the rule of recognition (Hart 1994, p. 147 ff.) and that judges may agree on the relevance of the tests provided by the rule of recognition as something defined by established judicial practice "even though they disagree as to what the tests require in particular cases" (Hart 1994, pp. 258 and 259). In short, a certain degree of uncertainty is compatible with the conventional nature of law.

[23] See Hart (1994).

semantic but about what kind of considerations are ultimately relevant (whether social or normative): the province of jurisprudential theories.

References

Almog J (1984) Semantic anthropology. Midwest Stud Philos 9:479–489

Bix B (1993) Law, language and legal determinacy. Clarendon Press, Oxford

Coleman J (2001) The practice of principle: in defence of a pragmatist approach to legal theory. Oxford University Press, Oxford

Coleman J, Simchen O (2003) Law. Legal Theory 9:1–41

Donnellan K (1970) Proper names and identifying descriptions. Synthese 21:335–358

Dworkin R (2006) Justice in Robes. Harvard University Press, Cambridge

Evans G (1973) The causal theory of names. Proc Aristot Soc 47:187–208

Frege G (1998a) El pensamiento. In: Ensayos de semántica y filosofía de la lógica. Tecnos, Madrid. Trans. Valdés Villanueva from Der Gedanke. Eine logische Untersuchung. In: Beiträge zur Philosophie des deutschen Idealismus, n. I, 1918, pp 58–77

Frege G (1998b) Sobre el sentido y la referencia. In: Ensayos de semántica y filosofía de la lógica. Tecnos, Madrid. Trans. Valdés Villanueva from Über Sinn und Bedeutung. In: Zeitschrift für Philosophie und philosophische Kritik, 1892, C, pp 25–50

Hart H (1994) The concept of law, 2nd edn. Clarendon Press, Oxford

Kripke S (1980) Naming and necessity. Harvard University Press, Cambridge

Marmor A (2005) Interpretation and legal theory, 2nd edn. Hart, Oxford

Marmor A (2009) Social conventions. from language to law. Princeton monographs in philosophy. Princeton University Press, Princeton

Martí G (2015) Reference without cognition. In: Bianchi A (ed) On reference. Oxford University Press, Oxford

Martí G, Ramírez-Ludeña L (2016) Legal disagreements and theories of reference. In: Capone A, Poggi F (eds) Pragmatics and law. Springer, Holland

Montiel J, Ramírez-Ludeña L (2010) De camareros estudiantes de biología a jueces biólogos. A propósito de la sentencia del BGH sobre los hongos alucinógenos y la deferencia a los expertos en el ámbito penal. Indret 1/2010: http://www.indret.com/pdf/691.pdf

Moore M (1985) A natural law theory of interpretation. South Calif Law Rev 58:277–398

Moore M (1994) Law as a functional kind. In: George R (ed) Natural law theories: contemporary essays. Clarendon Press, Oxford, pp 188–242

Moreso J (2001) In defense of inclusive legal positivism. In: Chiassoni P (ed) The legal ought. Giappichelli, Torino, pp 37–63

Moreso J (2010) Tomates, hongos y significado jurídico. In: Moreso J, Prieto Sanchís L, Ferrer Beltrán J (eds) Los desacuerdos en el derecho. Fundación coloquio jurídico europeo, Madrid, pp 15–47

Putnam H (1975) Mind, language and reality: philosophical papers, vol 2. Cambridge University Press, Cambridge

Raz J (1979) The authority of law. Clarendon Press, Oxford

Raz J (1994) Ethics in the public domain. Clarendon Press, Oxford

Raz J (2001) Two views of the nature of the theory of law. In: Coleman J (ed) Hart's postcript. Oxford University Press, Oxford, pp 1–37

Russell B (1905) On denoting. Mind 14:479–493

Russell B (1910–1911) Knowledge by acquaintance and knowledge by description. Proc Aristot Soc 11:108–128

Searle J (1958) Proper names. Mind 67:166–173

Shapiro S (1998a) On Hart's way out. Legal Theory 4:469–508

Shapiro S (1998b) The difference that rules make. In: Bix B (ed) Analyzing law. New essays in legal theory. Clarendon Press, Oxford, pp 33–64
Shapiro S (2011) Legality. Harvard University Press, Cambridge
Stavropoulos N (1996) Objectivity in law. Clarendon Press, Oxford
Vilajosana JM (2010) El derecho en acción. La dimensión social de las normas jurídicas. Marcial Pons, Barcelona
Waluchow W (1994) Inclusive legal positivism. Clarendon Press, Oxford

The Interpretation of Plans

Scott Shapiro

Abstract In his contribution, Scott Shapiro makes reference, within the framework of his theory of law as a plan, to the problem of legal disagreements. Shapiro emphasizes the relevance of social facts while refusing the requirement of interpretive conventions. Like Dworkin, he understands that, in order to provide an explanation for theoretical disagreements, it is essential to take into consideration the purpose of legal practice. In addition, both agree that the most appropriate interpretive methodology in a legal system depends on which best fits its objectives. But, unlike Dworkin, Shapiro does not accept that the attribution of a purpose requires an exercise in moral and political philosophy, but just an inquiry related to social facts. In this sense, the task of the legal interpreter is to detect the political objectives that were intended by the designers of the system, so that the relevant purposes are those that explain the practice and not those that justify; as a consequence, they may be morally deficient. To uncover these objectives, the interpreter must analyse the institutional structure and determine which objectives and values best explain the system. The correct interpretive methodology for the system will be the methodology that best harmonizes with the objectives of those who designed it.

1 Introduction

In *Law's Empire*, Ronald Dworkin set a challenge to all positivistic theories of law. As he pointed out, contemporary legal positivism accepts the idea that the criteria of legal validity—or in Dworkin's language, the "grounds of law"—are determined by consensus. A legal rule exists, and has the content it has, because it bears the properties that legal officials in the system in question accept as canonical and use in their official capacities.

However, as Dworkin pointed out, no such consensus need exists in legal systems, and typically does not exist. Officials often engage in what Dworkin termed

S. Shapiro (✉)
Law Faculty, Yale University, New Haven, CT, USA
e-mail: scott.shapiro@yale.edu

L. Ramírez-Ludeña, J. M. Vilajosana (eds.), *Legal Conventionalism*, Law and Philosophy Library 126, https://doi.org/10.1007/978-3-030-03571-6_11

"theoretical disagreements," namely, disagreements about which facts or properties determine the existence and content of the law. If so, then the grounds of law cannot be determined exclusively by consensus, for legal officials act as though there is law to find even when they know there is no consensus to be found.

Most legal positivists do not find Dworkin's argument compelling. However, I do. I think Dworkin has raised a serious challenge for positivistic theories of law. In this paper, I try to see whether the positivist can answer Dworkin's challenge.[1]

2 Accounting for Theoretical Disagreements

2.1 Looking for Social Facts

The first step in accounting for theoretical disagreements in a positivistic framework, I believe, is to concede that the plain-fact view, or any other account that privileges interpretive conventions as the sole source of proper methodology, ought to be rejected. Because theoretical disagreements abound in the law, interpretive methodology may be fixed in ways other than specific social agreement about which methodologies are proper.[2] The positivist should also agree with Dworkin that when theoretical disagreements abound, ascertaining proper interpretive methodology involves attributing a purpose to legal practice. One cannot understand disagreements over interpretive methodology unless one sees them as disputes about the point of engaging in the practice of law. Finally, the positivist should also maintain with Dworkin that in such cases proper interpretive methodology for a particular legal system is primarily a function of which methodology best harmonizes with the objectives of that system.

Here, however, the agreement must end. Although ascertaining interpretive methodology involves attributing a purpose to legal practice, the positivist cannot, of course, treat this attributive process in a Dworkinian manner, namely, as an exercise in moral and political philosophy. The positivist, rather, must seek *social facts*. The fact that some set of goals and values represents the purposes of a certain legal system must be a fact about certain social groups that is ascertainable by empirical, rather than moral, reasoning. Proper interpretive methodology would then be established by determining which methodology best harmonized with these goals and values. In this way, the positivist will have blunted Dworkin's critique: by claiming that interpretive methodology is a function of empirically derivable objectives, the positivist will have grounded the law in social fact. Moreover, the positivist will have established the social foundations of law in a manner that does not rely on

[1] For an extended explanation, see Shapiro (2011).

[2] It should be noted that sometimes courts settle theoretical disagreements. See, for example, *Edwards v. Canada* (Attorney General) [1930] A.C. 124, where the Privy Council rejected originalism as an appropriate method of constitutional interpretation. I thank Les Green for making this point to me.

specific conventions about proper interpretive methodology, thereby accounting for the possibility of theoretical disagreements. Theoretical disagreements would simply be a product of disputes over which purposes are in fact the objectives of the system or about which methodology best harmonizes with those objectives.

This proposed response, of course, is purely schematic, for it does not specify how the political objectives are to be ascertained. The proposal does not tell us, for example, whose objectives are relevant to determining the purposes of a legal system, nor how these objectives must be related to the actual behavior of legal participants. No doubt, these are questions that any adequate positivistic theory of legal interpretation must address. The above proposal, however, merely sets out a strategy: it claims that for the positivists to account for the possibility of theoretical disagreements, they should drop their conventionality requirement, concede that proper methodology is a function of systemic purpose, and yet maintain nevertheless that systemic purpose is a matter of social fact.

2.2 Settling on an Ideology

To be sure, it is not enough for positivists to advance a theory of legal interpretation that grounds interpretive methodology in social facts. Their account must be plausible as well. What, then, would a plausible positivist theory of legal interpretation look like? I will attempt to sketch the outlines of one such theory.

The proper task of the legal interpreter, I would like to suggest, is to impute to legal practice the political objectives that the current designers of the legal system sought to achieve.[3] The purposes that are legally relevant, in other words, are those that *explain*, rather than justify, the current practice. These objectives might be laudable ones, such as promoting democratic self-rule and protecting individual liberty, or they may be more morally suspect, such as seeking to implement the will of God or hastening the proletariat revolution. The proper methodology for a particular legal system would be the one that best harmonizes with the ideological objectives of those who designed the current system, regardless of the moral palatability of their ideology.

According to this proposal, proper interpretive methodology is grounded in social fact because the specific purposes of a legal system are matters of social fact. Whether a legal system ought to be understood as advancing some political goal G or realizing some value V depends on whether those with authority to design the system designed it to advance G or realize V. To uncover the political objectives of

[3] Because legal systems always contain mechanisms for revision, the designers of a system will change as the structure of the system is intentionally revised. The designers of the present American system include not only the framers and ratifiers of the Constitution of 1787, but the numerous agents over the past 200 years who have changed the complexion of the system. The framers and ratifiers of the 14th Amendment are as much the designers of the current regime as the framers and ratifiers of the original constitution. How the objectives of a system change as the institutional structure is revised is a complex question that I cannot explore here.

a legal system, the interpreter must analyze its institutional structure and determine which goals and values best explain why the legal system has its current shape. Thus, one might conclude that a system that made provisions for voting, representation, elections, and some protection for public deliberation is a system in which democratic self-rule is prized. By contrast, an institutional structure that empowered clerics to decide matters of principle and policy and minimized the degree to which secular forces can affect the direction of the law would be a system in which religious values are designed to be promoted.

It should be emphasized that the reason to privilege the objectives of legal designers in legal interpretation is not simply motivated by the desire to answer Dworkin's objections. More importantly, deference to the ideology of designers is necessary if designers are to do their job, *which is to settle questions about which specific objectives the group should pursue*.[4]

To see why this is so, let us start with the idea that the fundamental function of all legal systems is to achieve certain very general political and moral objectives. These objectives include the maintenance of order, the prevention of undesirable and wrongful behavior, the promotion of distributive justice, the protection of rights, the provision of facilities for private ordering, and the fair settling of disputes. How legal systems should go about attaining these objectives, of course, is likely to be a complex and contentious matter. What rights do individuals have and which deserve legal protection? Which distribution of goods is the just distribution? Against which moral metric is behavior to be assessed? These questions are apt to provoke serious doubts and disagreements. It is reasonable to suppose that without some mechanism for settling on which specific goals and values the legal system ought to pursue, there is a significant risk that the massive amount of coordinated behavior necessary for the law to achieve its moral mission will not take place.[5]

It is one of the primary functions of legal designers to resolve these very issues. They settle questions about specific political objectives through the process of institutional design, that is, by distributing rights and responsibilities in such a way that the exercise of the allocated powers and the observance of the assigned duties achieve the goals and realize the values they wish to promote. In this way, the

---

[4] Not every legal system has designers or has been designed. In some cases, the structure of a legal system, or some part thereof, is the result of custom. In these situations, there may be no ideology that underlies the system's institutional structure and thus no way to resolve theoretical disagreements (indeed, in these cases theoretical disagreements are not even possible). I say that there *may* be no ideology because legal officials may theorize previously untheorized customary aspects of a certain system and develop the system in the direction of this new ideology. These officials will then be considered designers, and theoretical disagreements can be resolved by reference to their ideology.

[5] Even in those rare instances where there is a very broad consensus in the community on which specific political objectives to pursue, how conflicts between them should be adjudicated, and how they ought to be implemented institutionally, there will still be a pressing need to have mechanisms that can quell dissent, should it arise. Given that in politics not everyone wins, there is always the threat that the loser will challenge the results, and without some way of settling these sorts of disputes, the ability of the legal system to achieve its fundamental ends will be significantly imperiled.

behavior of members of the community will be channeled in the direction of the selected objectives. This is not to say that the law's fundamental functions will be achieved simply through deference to the institutional structure designed by those in authority. Indeed, if the designers are untrustworthy and design the system poorly, the broad moral objectives mentioned earlier are guaranteed not to be met. The point, rather, is that if those in authority are basically trustworthy, which is what the law always supposes, deferring to the designers' judgments about how to attain the fundamental aims of the system is a highly effective strategy for actually attaining those ends.[6]

Once it is recognized that legal designers play this "settling" function, one can see why their resolutions concerning particular ends and values must be privileged when ascertaining interpretive methodology. For if members of the group are permitted to engage in moral and political philosophy to determine the proper justification for legal practice, they would effectively unsettle these matters. We might say that accounts of legal interpretation such as Dworkin's defeat the purpose of having legal authorities—they allow subjects to reopen the questions that authorities resolved by designing a legal system. After all, the judgments of designers are just more fodder for constructive interpretation. Their judgments will receive only the amount of deference that the Dworkinian interpreter deems to be morally appropriate in the light of current practice. To make that judgment, the interpreter will be forced to engage in abstract philosophical reflection and confront questions that have baffled humanity for the past few millennia.

Once we see the necessity of deferring to authoritative settlements about *which* particular objectives to pursue, the same argument counsels respect for decisions about *how* specifically they ought to be pursued. For authorities don't will just the *ends*, they will the *means* as well. It is also their task, in other words, to determine how to allocate rights and responsibilities based on their assessments of the competence and character of various members of the group. If, after having designed a particular institutional arrangement, those members were then to ask themselves afresh "Which assignment of power to me would best justify the practice?" they would be undoing precisely what the designers intended to do.

To preserve the ability of legal designers to design (and redesign) a legal system, the interpreter must defer not merely to the designers' decisions about specific political objectives, but also to those decisions concerning roles and trust.

Thus, the interpreter must figure out how those with authority to design the system divided labor and which roles they entrusted to various participants. She must also determine which judgments or claims of trust and distrust underwrite such a division of labor. Thus, for example, broad grants of power to certain participants, with comparatively few attendant duties, might evidence high degrees of confidence in the competence and character of those individuals, whereas highly diffused dis-

[6] It should be clear that this argument does not entail that members of the community are always morally obligated to defer to the system designers. For when those in authority are not trustworthy, or otherwise not entitled to deference, there may be no reason to defer to their judgments about fundamental aims.

tribution of power, with few opportunities for the exercise of discretion, might suggest low degrees of trust instead.

How should an interpreter process this information about ends and means? The interpreter might begin by drawing up a list of possible interpretive methodologies and attempting to ascertain their basic properties. She should try to discover, for example, whether certain methodologies require a great deal of expertise to implement or comparatively little, and whether they are easy to abuse or hard to manipulate. Having ascertained the basic properties of the candidate methodologies, the interpreter should then attempt to extract certain information from the institutional structure of the legal system in question. She ought to ascertain the attitudes of those who designed the system regarding the competence and character of certain participants, as well as the objectives that they are entrusted to promote. Finally, the interpreter should apply the information culled from the first two tasks to determine proper interpretive methodology. She must try to figure out which interpretive methodologies best further the extracted goals in the light of the extracted attitudes of trust. The relationship between interpretive method and systemic ideology can often be quite complex, but it can also be rather simple. Here is an example of a straightforward connection: an interpretive methodology that requires for its effective implementation a high degree of competence or moral character will be inappropriate for systems where high degrees of trust are inappropriate; instead, hermeneutic procedures that are easier to apply and less subject to abuse—perhaps ones that defer to plain meaning, instead of purpose—would be more fitting.

As mentioned previously, a virtue of this type of proposal is that, insofar as interpretive methodology is not determined by a specific convention about proper interpretive methodology, it is able to account for the possibility of theoretical disagreements. Participants in a practice can disagree over proper interpretive methodology because they disagree about any of the steps mentioned above. They might disagree about the demands imposed by particular methodologies, the ideological purposes of the system, its distribution of trust and distrust, or which methodology best harmonizes with such purposes and judgments of competence and character.

Notice further that this theory is strongly positivistic. Because it takes a regime's animating ideology as its touchstone, this account may end up recommending an interpretive methodology based on a morally questionable set of beliefs and values. The legal system in question, for example, may exist to promote racial inequality or religious intolerance; it may embody ridiculous views about human nature and the limits of cognition. Nevertheless, the positivist interpreter takes this ideology as given and seeks to determine which interpretive methodology best harmonizes with it.

This account of legal interpretation is positivistic in the most important sense, namely, it roots interpretive methodology in *social facts*. That a legal system has a certain ideology is a fact about the behavior and attitudes of social groups. The account privileges social facts, as mentioned earlier, not out of fanatical desire to save positivism at all cost, but because the alternative would render legal systems incoherent. Imputing to legal systems purposes, division of roles, and judgments of trustworthiness that are morally justified undercuts the basic division of labor between those with authority to settle such matters and those under a duty to implement such settlements.

It is possible, then, for the positivist to maintain that the grounds of law are determined by social facts *and* to account for theoretical disagreements about those very grounds, Dworkin's contention in *Law's Empire* notwithstanding. The commitment to the social foundations of law, I have tried to show, can be satisfied in the absence of a specific convention about proper interpretive methodology just in case a consensus exists about the factors that ultimately determine interpretive methodology. The law will be grounded in social facts, that is, if the current designers agree about the basic objectives of the system, the competence and character of participants, and the proper distribution of roles.[7] The fact that interpretive methodology is determined by these factors not only renders theoretical disagreements possible, it explains why they are so prevalent. For it is highly likely that participants will disagree with one another about what these shared understandings are and which methodologies are best supported by them.

To be sure, it is a consequence of this approach that, in the absence of these shared understandings, disagreements about proper interpretive methodology will be irresolvable. And even if shared understandings do exist, they may be quite thin and thus will provide neither side much leverage in interpretive debates. I am not sure, however, that these implications undermine the solution I am offering. First, although thin shared understandings may not determine a unique methodology, they might nevertheless rule out certain interpretive stances. There may be no right answer to these disputes, but there are usually wrong ones. Second, and more important, a theory of law should account for the *intelligibility* of theoretical disagreements, not necessarily provide a resolution of them. An adequate theory, in other words, ought to show that it makes sense for participants to disagree with each other about the grounds of law. Whether a unique solution to these disputes actually exists is an entirely different, and contingent, matter, and a jurisprudential theory should not, indeed must not, demand one just because participants think that there is one.

3 The Future of the Hart-Dworkin Debate

In his article, "Beyond the Hart-Dworkin Debate," Brian Leiter makes the following provocative claim:

> The moment now seems opportune to step back and ask whether the Hart/Dworkin debate deserves to play the same organizing role in the jurisprudential curriculum of the twenty-first century that it played at the close of the twentieth. I am inclined to answer that question in the negative, though not, to be sure, because I can envision a jurisprudential future without Hart's masterful work at its center. Rather, it seems to me – and, I venture, many others by now – that on the particulars of the Hart/Dworkin debate, there has been a clear victor,

[7] Similarly, there must exist a shared understanding among participants in the system about who the designers are and which institutional structures they have created.

so much so that even the heuristic value of the Dworkinian criticisms of Hart may now be in doubt.[8]

Needless to say, Leiter thinks that Hart has been the clear winner and that, given this resounding victory, the Hart-Dworkin debate no longer deserves the scholarly and pedagogical pride of place that it has been accorded for the past four decades.

To some extent, I agree with Leiter. If we identify the Hart-Dworkin debate solely by Dworkin's criticisms in "The Model of Rules I" and the discussion generated by them, which is how Leiter and many others understand it, then I think that the positivists clearly have "won," at least in the sense that they have successfully parried Dworkin's challenge. Narrowly construed, the Hart-Dworkin debate is indeed past its intellectual sell-by date. For whether positivism can account for the fact that judges are often required to apply nonpedigreed principles in hard cases is a question that, as lawyers say, has been asked and answered.

Yet Dworkin's critique of Hart and legal positivism did not end with "The Model of Rules I." His challenge evolved over time and, in the process, became resistant to the existing positivistic defenses. Thus, I part company with Leiter when he writes that "The point is not, I hasten to add, that there remain no challenges to legal positivism, but rather that the significant issues that face legal positivists are now different, often in kind, from the ones Dworkin made famous." However, positivism is particularly vulnerable to Dworkin's critique in *Law's Empire*. To overlook this challenge, which most positivists have done, is to ignore the most serious threat facing legal positivism at the beginning of the twenty-first century.

Reports of the demise of the Hart-Dworkin debate, therefore, would be greatly exaggerated. The particulars have changed, but the basic issue, and its fundamental importance, remains the same today as it did 50 years ago. Is the law ultimately grounded in social facts alone, or do moral facts also determine the existence and content of the law? Only the future will tell who has the right to claim victory in this debate.

References

Leiter B (2003) Beyond the Hart/Dworkin debate: the methodology problem in jurisprudence. Am J Jurisprud 48(1):17–51

Shapiro S (2011) Legality. Harvard University Press, Cambridge

[8] Leiter (2003), p. 18.

The manufacturer's authorised representative in the EU is Springer Nature Customer Service Centre GmbH, Europaplatz 3, 69115 Heidelberg, Germany. If you have any concerns regarding our products, please contact ProductSafety@springernature.com

Printed and bound by CPI Group (UK) Ltd, Croydon, CR0 4YY
05/10/2026
02228131-0002